Modern French Literary Studies in the Classroom

Teaching Languages, Literatures, and Cultures

MODERN LANGUAGE ASSOCIATION OF AMERICA

Learning Foreign and Second Languages: Perspectives in Research and Scholarship. Ed. Heidi Byrnes. 1998.

Cultural Studies in the Curriculum: Teaching Latin America. Ed. Danny J. Anderson and Jill S. Kuhnheim. 2003.

Modern French Literary Studies in the Classroom: Pedagogical Strategies. Ed. Charles J. Stivale. 2004.

Modern French Literary Studies in the Classroom

Pedagogical Strategies

Edited by

Charles J. Stivale

THE MODERN LANGUAGE ASSOCIATION OF AMERICA
New York 2004

Library of Congress Cataloging-in-Publication Data

Modern French literary studies in the classroom : pedagogical strategies / edited by Charles J. Stivale.
p. cm. — (Teaching languages, literatures, and cultures)
Includes bibliographical references and index.
ISBN 0-87352-804-2 (hardcover : alk. paper) — ISBN 0-87352-805-0 (pbk. : alk. paper)
1. French literature—Study and teaching. 2. French language—Study and teaching. I. Stivale, Charles J. II. Series.
PQ53.M58 2004
840'.71—dc22 2004014631
ISSN 1092-3225

Printed on recycled paper

Published by The Modern Language Association of America
26 Broadway, New York, New York 10004-1789
www.mla.org

CONTENTS

PREFACE TO THE SERIES

The Teaching Languages, Literatures, and Cultures series was created in response to recent transformative changes in these three areas. By curricular necessity or personal choice, many teachers work in more than one area of specialization. Current theories and methodologies encourage them to incorporate multiple perspectives in their courses. This series aims to help teachers meet new challenges by examining how teaching different languages, literatures, and cultures intersects in theory, research, curriculum and program design, and pedagogical practices. The series is intended to reach specialists and nonspecialists and to create cross-specialty dialogue among members of the profession engaged in what were previously separate efforts.

Series Editors

ACKNOWLEDGMENTS

A volume such as this one owes its existence to contributions from teachers and scholars; collaboration among conference presenters, organizers, and audiences; and the continued support of a press and its editors. Hence I thank all the volume contributors for their patience with my editing efforts and especially Doris Y. Kadish, who co-organized the first panel on the volume's topic and who helped me at every step. I also thank the panelists at the different conferences at which we reflected on teaching and the organizers of five conferences in particular for making space and time for an uncommon session format—Kathryn Grossman, Benedicte Monicat, and Willa Silverman (Pennsylvania State Univ.); Clive Thompson (Univ. of Western Ontario); Gerald Prince (Univ. of Pennsylvania); Lawrence Schehr (Univ. of Illinois, Urbana); and Peter Schofer (Univ. of Wisconsin). Finally, I owe special thanks to Theresa Antes, Lisa Vollendorf, Martha Noel Evans, and David G. Nicholls, who gave me important advice and provided encouragement about developing this volume.

CJS

Charles J. Stivale

Introduction

The operative principle that inspires this volume is succinct and deserves all the emphasis one can muster: TEACHING MATTERS. To state this so baldly might appear to be an exercise of crashing through already opened doors. However, I state it in this way to focus on students, who are the most important factor in teaching practices. Ideally, teaching involves a rewarding dialogue between young adults, who are hungry for knowledge and guidance, and a teacher-mentor deeply involved in a particular field of study. Yet teachers are confronted all too frequently with conflicting demands, starting with that of students, who just want to learn the "facts." This attitude may be reinforced by an implicit or even explicit institutional message that equates students with customers. Moreover, competition in the domain of research requires us to publish ever more original, singular, and creative work at increasingly earlier phases of the career arc, and to do so in a context of scrutiny and verification that would lend legitimacy, however relative, to what has come to be known as scholarly production. Similarly, peer review, student evaluations, and teaching portfolios seek to assess excellence, originality, and innovation in all classroom work, yet these presumed sources of objectivity evaluate a volatile, subjective process—the teaching exchange.

While faced with these developments, we must remain concerned about implementing a curriculum to train students in the necessary skills of critical and creative thinking. The tensions between curricular challenges and professional and institutional demands are particularly pronounced in foreign language and culture programs, where literature is an increasingly demonized subject that has become incompatible with attracting majors. Such a conflict, combined with decreasing enrollments (except for Spanish in most institutions), creates the impression of crisis in foreign language and literature study. Yet a steadfast commitment to the teaching process and to examining that process in practical terms is necessary to maintain our integrity as educators. As Elaine Showalter reminds us, "Although we talk a lot about *what* we teach, we are embarrassed or afraid to ask *why* and *how* we teach" (vii).

The essays in this volume lie at the intersection of these tensions. The authors share a commitment to developing new strategies for teaching French, especially French literature, and to pursuing possibilities for students to learn in the face of conflicting, sometimes confusing, institutional demands. This collective concern animates an optimistic resolve for the growth of French studies in North America, nourished not only by the principle that teaching matters but also by an active and committed belief that the understanding of foreign cultures matters now more than ever. Rather than impede our critical engagement, the aforementioned tensions provide an incentive to undertake a multifaceted reflection on pedagogical practices in a particular disciplinary field and, by extension, in adjacent domains—literary, cultural, and foreign language studies.

This commitment to develop pedagogical strategies was not made in a vacuum. During the 1990s, the field of French studies underwent considerable transformation and even turmoil in North American higher education. The decline in enrollment and majors in French corresponded to the waning of French hegemony in intellectual and theoretical matters. As Jean-Philippe Mathy has noted:

> The passion for theory has largely subsided today, or rather it has taken on new forms, moving away from its initial association with the postwar French philosophies of meaning and desire into a decidedly more nativistic terrain, that of the culture wars involving issues of gender, sexuality, race, nationality, teaching and canonicity that are distinctly American. (8)

Within French studies, the clash between these "distinctly American" issues and Continental perspectives produced a lively polemic in the early 1990s. Ostensibly focused on revisions to the traditional literary canon, this debate also raised explicit pedagogical questions. The focal issue was whether French literary studies as traditionally conceptualized is well served by the numerous attempts to broaden the canon to include women as well as nonmetropolitan French writers.[1] While this question is certainly legitimate and likely to promote ongoing dialogue, the terms in which it was posed and debated raised further issues about whether the field of North American French studies had been unduly influenced by the current social and political agenda, even by a certain homegrown political correctness that created a demand for a broad, interdisciplinary revision of the canon. This complaint was exacerbated by two factors. First, the opponents of the canonical revision implied that the North American circumstances were somehow exceptional in relation to the movement of French literary history, as if the French canon itself was not formed by political and social processes in France during the nineteenth century. Second, the concurrence of this exchange with the full-scale conservative attack on the humanities in the United States, known as the culture wars, contributed to polarizing the discussion into distinct camps without reaching any clear resolution.[2]

Following this exchange was another debate in certain quarters of French studies that concerned the perceived threat posed by the presumably rival field of cultural studies.[3] Instead of reaching an apparent stalemate as did the French culture wars *différend,* this discussion has moved away from initial tentative and fretful musings about possible threats to the field toward a thorough critical overhaul of the very bases on which French studies might proceed. Through conferences, working groups and institutes, special journal issues and other publications, discussions during the 1990s led the field toward some exciting critical horizons in and related to literary studies.[4]

This is the sociocultural and intellectual context in which we have developed the essays in the present volume. Their origin lies in a series of dynamic discussions on teaching literary and cultural studies that have occurred since 1998 at colloquia on nineteenth- and twentieth-century French studies.[5] Two aspects of these discussions made them so important for all participants: first, in contrast to the usual focus on formal presentations of literary critical subjects, these round tables on topics related to teaching French literature attracted significant audience participation and convinced the conference organizers of the need for such a panel at successive colloquia. Second, by making available on the World Wide Web the texts to be discussed before the colloquia, the round tables allowed participants to devote themselves almost solely to actual discussion. A Web site created for this volume will continue to make available, when appropriate, supplementary materials related to topics discussed by different authors. This site also provides the possibility for subsequent dialogue between readers and the volume's contributors (see *Web Support*).[6]

The teaching practices considered here are respond to the debates of the 1990s as well as to mounting curricular and institutional pressures that face us today, including distance education and digital technologies. However, rather than attempt to cover too general a range of topics, we limit ourselves to the domain of nineteenth- and twentieth-century French studies. This post-revolutionary period contains ample issues that need to be addressed from pedagogical perspectives. Indeed, given that most French programs include required courses in French literature and culture after 1789, the need is all the more vital to develop different strategies for studying texts and contexts on the period's movements, themes, and authors. Moreover, modern and postmodern literary and cultural studies have created teaching opportunities—notably, for discussion, textual analysis, and students' own research—that are distinct from those available for texts originating in earlier centuries. This observation in no way diminishes either the importance or the lively scholarship and teaching that occur in medieval, Renaissance, and early modern studies.

The essays in this volume describe strategies developed by teachers in a broad range of institutional settings that respond to varied pedagogical demands, course levels, and audiences. Contributors also cover a wide array of texts and give different definitions to the term *texts*. Depending on the curricular circumstances, we may define *texts* in a strict fashion as canonical literature or more broadly as written, aural, and visual texts. The common purpose of any such definition is to help students develop an understanding of the many complex cultural topics and conjunctures. These texts and the ways in which we define them also help us attract new students to our programs. The contributors to this volume agree that we must be attentive to these dual concerns—how we select texts and how we use them in the classroom—given the need to develop curricular offerings in response to the unremitting pressures on foreign language programs.

Furthermore, the process of dialogue through which these essays developed has moved the discussions in directions that engage important concerns related to pedagogy in foreign languages and in literary and cultural studies. While these foci vary—on marginal texts, sexuality, online reading and writing, study abroad, and cross-disciplinary curricular planning—the authors maintain the primary emphasis on how we teachers of literature in the foreign languages can best bring our fields to the attention and interest of our students, against the odds of contemporary reduced cultural and literary awareness. We thus seek to share information on the pedagogical tasks that we pursue with different texts and to consider many issues of interdisciplinarity. Finally, the contributors make common cause with our colleagues in all foreign language programs. Our purpose is to create a useful resource for teachers in French studies and for the broad contingent of our colleagues—those with teaching interests in literature and cultural studies, whatever the national language or the literary period may be.

In part 1, "Instructing Readers: Linguistic and Literary Frameworks," the authors link our concern with language instruction to the selection and uses of texts. The first two essays, by Kate Paesani and David A. Powell, situate literary study in relation to language learning. Paesani maintains that reading literary texts at as early an age as possible is important for acquiring a foreign language. Providing insight about research on both top-down and bottom-up approaches to teaching reading practices, Paesani argues for establishing an interactive bridge between literary content and the linguistic vehicle of literature. Powell takes this task to heart by situating the important facets of phonetics, translation, and grammar as bases for helping students come to terms with stylistic and structural elements in, and thereby enlivening, literary texts.

In the second pair of essays, the authors consider how to inspire our students' creative engagement with language through reading and writing. Gayle A. Levy confronts the notoriously resistant poem by Stéphane Mallarmé, *Un coup de dés*. By introducing students gradually to different typographic and lexical details, Levy enables students to read the poem "dans tous les sens," in all directions and toward many if not all meanings, thereby engaging the virtual text with the actual poem under consideration. This emphasis on inspiring student creativity constitutes the primary focus of the collaborative essay with which the first section closes. Laurence M. Porter, Anita Alkhas, and Larry Kuiper consider how to employ texts as tools to develop creative thinking and writing. This task is especially important when students make the leap from undergraduate to graduate study, often confronting texts of literary criticism for the first time. The authors argue that teachers should empower students with self-confidence, make them aware of how structures with dynamic potential can help them develop their thought, and free them from the hegemony of established critics. The purpose of these pedagogical strategies is to help students find their own voice as they refine their critical insights.

In part 2, "Exploring the Cultural: Pedagogical Devices," the authors address the domain of culture studies by presenting innovative approaches for teaching a diverse range of texts. Anne E. McCall confronts the problem of developing the undergraduate civilization course. Her approach is to help students develop a better understanding of both textual production and the cultural context in which texts are produced. To do this, she pairs selected short readings in French and English in a semester-long common class project centering on an individual text. McCall argues that this common experience of cultural construction and criticism yields a course that is intellectually rigorous, despite the drift away from strict use of the target language. Examining a related challenge, Adrianna M. Paliyenko links literature to culture in an effort to draw in culture-track and literary-track majors, a dual strategy requiring that Paliyenko attend to the needs of each group in a single course. Her essay recounts how, in class presentations, discussions, and individual projects, students related the literary and the visual and thus sharpened their understanding of the connection between seeing what is read and reading what is seen. Paliyenko enhanced classroom presentations by using PowerPoint in her lectures. She also encouraged students to use it in their own research into French culture.

In this section's second pair of essays, the authors consider how to employ specific texts through diverse visual and electronic media. Kathryn M. Grossman takes up Victor Hugo's tome *Notre-Dame de Paris*, with pedagogical and technological brio. She shows how course materials can be aimed at more than one kind of student audience, particularly with electronic classroom capabilities that can enrich the study of the text through videos, CD-ROMs, and the Internet. Véronique Flambard-Weisbart pursues this research into the intersection of cultural and literary texts and technology by considering how role play may serve textual studies. Flambard-Weisbart develops global-simulation exercises to help students engage in online textual constructions in the parameters of specific narratives and cultural settings.

The section's last two essays envisage literary texts in terms of the margins and centers of French sociocultural or critical contexts. John Anzalone directs his attention to so-called marginal movements by raising the problems—linguistic, literary, cultural, curricular—posed by nineteenth-century fin de siècle texts. Michael Garval describes an original approach for introducing students to issues in contemporary French culture. Adopting a cultural manual destined for children's education during the early Third Republic era (1875–1906) as a core text for an intermediate French culture course, Garval shows how the "common sense" formulas of Third Republic ideology offer insights to students as they engage with contemporary textual and cultural practices.

In part 3, "Expanding Horizons: Interdisciplinary Challenges," the authors approach the curricular demands to develop students' interdisciplinary acumen. My contribution to the volume consists of finding models for gently drawing students—undergraduate and graduate alike—into the realm of the other tongue known succinctly as theory. I reference selected syllabi on the volume's Web site and emphasize the (always relative) failures as well as successes that I have experienced introducing students to primary literary texts while engaging their attention critically with different theoretical approaches. Then, shifting focus toward sexuality and racial issues, the next two authors consider how we must continue to place into question received notions of canonicity and teaching. Garett R. Heysel examines the role that "professing sexuality"—notably, gay sexuality—can play in designing courses and analyzing literary texts in undergraduate courses. Doris Y. Kadish considers the effect that the expanded concept of francophone studies can and should have on literary studies before 1950, especially in nineteenth-century studies. Heysel and Kadish supplement their arguments and analyses with such documentation as syllabi, bibliographies, and resources from the Web.

In the section's fourth essay, Marie Lathers raises an important issue by reassessing an interdisciplinary practice that reads literary and visual texts in tandem. Not satisfied that students will immediately grasp the significance of juxtaposing literary texts with visual examples, Lathers explores how the metaphors of the writer sculpting a literary work and, conversely, of the spectator reading a statue form the matrix around which a course or course unit may be envisioned. Lathers thus seeks to move the students' engagement with these works from cross-disciplinarity to true interdisciplinarity. Cynthia Running-Johnson and Judith F. Stone complement Lathers's perspective by describing their successful collaboration in developing a cross-disciplinary course in twentieth-century French history and film studies. Their testimony and teaching strategies address the practical issues that many of us face in response to institutional demands for teaching across departmental borders.

The students from French, history, and film studies benefited from the exchanges and expertise that Johnson and Stone could provide.

The title of part 4, "Stitching the Quilt: Institutional Demands, Curricular Strategies," emphasizes issues that academic professionals confront in different institutional contexts. In the first two essays, the authors consider issues related to undergraduate studies as they intersect with specific institutional structures—notably, general education and the articulation of undergraduate studies with graduate education. E. Nicole Meyer examines the interdisciplinary context of a state institution where she teaches courses in French and English to a broad range of undergraduate students. These courses are intended to meet the diverse needs of the humanities department and to fulfill general education requirements. Meyer explains how she has been able to respond to institutional needs and stay true to her own interests in nineteenth-century French literature, expanding both the course content and her own expertise in the process. Deborah Harter addresses the issues of how to meet the needs of graduate students who enroll for credit in undergraduate seminars and of how to hold onto outstanding undergraduates who enroll in graduate seminars. The goal here is to prepare a course that neither overwhelms the undergraduates nor underserves graduate students by diminishing academic rigor. Both Meyer and Harter anchor their discussions by outlining the syllabi each conceived and sharing strategies they have devised over the years.

Gayle Zachmann unites language teaching and globalization in the context of a successful summer study-abroad program. Providing insights about links between administrative logistics and curricular planning, Zachmann analyzes the creation and structure of the University of Florida's programs in Avignon and Aix-en-Provence as a response to local, national, and international pressures and realities. Zachmann considers study abroad a means to address the curricular demands that teachers face in developing pedagogically viable and intellectually vital French programs and the institutional pressures that departments face to attract greater numbers of majors and minors.

The two final essays both focus on globalization but provide distinct perspectives, from the private and public sectors of higher education. Nathalie Rachlin articulates the grounds on which we can still argue for the proposition that French studies in particular and foreign language and cultural studies in general still matter. She contends that by teaching the current debates about American-led globalization and the strong reservations that have emerged from that debate, we can help our students understand the extent to which these global issues determine the links between past and present foreign cultures and students' own circumstances in the world today. Melanie Hawthorne considers the stakes for responding to institutional calls for *globalization*, a frequently used term that functions as a synonym for "domesticating the foreign." From the perspective of what she calls a "new regionalism," Hawthorne argues for facing the challenges this domestication poses for French studies, including linguistic domination by English. Drawing from examples of interdisciplinary courses at the state institution where she teaches, she cautions readers about the difficulties of selling French studies.

The contributors to this volume raise myriad questions about and provide a range of answers to our twofold pedagogical task: first, of selecting French literary texts that will attract our students, and, second, of developing pedagogical and institutional strategies that encourage students to engage fully with the literary, critical, and cultural facets of each course. We believe that this volume responds to the growing emphasis in private and public, small and large institutions on the true mission of the humanities: teaching as the primary means to conjoin pedagogical, institutional, global, and research goals. The interests of the contributors to this volume coincide with that emphasis in practical ways, most notably because contributors discover how to stimulate our students' interest in French language, literature, and culture and how to think about these subjects, these passions of ours, through engaged practices of dynamic dialogue.

NOTES

1. The key texts in this debate are Apostolidès; Compagnon ("Diminishing Canon"); Hullot-Kentor; Pavel ("Profession Forum"); Schor ("Righting," "Reply to Hullot-Kentor," and "Reply to Pavel"). One volume in particular, by Hollier, provides a culturally based approach to French literary history as an alternative to traditional French literary anthologies, which raised the ire of some commentators (most notably, Compagnon, "Diminishing Canon").
2. See Le Hir ("Bridging") and Stanton for reviews of French and American perspectives in French studies; see Compagnon ("A la recherche") for a concise overview of French studies in the United States.
3. Besides Mathy, see Fourny and Schehr; Klein; and Schehr, Introduction. I summarize the shifts of opinion and nuances in the discussions about French cultural studies in *Disenchanting Les Bons Temps* (14–20).
4. For different positions on French cultural studies, see Goux and Wood; Le Hir and Strand; Marks and McCaffery; Schehr and Weiss; David F. Bell; Chambers, "Cultural Studies," "Nexus"; Conley, "Afterword," "Putting French"; Furman; Kelly; Kritzman; Le Hir, "French Cultural Studies," "The 'Popular,' " "Transatlantic Solidarity"; Pavel,

"Les études culturelles," Letter in *PMLA*; Petrey, "French Studies," "When Did Literature"; Rosello, *Declining*, "Rap Music," *Postcolonial*; Stivale, "Cultural Lessons," "A la recherche"; Strand; and Yaari, "Culture Studies," "Cultural Curriculum." See also Cusset for a French perspective on American French theory.

5. These panels began at the annual Nineteenth-Century French Studies Colloquium, held at Pennsylvania State University in October 1998; one panel was also organized at the 2000 Twentieth-Century French Studies Colloquium, at the University of Pennsylvania. See links to these panels and papers presented there at http://www.langlab.wayne.edu/CStivale/index.html.
6. I will maintain and update the contents of this Web site, which is available through my faculty-member home page at Wayne State University.

PART ONE

Instructing Readers: Linguistic and Literary Frameworks

Kate Paesani

Using Literature to Develop Foreign Language Proficiency: Toward an Interactive Classroom

Traditionally, in many foreign language departments, the development of language proficiency and the teaching of literature have been divorced from each other. Communicative-based foreign language courses have focused on skills development (speaking, listening, reading, writing, and culture) and interaction among students. Foreign language literature courses have focused on literary analysis, often to the exclusion of skills development, and even in courses with class discussion, interaction among students remains largely teacher dominated. Although attitudes about the split between so-called proficiency- and content-oriented courses have improved, the problem continues to plague foreign language departments in the United States. Despite numerous hurdles, a growing number of researchers (e.g., Barnett, "Language"; Hoffman and James; Swaffar; Swaffar, Arens, and Byrnes; Jean Marie Schultz; Schulz) recognize the important link between the development of language proficiency and of expertise in content. Most notably, in an effort to bridge the gap between language and literature, researchers in applied linguistics have underlined the importance of introducing authentic texts—in particular, literary texts—at the beginning and intermediate levels of language study.[1]

The changing face of foreign language education and the needs of current foreign language majors and minors demand that we revamp our curricula and question the traditional mission of foreign language departments (*Standards*; Swaffar 35). Gwendolyn Barnes-Karol points out that fewer students are pursuing foreign language study with the goal of becoming teachers or of advancing to graduate work in literature. Instead, more students are double majoring in foreign language and a field such as business, biology, or engineering. These changes in student demographics require that we question the goal of teaching literature at the advanced level:

> [Is] it to only produce future professional literary historians or critics? Or [is] it to help students develop greater linguistic and cultural fluency, to enrich their understanding of the [target culture], and to prepare them for interactions ranging from face-to-face conversational exchanges to dialogues with interlocutors across time and national borders? (45)

An approach to foreign language instruction that addresses these curricular needs and introduces literary texts from the start of language instruction better prepares students for what lies ahead, thus easing the transition from language to literature courses.

In recent research on reading, authors from different perspectives have emphasized two important discoveries: that literary texts provide excellent input for the development of reading and general language proficiency and that interactive models of reading are most effective in helping learners develop this proficiency. Furthermore, interactive reading models that place equal importance on textual information and on readers' mental activities used in comprehending a literary text may also help beginning and intermediate language students develop skills in literary analysis that are vital at the advanced level of instruction. Content, and more specifically literature, across the curriculum is an important topic of current second language acquisition research and foreign language pedagogy.

In this essay, I examine the relevant research on the link between language and literature and explore the idea that, although the teaching of literature at all levels of language instruction is extremely valuable, equally valuable is a focus on proficiency development at all levels of instruction. As Janet K. Swaffar writes, "Spiraling both content and language in a systematic and meaningful program necessitates a holistic curriculum in which the right hand knows what the left hand is doing and where all the activities of the typical department are conceived of as a coherent package" (35). This spiraling, or intertwining, of content and language is essential since language learning is an ongoing process. Research on the link between language and literature clearly demonstrates that we cannot abandon the development of skills in literary analysis for the sake of language proficiency. Conversely, we cannot abandon the development of skills in language proficiency for the sake of literary analysis. I argue that this spiraling of language and content must be achieved through an interactive approach to the study of literature. Interactive reading models, which are typically reserved for proficiency-oriented beginning and intermediate language learning contexts, must extend beyond language courses to apply to the teaching of literature. To explore the role and purpose of using literary texts in the beginning language classroom, I first establish a theoretical basis for the teaching and processing of textual information.

MODELS OF FOREIGN LANGUAGE READING

Research on reading processes has played an important role in linguistic literature for decades. The goal of foreign language reading is to construct meaning. Interaction between the text and the reader on multiple levels contributes to the construction of meaning. The ways in which this interaction is defined are based on three types of reading models examined here: bottom-up, top-down, and interactive.

Before the widespread adoption of communicative language teaching, texts used in the beginning language classroom were generally approached from a bottom-up perspective. Bottom-up reading processes are text-driven; learners employ reading strategies such as decoding, word recognition, and syntactic feature recognition and therefore construct textual meaning through letters, words, phrases, and sentences. According to Marva A. Barnett, "bottom-up models analyze reading as a process in which small chunks of text are absorbed, analyzed, and gradually added to the next chunks until they become meaningful" (*More* 13). Comprehension is often equated with a learner's ability to recall a text; provide summaries; or translate specific words, phrases, or passages. Although learners who approach texts from a bottom-up perspective may certainly construct meaning, exclusive use of such strategies poses a number of problems. Readers who use these strategies tend to rely heavily on the dictionary and to focus on surface details rather than on meaningful interpretation. In addition, bottom-up processing of texts undermines strategies such as skimming and scanning (Swaffar, Arens, and Byrnes 24).

Top-down models of reading processes, however, are reader-driven; readers construct meaning by accessing background information and drawing inferences about the content, organization, and rhetorical structure of texts. A large part of textual meaning is constructed from the reader's background knowledge and personal experiences, or schemata. According to Claire Kramsch, "schema theories of reading stress the fact that readers make sense out of a text by constructing schemata or universes of discourse based on their knowledge of the world and the totality of their experience" (357). In the top-down processing of a text, readers match the content of the text with their existing schemata to construct meaning. In such models, then, what the reader contributes to the construction of textual meaning takes precedence over the words and sentences of the text itself.

Swaffar, Katherine M. Arens, and Heidi Byrnes argue that both types of processing are necessary to comprehend a text. Failure to understand textual detail through bottom-up processing may lead to miscomprehension of overall textual meaning; failure to activate reader schemata may lead to miscomprehension of new linguistic information in the text (27). Moreover, if readers rely heavily on one type of processing over the other, it may lead to "unidirectional bias" (Carrell 103).

> If the bias is knowledge-based, the reader tends to fill in details not motivated by the text and make unsupported inferences. If the bias is text-based, readers tend to exclude inferential thinking. Either bias leads to inaccurate comprehension.
>
> (Swaffar, Arens, and Byrnes 29)

This line of argumentation, as well as continued research in schema theories, has contributed to the development of a third, hybrid approach, interactive models of reading processes.

In interactive models, text-based and reader-based factors contribute to comprehension. Although bottom-up and top-down models view reading as a linear or sequential process, interactive models propose that text-based and reader-based variables operate simultaneously in the construction of textual meaning. According to Barnett:

> [Interactive reading models] are not linear but rather cyclical views of the reading process in which textual information and the reader's mental activities (including the processing of graphic, syntactic, lexical, semantic, and pragmatic information) have a simultaneous and equally important impact on comprehension. That is, as in top-down models, the reader uses his or her expectations and previous under-

> standing to guess about text content, but, as in bottom-up models, the reader is still dependent on what is in the text. (*More* 13)

Swaffar, Arens, and Byrnes identify eight distinct text- and reader-based variables that play a role in the interactive processing of texts. These include top-down variables such as reader background, reader perspective, text schema, text structure, and episodic sequence and bottom-up variables such as illustrative detail, surface-language features of the text, and reader language proficiency (24).[2] These variables interact to allow the reader to construct the meaning necessary to comprehend a text.

An approach to the teaching of reading that promotes interactive processing is essential to develop reading skills and general language proficiency in beginning language instruction. Swaffar, Arens, and Byrnes insist on the importance of "supersentential reading and writing," that is, reading and writing tasks that go beyond a focus on grammar and sentence structure toward more complex meaning construction. They argue that "when supersentential reading and writing are absent in beginning language instruction, students have trouble adjusting to these tasks at a later time" (38). One way in which to promote supersentential reading and interactive processing is through the use of authentic texts, including literature, at all levels of language instruction.

LITERATURE IN THE PROFICIENCY-ORIENTED CLASSROOM

One of the main goals of foreign language education is to foster an appreciation for and understanding of the literature of target language cultures. Yet the transition from language to literature courses is a major problem facing foreign language pedagogy (Schulz 43). Given declining enrollments in advanced-level language courses and the frustrations students encounter when facing full-length literary texts for the first time, it is clear that we are not adequately preparing our students to advance through their foreign language studies. One reason for this failure is the continued division between so-called proficiency- and content-oriented courses. According to Jean-Marie Schultz, "adherence to fixed lines of demarcation between language and literature study makes advanced work on literature at the undergraduate level accessible to fewer and fewer students" (6).

For decades, reading instruction in the foreign language classroom has been based on a hierarchy of tasks and text types. Students typically move from basic comprehension of short, authentic texts relating to real-world experiences in beginning-level courses to the interpretation of expository texts or literary excerpts on topics related to history or culture in intermediate-level courses and, finally, to the close analysis of full-length works of literature in advanced-level courses. This traditional development of reading skills, moving from bottom-up to top-down processing tasks and from short texts to works of literature, has created obstacles for students moving from proficiency- to content-oriented courses. Moreover, traditional approaches to literary study have been primarily teacher-focused, and students have played a passive role, even when whole-class discussion is a component of the course. This classroom experience is contrary to what students have been exposed to in language courses, where the instructor is an active facilitator of learning and students are active participants in the learning process. Of course, the pedagogical essays in this volume suggest precisely this interactive emphasis in the advanced literature classroom. Still, I argue that it is in the active learning environment of proficiency-oriented courses that increased exposure to literature may help students overcome obstacles to learning and produce significant benefits.

When integrated into the curriculum with well-designed reading tasks, literature becomes accessible to beginning learners. David J. Shook argues that beginning language learners benefit from early exposure to literature because literary texts possess characteristics absent from other types of texts. Literature is compelling, evocative, creative, and memorable. Because of these traits, Shook argues, literary works may interest readers, evoke thought and discussion, offer insight into the complex nature of the target culture, provide a model for innovative language use, and leave a lasting impression on language learners (206–07). Peter Schofer also identifies many benefits to bringing literature into the beginning language classroom. First, literature is an authentic representation of language and society. Second, from a programmatic perspective, integrating literature across the language curriculum may lead to more efficient program articulation and to increased collaboration among professors of language and literature. Finally, the introduction of literature in beginning language classes better prepares students for advanced study in foreign language and increases student enjoyment of literature (326–27).

Introducing literature into the beginning language classroom, then, fosters the development of language and literary-analysis skills and helps bridge the gap between proficiency- and content-oriented courses. In fact, much of the research on the use of literature in beginning language instruction (e.g., Jean-Marie Schultz; Swaffar, Arens, and Byrnes) focuses on promoting skills in literary analysis and critical thinking to help bridge this gap. This research shows that if students start developing skills in literary analysis at the beginning of language study, they will be more successful students of literature at the advanced level. Initiation into these kinds of skills is often lacking before advanced-level courses in which the focus is on the discussion and interpretation of full-length literary works.

Despite the benefits of teaching literature across the curriculum, language programs that aim to introduce literature from the start of language instruction face several challenges, which include the proficiency level of beginning foreign language students, the selection of appropriate literary texts, and the development of suitable reading activities. A frequent argument against using literary texts has been the low proficiency level of beginning-level students. Many instructors base this argument on the assumptions that language learning involves the mastery of discrete grammar points and the building of a basic lexicon and that the difficulty of reading tasks and texts increases in a hierarchical fashion. According to Swaffar, Arens, and Byrnes, however, proficiency level does not dictate whether students can begin to read literature for meaning. Reading for meaning is both possible and necessary at beginning levels of instruction. Instead, proficiency level dictates when students can graduate from reading about familiar subject matter to reading about unfamiliar subject matter. Language level, then, "helps predict the extent to which students will have to rely on prior knowledge and command of encoding strategies (top-down processing) to comprehend the gist and the degree to which they will probably encounter problems with textual detail (bottom-up processing)" (54). According to this view, the schemata, the background knowledge and personal experiences that readers bring to a text, influence their ability to construct meaning as much as or more than their level of language proficiency.

Since schemata play a pivotal role in the comprehension of texts at beginning levels, it is important to select literary works that are accessible to students. Not only must texts treat topics that are familiar to beginning language students, they must also have a substantive plot, a clear sequential development, well-marked transitions, a minimal amount of description, and unambiguous intent (Swaffar, Arens, and Byrnes 137–39). According to Schofer (330), excerpts of narrative texts such as fairy tales and short stories satisfy these requirements and provide appropriate input for beginning language learners. Swaffar, Arens, and Byrnes (58) also point out that students may not necessarily benefit from reading shorter texts. Such texts lend themselves more easily to word-for-word reading strategies (bottom-up processing) because students place more attention on details. Longer literary excerpts are contextualized and are therefore more cohesive and interesting to the learner, thus facilitating text-level reading strategies (top-down processing).

Careful selection of literary texts does not ensure that learners will construct meaning from a text or that they will go beyond summarizing the plot to engage in in-depth literary analysis. Beginning language students must be given adequate preparation to read these texts, strategies that reflect the interactive process of reading. In particular, prereading tasks that activate readers' schemata, reading tasks that guide comprehension and interpretation, and postreading tasks that allow readers to reconstruct meaning and personalize texts help ensure that beginning learners will construct meaning and go beyond simple plot summary. Sandra N. Harper outlines an approach to teaching literature at the beginning and intermediate levels that is student focused and communicatively oriented. To encourage students to understand and appreciate literary texts, she incorporates interactive reading strategies that allow for preinterpretation (prereading tasks), guided interpretation (reading tasks), and synthesis (postreading tasks) of written texts. According to Harper, these strategies

> (1) allow individualization of learning; (2) incorporate the multiple perspectives and experiences of students into the teaching/learning process; and (3) provide structured, sequenced activities that facilitate reading and comprehension and instruct students in various strategies involved in deciphering a text. (403)

A reading activity developed for an excerpt of Jules Verne's *Le tour du monde en 80 jours* exemplifies this approach to treating literary texts in the elementary classroom. The excerpt, selected because it contains references to modes of transportation, international travel, and time, treats subject matter that is familiar to students and has a clear sequential development. Prereading tasks activate students' background knowledge. Students talk about their own experiences traveling, including where they went and how they got there. Then, to relate their personal experience to the novel, students brainstorm how the modes of transportation and travel destinations might differ if the trip were to take place in 1872. Reading tasks include individual, small-group, and whole-class activities. Students first read the excerpt individually to identify cognates in the text. Next, in small groups, students reread the text and answer a series of questions about its content (e.g., geographical location, chronology of events, characters). Finally, to encourage more detailed examination of the text, the instructor leads a whole-class decoding activity that targets relevant vocabulary and structures. A postreading activity requires students to write a short paragraph describing their own trip around the world in eighty days. This kind of sequenced, interactive, and meaning-based treatment of literary texts, focusing on proficiency development and literary analysis, is essential at all levels of language instruction. It is this notion of spiraling content and proficiency across the curriculum to which I now turn.

PROFICIENCY DEVELOPMENT IN THE LITERATURE CLASSROOM: AN INTERACTIVE APPROACH

The research presented thus far demonstrates a clear need for developing skills in literary analysis in proficiency-oriented language courses. In this last section, I show that there is an equally clear need for developing proficiency skills in content-oriented literature courses. Not only does a focus on language proficiency across the curriculum better equip students to carry out more sophisticated literary analysis, it narrows the traditional split between language and literature in foreign language departments. A growing body of research supports this claim. Daniel B. Soneson argues that "techniques for fostering communicative competence with proficiency as a goal can and must be continued at the upper level in order to nourish student interest and enthusiasm" (31). Schofer echoes this belief: "Considerable work needs to be done in introductory literature courses, where all too often, little attention is paid to students' language needs" (332). Furthermore, according to Kamakshi Murti, "student involvement, activation, and participation cannot be limited to the elementary and intermediate levels of language learning. . . . [This awareness] needs to be translated into more tangible forms for classroom use by those who teach literature at the advanced levels" (41).

The need for continued proficiency development in content-oriented courses is supported by recent research on proficiency levels at various levels of instruction. This research stresses that we cannot assume learners possess an advanced level of language proficiency once they enter advanced courses.

As Barnett points out, "tests, research studies, and personal experience confirm that mastering a language is an ongoing phenomenon" (*Language* 8). Yet instructors at the advanced level are often disappointed or frustrated to find their assumption that students have mastered the linguistic code is incorrect. Ernst Fedor Hoffmann and Dorothy James (30) explain that ACTFL proficiency testing reveals that students entering intermediate- or advanced-level study after a two- or three-semester beginning-level foreign language requirement usually rate Intermediate-Mid or Intermediate-High. According to the *ACTFL Proficiency Guidelines: Speaking* (American Council 4), learners at this level are at best able to describe, report, and narrate but do so with varying levels of consistency. Moreover, foreign language majors generally rate at Advanced-Low or Advanced-Mid levels only at the end of four years of college-level language study. Nevertheless, students entering advanced-level courses where the focus is on literary analysis are often asked to carry out Advanced- or Superior-level tasks, such as explaining and supporting opinions, developing hypotheses, and providing lengthy and coherent narrations (American Council 3). The facts regarding proficiency level throughout language instruction underscore the need to spiral language and content and to develop linguistic proficiency and literary expertise across the curriculum. Swaffar writes, "Foreign language departments must teach processes, not products. To do so . . . faculty members must spiral . . . topics, learner strategies, and articulatory roles, repeating them at different levels across the curriculum" (37).

I propose that the most effective way to spiral language and content at the advanced level is to incorporate interactive reading strategies into the literature classroom. As other essays in this volume suggest, this approach transforms the study of literature into a student-focused process by using communicative strategies that examine texts from both top-down and bottom-up perspectives. The link between proficiency development and interactive processing strategies at the advanced level is intuitive. Both represent an intertwining of two elements where each element has a simultaneous and equally important effect; proficiency development at the advanced level intertwines language and content, and interactive reading at the advanced level intertwines top-down and bottom-up processes. To help implement effective reading strategies in the literature classroom, instructors need to continue their role as facilitators of learning and to develop tasks that encourage interactive processing of literary texts.

Teachers may act as facilitators in the study of literary texts, just as they act as facilitators in the development of language proficiency. Swaffar, Arens, and Byrnes claim that beginning and intermediate language classroom teachers "have a fourfold task: (1) to activate reader schemata, (2) to guide students to an awareness of text structure, (3) to assist in strategy development, and (4) to promote relaxed interaction between students and text" (70–71). Even at the advanced level, where students are focused on developing expertise in literary analysis and content knowledge, teachers can continue to play this facilitative role and to promote interactive processing of texts. The difference between studying literature at the beginning and intermediate levels and at the advanced level is the way in which instructors facilitate this interaction.

Strategies that focus simultaneously on bottom-up and top-down processes are easily integrated into prereading, reading, and postreading tasks at the advanced level, where background information continues to play a pivotal role in how learners interpret new information and construct textual meaning. In the context of the literature classroom, students may activate schemata by reading cultural, historical, or political texts before reading an assigned work of literature. This exercise provides learners with a context that goes beyond personal experiences and lays the groundwork for in-depth literary analysis. Instructors can encourage students to think critically about the concepts inherent in these background texts and how they might apply to a work of literature. Reading tasks can then be designed to focus first on global and then on detailed comprehension of the literary text. Global-comprehension strategies include identifying the episodic structure of a text through scanning (top-down processing) or recognizing discourse markers (bottom-up processing); an example of a detailed comprehension strategy is to relate specific sentences to the main episodes of the text (top-down processing) (Swaffar, Arens, and Byrnes 77). Postreading tasks allow learners to further interact with the text in more creative ways. Instructors might guide students in reconstructing a text from a different perspective (top-down processing). To encourage personalized postreading tasks, instructors might have students use specific language examples to confirm or reject students' opinions about the literary text (bottom-up and top-down processing).

I return to *Le tour du monde en 80 jours* as a concrete example of the spiraling of language and literature at the advanced level. In prereading activities, students activate schemata through an introduction to the genre of travel literature and to the travel literature of Jules Verne. Next, students examine the table of contents and chapter titles to brainstorm ideas about the content of the novel, the author's style, and the text structure. Students can then read the first chapter of the text in class and work in small groups to prepare brief character portraits of Phileas Fogg and Passepartout, the novel's protagonists. This background information provides a context for discussing the novel and for understanding its episodic structure. A take-home reading guide leads students through the text, develops reading strategies, and fosters global comprehension. This out-of-class reading is complemented by in-class, small-group discussion of information gleaned from the reading. According to Barnes-Karol (46–47), who employs similar strategies in a Spanish novel course, whole-class discussion activities such as drawing conclusions and suggesting topics for further analysis allow students to gain a more detailed understanding of the text. Postreading tasks take numerous forms, including role-play in which small groups of students act out different chapters of the text or short writing activities in which students retell parts of the novel from the perspective of one of its characters. To explore and analyze the genre of travel literature in more detail, students develop a paper contrasting the novel with popular travel guides such as Hachette's Guide bleu series, using Barthes's essay "Le guide bleu" (121–25) to anchor their arguments. The tasks outlined here clearly focus on language and content while using top-down and bottom-up processing strategies to construct meaning from literary texts.

Many innovative programs that spiral language and content are implementing curricular change to reflect current research on the use of literary texts at all levels of language instruction and, more generally, on content across the curriculum. If we are to effectively execute change that reflects this trend, however, we must consider the equally important need for continued proficiency development throughout foreign language study. Our success as foreign language departments can best be measured by a strategic combination of elements, both the knowledge about literary interpretation or criticism that students possess and their proficiency in communicating this knowledge in a skilled way. This dynamic model integrates language proficiency and content and thus offers a way to prepare students, who may enter careers in which expertise in both aspects of language will play a significant role.

NOTES

1. I use the term *beginning language study* to refer to the first year of university-level foreign language instruction. At some universities, this year of instruction spans

three semesters. I use the term *intermediate language study* to refer to the second year of foreign language instruction. At some universities, intermediate language courses are referred to as bridge courses. Finally, I use the term *advanced language study* to refer to all undergraduate language (conversation, composition, grammar, etc.) and content (literature, culture, linguistics, etc.) courses after the intermediate sequence.

2. In Swaffar, Arens, and Byrnes's interactive reading model, top-down variables reflect both text- and reader-based factors. Among their top-down variables, reader background (schemata) and reader perspective (strategies) are reader-based, whereas text schema (topic), text structure (organization), and episodic sequence (subsets of topic and organization) are text-based. Likewise, bottom-up variables reflect text- and reader-based factors. Among the bottom-up variables cited, reader language proficiency is reader-based, but illustrative detail (text samples representative of the main topics) and surface language features of the text (letters, words, sentences) are text-based (24, 77).

David A. Powell

Linguistic Contexts for Studying Literary Texts

Those of us in small departments who have the good fortune to teach the gamut of the curriculum experience firsthand the pedagogical intersections between intermediate language courses and advanced literature and culture courses. For a long time, I've been exploring curricular junctures that would benefit from exploiting these intersections. By sowing a passive appreciation of cultural and linguistic markers in intermediate language courses, we can harvest the fruits of such subliminal information in advanced courses. I focus here on a sampling of matters that all teachers of French—indeed, teachers of all languages—incorporate into their language courses. It is beneficial to articulate and discuss these issues, especially in the light of curricular changes many of us are facing. In addition, the current student population's steadily diminishing cultural background demands that we seek better sequential pedagogical tactics.

I arrange my comments in three groups that represent the bulk of my intermediate teaching: phonetics, grammar, and translation. Although I address culture throughout, I do not present it as a separate unit, since culture elements are found at all levels of the curriculum; this is an especially important consideration for some colleges where no isolated course is devoted to culture. I propose only a few examples from each group to demonstrate how lessons that may remain latent or abstract in early stages can benefit students in advanced courses. My comments, though not exhaustive, demonstrate the answer to the eternal questions, Do we have to know this? Will it be on the test? For, in fact, the elements I discuss will always be involved at some level on every test a student ever takes, from the intermediate level through advanced courses, to graduate school, and indeed throughout the first years of teaching.

PHONETICS

Although a course in French phonetics often teeters between an introductory course in theoretical linguistics, on the one hand, and a practical or remedial course in pronunciation, on the other, there are multiple opportunities in such a course to introduce important decoding tactics to intermediate students. Let me begin with vowels. Teaching the French vowel system—apart from the important and arduous task of stressing the tension of pure vowels—eventually leads to syllabification and rhyme. Obviously, the importance of syllabification affects many aspects of spoken French—for instance, the nasality or orality of initial vowels + n/m (e.g., the distinction of *important* and *immédiat*). Another example is the unstable-e. The matter of whether to pronounce the so-called mute-e can branch off with varying degrees of subtlety into a discussion of levels of discourse. In a single lesson where students become familiarized with these nuances (e.g., the effects of pronouncing *maintenant* in either two or three syllables), we can sensitize them to the various types of French they might hear in different situations and, with some hope, expand and nuance their use of spoken French. With a view to training analysts of French literature, we obviously have to teach students to count syllables for parsing poetic texts. Just a few examples of alexandrines at the intermediate level, where everyone in the class counts syllables on their fingers, can exhibit the importance of syllabification in a way that may not seem pertinent to students at the time but that will come back to them in an introduction to textual analysis.[1]

The study of French vowels can also lead to a discussion on assonance and rhyme. It's especially important for English-speaking students to hear, recognize, and distinguish between vowel sounds that are not clearly different to the untrained, non-French ear. Besides the usual difficulties (e.g., oral versus nasal, open versus closed vowels), students must master the eminent problem of /e/ and /ɛ/, so central to classical French verse and in *langue recherchée*. But at the same time they must learn that these are allophones for many French speakers. Similarly, the variance in /œ̃/ and /ɛ̃/ for the nasal vowel spelled "un" or "um" (here the typical example is *lundi* as either /lœ̃di/ or /lɛ̃di/) should be introduced, once again illustrating levels of discourse and variance among speakers. It is important to sensitize students to these nuances and train them to recognize and accept variants, which may be voluntary and selective or automatic and constant for the native speaker of French. At the same time, the discussion of variants provides the opportunity to discuss a tolerance for difference, which is a lesson whose far-reaching benefits I need not point out here.

This brings me to the vague notion of accent. A discussion of different accents could be considered an unnecessary diversion for the intermediate student. But it is important to make students aware of the variety of accents that make up a language nation.[2] It might be useful for students to articulate different accents of United States and British English and other English-language accents and to encourage them to embrace these differences with the specific goal of debunking the so-called standard of a specific metropolitan French as the only acceptable French—no more hegemony of Tourangeau French in the twenty-first century! Students should be given films and language-lab exercises that expose them to a variety of accents, which can then be discussed in terms of what these phonetic and sociocultural markers might indicate. United States students immediately recognize the underlying connotation of a stereotypical southern accent in the midst of a discourse among Yankee speakers. Similar examples are easy enough to find in French film, and students' awareness of the stereotype that is being evoked should be heightened to encourage an appreciation of irony. From a recognition of differences in accent to a realization of prejudice triggered by a different accent, the student is sensitized to awareness and tolerance.

Students will also need to be prepared for encountering literary representations of class and dialectic phonetic differences, such as Honoré de Balzac's ironic use of Teutonic French in *Le Cousin Pons*, in which the Germanic accent of the character of Schmucke (not to mention his name) bears a significant portion of the character's narrative force, or the working-class dialects of Émile Zola's characters. Other variants that could indicate class or discourse differences and that could leave the neophyte oblivious should also be introduced at this point, enabling students to retrieve the information later. For instance, the often-neglected vowel /ɑ/ (the open-a) is not commonly used in modern standard French. But what of the comedic use of it in linguistic frolicking?

The French indulge in this particular game often and seriously, and it is therefore a significant cultural practice students should know about. An example of such a use follows (and this example should be read with the most caricatured accent possible and using the open-a): "C'est un monsieur prétentieux, un homme d'un certain *âge*, qui adore manger des *gâteaux* dans son *château*."[3] This affectation is communicated in comic books by several *â* in a row, *gââteaux*, or sometimes with several circumflexes superimposed over a single "a." Or take the example of the *paysan* speaker, whose dialect a student might encounter in film or in a text, who pronounces, "C'est pas moi" as / s e p ɑ m w ɑ / or even / s e p ɑ m w *e* /. Another example along these lines is the variants of "r." The uvular "r," /ʀ/, is usually a focal point in the lesson on French consonants. But we do our students a disservice if we are content with that standard uvular pronunciation. There are several regions in metropolitan France where /*r*/ and /r̄/ are standard, as well as in Québec and in some Caribbean accents.[4]

Notions of accent, regionalism, social class, education, and socioeconomic levels can lead to a murky and dangerous but highly necessary aspect of phonetics. It would be irresponsible for us to pretend there is only one French phonetic system. Here I will use French Canadian examples as my point of reference in the interest of citing a nonmetropolitan version of French with which I am familiar. These examples demonstrate tension in French vowels, which is not as constant in Québec as in the Hexagon. The topic of vowel tension introduces the problematic matter of standardization, since even in metropolitan France its use is not consistent, depending on the region, the level of speech, the level of the speaker's education, and the nature of the speaker's affect. In Quebecers' speech, vowel tension is often a marker. The evenly measured stress of multisyllabic words or of a series of syllables in a single breath group that characterizes metropolitan French speech often falls away in Québec because of the frequent use of weak vowels and stressed syllables, for example, *administration*:

/æ̱d mɪ̱ nɪ̱ 'stRɑ̱ tsjõ/[5]

In this example, in addition to the open-a, we notice the weakening of certain vowels in unstressed syllables, the weak-i or the /ɪ̱/ that is also typical of standard English. Note also the /æ/, which is typical of English but which does not exist, to my knowledge, in any dialect of metropolitan French. Also, in this example, I have marked the fourth syllable with a stress, the same syllable that would carry the stress in English. Another example provides further important samples of variants: *l'objectif du candidat*:

/lɔb jɛk 'tsɪf ʤy kã tsɪ 'da/

In addition to the weak /ɪ/, we observe the common occurrence of the alveolar /ʤ/ and /ts/ that characterize many Quebecers' articulation. I should also highlight the intrusive "t" that punctuates some French Canadian's speech, for example, "y'es venu jusqu'icitte?" (Tremblay, *Thérèse* 98):

/je vny ʤys kɪ tsɪt/[6]

Here, we also notice the characteristic /i/ or /j/ in the place of /il/, characteristic of French-speaking Canada as well as metropolitan France.

The alternate vowels /e/ and /ɛ/ and /a/ and /ɑ/ occur in Québec, but with different effects than in the Hexagon. Witness this example: *ces affaires-là*:

/se za feɪʀ lɑ/

Note the characteristic open *a* of *là* and the diphthong in *affaires*. Students should be taught the existence of this particular diphthong as fairly standard pronunciation for many speakers in Québec. Note, in contrast, the example of *atmosphère*:

/at mɔs feɪʀ/

This is standard pronunciation for many speakers in Québec, but would have a comic reference in the Hexagon: "Atmosphère? Atmosphère? Est-ce que j'ai une gueule d'atmosphère?" (Arletty from the film *Hôtel du Nord*). I use this comparison purposely to elicit cries of outrage from some readers who might see here a brutal case of bias, since they suppose I am linking a lower-class Parisian accent with a standard Québécois pronunciation. It is precisely this sort of prejudiced response we encourage in our students when we do not expose them to variants and explain differences of discourse. This follows from the earlier example of southern American speech I cited, where most American students are already culturally trained for a prejudice against certain accents. In teaching foreign language, we should point out the prejudice and then debunk it, especially when pronunciation that is conventionally denigrated in metropolitan France is close to the standard pronunciation in other regions, such as Québec.

GRAMMAR

Some intermediate-level grammar items may illustrate the importance of nuances that will become clear to students only at a higher level. An essential element of French grammar, and one that causes decided problems for English-speaking students, is agreement in gender and number. Identifying grammatical and syntactic relations by the use of agreement is important for clarifying meaning in spoken French and even more so for following poetic and prose syntax. Students traditionally have difficulty locating the subject of a verb, the antecedent of a pronoun, or the direct or indirect object of a verb. Mastery of agreement rules will help. Another important topic is the feminization of nouns for which there once existed only masculine forms—for example, *la ministre, la maire,* and *la professeur(e)*. This provides an excellent opportunity to discuss the state of feminism in French culture and its advent in "official" discourse. A comparison with standard Québécois usage reveals even more interesting cultural differences, as students become aware that feminine forms such as *une écrivaine* and *une auteure* have been widely accepted in French-speaking Canada for over a decade. Understanding the connotations of gay men's discourse is also dependent on agreement between feminine pronouns and adjectives, for example, in some of Michel Tremblay's writing, such as the following line from *Des nouvelles d'Édouard,* where one drag queen says to another, "On est toutes vieilles pis fatiguées, le samedi soir à deux heures du matin" (126). Similar feminine agreements and pronouns can be heard among gay men—not just drag queens—in informal situations in France and Québec and elsewhere.

Verb tense also raises questions for advanced students. Classes constantly struggle not only with the *passé composé–imparfait* distinction but also with the *passé simple.*[7] Passive recognition of the *passé simple* is essential, and students should be encouraged to learn the forms. They will soon need to recognize *elle fit* and not to confuse it with *elle fut*; further, they will need to distinguish between *dit-elle* as a present and as a *passé simple.* I have found that paragraphs from literary texts where students have to change the *passé simple* to *passé composé* provide an opportunity to discuss and point out the forms while emphasizing the usage of a punctual past.[8] The discussion of

Proust's "Longtemps je me suis couché de bonne heure" will be meaningful and enriching only if the groundwork of verbal nuances has been laid in an intermediate grammar course. Other verb tenses, whose structures logically follow the forms intermediate students are already learning—such as the *passé surcomposé*, the *imparfait du subjonctif*, and the *plus-que-parfait du subjonctif* and its analogue the *conditionnel passé seconde forme*—can be introduced early on for passive recognition. This passive knowledge can be resurrected later for the purpose of textual analysis.

TRANSLATION

The links between grammar and translation, and their importance for textual analysis, are obvious. The links with phonetics are less obvious but can also be exploited at the beginning level. Translation affords a forum for exhibiting the importance of language in analyzing not only literature but also French culture. Verb tenses are often the focus of translation exercises. And the problems of levels of discourse become a necessary and sometimes philosophical discussion before we can settle on an adequate translation. Tense and levels of discourse are issues that students will encounter in subsequent courses, and this repetition parallels other pedagogic repetitions; both tense and discourse level show up on test after test.

Idioms offer an endless source of material for the translation course. Apart from the benefit of their being amusing to students, they serve the very useful purpose of driving home the need to understand fully an expression in one language before attempting to translate it into another, and thus students learn to be more aware of structure and meaning. First are those idioms that are almost identical to English, such as, "Tout est bien qui finit bien." "Quand le chat dort, les souris dansent." "Rira mieux qui rira le dernier." "Il faut casser des œufs pour faire une omelette." Next come those with similar content but different metaphors or referents: "L'habit ne fait pas le moine." "Je me suis levé du mauvais pied ce matin." "Faire d'une pierre deux coups." Another type of idiom requires, on the contrary, a blind acceptance of usage, the essential nature of an idiomatic expression. One sphere of idiom that provides several good illustrations of such seemingly nonsensical expressions is numbers. In "to be at sixes and sevens" or "to be dressed to the nines," the numbers have no more semantic significance than in the following French expressions: "Il n'y a pas trente-six solutions!" "22! V'là les flics!"[9]

These are not to be confused, of course, with the idiomatic use of numbers where the *signifié* of the number is clear, for example, "La semaine des quatre jeudis."

Translation exercises can lead to fruitful cultural commentary. For example, translating the English imperative provides an excellent opportunity to discuss the French avoidance of direct commands. "Close the door, please" can be rendered as "Peux-tu fermer la porte?" or "Veux-tu fermer la porte?" or "Tu fermeras la porte, s'il te plaît" or even "Tu seras/serais gentil de fermer la porte, merci." All such renderings avoid the imperative. The conditional typically used politely in both English and French can sometimes sound condescending and thus requires careful consideration. Finally, the infinitive can be used for commands, as in the ubiquitous "Rayer la mention inutile"—a formula that can open up a cultural commentary on French bureaucracy.

Intonation also plays an important part in students' language learning. It's an element that is hard to convey in translation courses, which usually focus on written language. Dialogue in prose fiction and drama often presents particular comprehension and therefore translation problems. The nuances among "*I* could help you if you like" and "I could *help* you if you like" and "I could help *you* if you like" will test a student's ability to express the differences in French, where more than simple word stress is needed.

Finally, context in translation exercises is best presented by offering examples of why a particular and ostensibly correct translation for a term does not fit. For example, why doesn't *bouche* communicate appropriately in a translation of "Shut up!" or even "Shut your mouth!"? Students should learn "Tais-toi!" or "Ferme ta gueule!" or "Ferme la!"—all of which adequately communicate the sentiment without recourse to the expression favored by American high school students, "Fermez la bouche!" To take this example one step further, a translation exercise that helps students distinguish the dialogic context of word usage will help them understand the difference between "C'est une putain" and "Putain! ça fait mal!"

A further point in this category would be the distinctions among "to put," "to put on" ("to put on your shoes" or "to put someone on"), "to put up" ("to put something up on the shelf" or "to put someone up for the night"), and "to put up with," all of which will require different verbs in French. For the English speaker this is a more difficult obstacle than the analogous problem of translating the various uses of *faire* or *mettre*. Consider: "Quel temps fait-il?"; "Elle m'a fait à manger"; "Elle m'a fait comprendre que non!" Then consider: "Qu'est-ce que tu vas mettre pour sortir ce soir?"; "Combien pouvez-vous mettre dans cette affaire?"; "Dans sa lettre, il met que tout va bien."

EXPLOITING ENGLISH

The axiomatic premise of my exposé is that students need to be sensitized to language, the function of language, and the versatility of language throughout the curriculum. Many subtle elements of textual analysis and cultural awareness can be cultivated at the early levels of their training. When students need to understand French rhyme schemes and the differences among "rimes riches, suffisantes et pauvres," "rimes embrassées, croisées et plates," and "rimes féminines et masculines," it's better that they already know how to determine whether words rhyme or not. One way to point out important details, which might otherwise go misunderstood or underappreciated because students memorize them thoughtlessly, is to provide analogous examples in English.[10] Some pedagogues proscribe this practice as interfering with natural language learning. Although I also eschew using English in straightforward language learning at the elementary level, intermediate courses move into the self-reflective and metalinguistic area of language learning. Intermediate students need to be able to discuss why a verb tense functions, just as they need to show how it functions. A basic problem with students' inability to move smoothly into textual analysis is often the lack of discursive vocabulary or linguistic terminology necessary for discussing language functions, a basic element of explication de texte.

In phonetics, for example, once English speakers can articulate the importance of and distinguish between the variants /d/ and /t/ to indicate the past tense of regular English verbs or the variants /s/ and /z/ to indicate the plural, they are well on their way to understanding the significance of discriminate phonemes. Similarly, if they can recognize the alternates /waʃ/ and /wɔɹʃ/ for *wash* and /s/ and /z/ for *greasy*, they are in a position to appreciate and accept variations of standard French.

In grammar, once students can see the difference between "I saw" and "I seen" and can appreciate the function of these two statements as an indicator of education and social class, they are better equipped to recognize verbal cues in spoken and written French: "je vas" has its place, which needs to be understood. Another problem that comes up in students' writing in English, as well as in foreigners' use of English, is the incorrect use of pronouns, especially pronoun agreement. Demonstrating this error in English can underscore the importance of pronouns and agreement in French.[11]

Another element of English that is natural for native speakers but poses a problem for beginning students of English as a foreign language is the use of tags, such as, "They can do it, *can't they*?" Although it is sometimes difficult for English speakers to understand why this presents such a problem for foreigners, pointing it out to our students can be a way of encouraging them to think about apparently simple linguistic functions. This exercise prepares students for the problems such ostensibly simple functions might pose for translation. It also prepares them to accept without logical explanation structures that seem incomprehensible to them in the foreign language. From this realization, they will learn not only tolerance for foreigners speaking English but also the importance of paying attention to detail and to their own use of pronouns, pronoun placement, and past tenses, to name just a few areas of common errors in spoken French. At the same time that students begin to realize the automatic nature of tags in English, they should be learning not to succumb to an automatic "n'est-ce pas" at the end of every declarative statement in French. And let us not forget the ever-popular problem of verb tenses with *depuis*, and inversely the English translations for *depuis*—the famous "for, since, and ago" that French students of English chant to the bewilderment of English speakers. These expressions occur so frequently in spoken language that they need to become automatic, and these habits are best instilled in the early stages of language learning.

None of what I have presented here comes as a surprise. All French teachers are used to the need for various techniques and strategies for helping students to negotiate the hurdles of language learning and to make the transition from intermediate to advanced levels. But how long did it take us to articulate and develop these strategies? How many students did we helplessly watch struggling before we remembered our own linguistic anguish? Wouldn't it be a good idea to share these tricks with student teachers or with teaching assistants in graduate school? These tricks are another rarely articulated aspect of the profession.

We all encounter these and other problems teaching language. Since our main goal is to teach our students how to read, the challenges are pertinent to teachers of all levels of French. There are, however, particular problems for students of medieval and Renaissance literature that differ from those of classical literature or literature of the Enlightenment. But nineteenth- and twentieth-century literature also carries cultural and sociological meanings closely linked with history, geography, politics, society, and so on, requiring particular attention. The *parler* of Annie Ernaux is no more similar to that of George Sand than Balzac's is to Rousseau's. Certain verb tenses Gustave Flaubert used are not to be found in Hervé Guibert. The use of *être* for the *passé composé* of some verbs in the work of Jean Echenoz will not always mirror Victor Hugo's usage. The issues I raise here are relevant for teachers of all periods, indeed for teachers of all languages.

The most important message I'd like to communicate is that we need to be aware of our students' struggles and of their ability, with our help, to overcome them. Our job as pedagogues is to prepare students to solve a variety of problems but not to overwhelm students with too much information all at once. If we can initially provide essentials in a subliminal way and then access them again later, students will have a better chance of assimilating and applying them as well as progressing to advanced stages. My pedagogical goal is to illustrate the interactive nature of the skills students learn throughout the curriculum. Just as we hope to bring to light the value of reassembling a text after having examined its constitutive parts in the exercise of explication de texte, so should we hope to convince students that harvesting techniques and information throughout the curriculum produces a well-proportioned cornucopia. In this cornucopia, some of the crop seems to hide in the slender part, whereas, in actual fact, it supports and completes the rest of the yield. And thus we can "cultiver notre jardin pédagogique."

NOTES

1. Students often take an introduction to textual analysis concurrently with intermediate language courses such as phonetics. This combination provides an especially propitious opportunity for such details to be reinforced.
2. There is no political connotation to the term *nation* here, since I use it to encompass all of francophonie in addition to all the various accents of the Hexagon.
3. Some may remember this as a Marie-Chantal-style affectation.
4. Since I am not familiar enough with it to make pertinent remarks, I do not discuss the common pronunciation of many sub-Saharan Africans, who use /w/ for the "r."
5. In my examples I underline the elements that are not traditionally considered characteristic of standard, metropolitan French.
6. I take this citation from Michel Tremblay's *Thérèse et Pierrette à l'école des Saints-Anges*.
7. I get no sympathy from my colleagues in Spanish and especially in Italian, whose students must learn half again as many verbs tenses as do mine, and at an earlier stage.
8. This exercise naturally disregards the *passé composé–passé simple* distinction. That

distinction must be left to more advanced grammar or stylistic, indeed perhaps graduate, courses.

9. There is probably a cultural etymology for the use of these specific numbers. I leave the job of finding the origins to lexicographers, since my point here is the apparent nonsensical *signifiant* of the idiom and its challenge to the translator.
10. In this section, as elsewhere, I presume the native tongue of the student to be English, which is obviously not universal. But given the vast majority of English speakers in our classrooms and because students must function in English elsewhere in the university, I hope my assumption will be seen as productive.
11. The recent trend in spoken and written English of using a plural pronoun to refer to a singular antecedent to avoid the use of a universal masculine presents a complex problem that goes beyond the scope of my essay. However, an appreciation for the ambiguous use of "une personne" and a feminine pronoun as referent can be introduced at this point.

Reading *dans Tous les Sens*: Thoughts on Teaching *Un coup de dés*

Gayle A. Levy

For some bewildering, partly sadistic, partly masochistic reason, I take great pleasure in reading Stéphane Mallarmé's masterpiece *Un coup de dés jamais n'abolira le hasard* with my students. Over the past six years, I have presented this poem in five different courses—two were introductions to French literature and the other three were advanced seminars. The students all responded in the same way when confronted by this poem for the first time: utter disbelief. "How are we supposed to read this?" "What does this mean?" "Is this poetry?" ring out from the classroom. I realized that these questions grew out of the context in which the students were asked to read this poem—nineteenth-century poetry or other literature—and not out of their own experiences of contemporary popular and high culture. They were, for once, perhaps unfortunately for their mastery of the poem, responding like nineteenth-century readers, not like late twentieth-century viewers. For most of my literature classes, I do not want my students to read anachronistically; I teach them to be sensitive to historical context and intertextuality. However, Mallarmé's goals—to create a radically new book, to make the object and the poet disappear completely, to bring the materiality of poetry and space into the foreground—are all objectives that our students understand, although certainly understand with a different vocabulary. In this essay, I explain how I draw on skills students already possess to encourage their inherent understanding of *Un coup de dés*, a text usually deemed difficult.

READING THE HISTORY

To teach *Un coup de dés,* one needs to recall some of the historical and genetic details concerning this poem. Mallarmé envisioned his greatest work, *L'œuvre,* as early as 1866 and wrote about it in a letter to Auguste Villiers de l'Isle-Adam, in which he stated that he finally understood "la corrélation intime de la Poésie avec l'Univers" and that he intended to link that with "la sortir du Rêve et du Hasard" (Davies 23).[1] In 1881, in a letter to Paul Verlaine, Mallarmé expanded his ideas and brought them closer into line with the work that would ultimately become *Un coup de dés*: "un livre qui soit un livre, architectural et prémédité, et non un recueil des inspirations de hasard. . . . J'irai plus loin, je dirai : le Livre, persuadé qu'au fond il n'y en a qu'un . . ." (Davies 23). Finally, in 1897, Mallarmé finished *Un coup de dés,* which appeared in the review *Cosmopolis* along with a preface written by him. Paul Valéry's powerful response to the text, which he saw at Mallarmé's home before its publication, is worth rereading: "Il me sembla de voir la figure d'une pensée, pour la première fois placée dans notre espace. . . . Ici, véritablement, l'étendue parlait, songeait, enfantait des formes temporelles . . ." (Mallarmé, *Œuvres* 1582). The *Cosmopolis* version of the poem was the only one published by Mallarmé during his lifetime. At the end of his life, he was preparing an edition that was to be illustrated by Odilon Redon. Sadly, it was never completed, and we can only imagine how beautiful that work would have been. Instead, *Un coup de dés* was published separately in 1914, sixteen years after the poet's death.

It is difficult to discuss *Un coup de dés* without recourse to "Igitur," its intertext and genetic forefather. As I have shown in *Refiguring the Muse,* the subject of the poem, the character Igitur, represents the poet as he tries to resolve his creative sterility, the writer's block, or "page blanche," that haunted Mallarmé periodically through his life. "Igitur" is difficult to understand, but not solely because of the conscious encryption that is Mallarmé's stylistic practice. Rather, "Igitur" was never meant to be published. According to Edmond Bonniot, Mallarmé's son-in-law and posthumous editor, the poet had marked the pages on which the text was written as "déchet," indicating that he intended to bury it along with many other notes after he had completed his *Œuvre* (Mallarmé, *Œuvres* 423). This never happened, and in 1925 Bonniot published a rough draft of this text.

In the story, Igitur, the last representative of his race or family, must throw the dice at midnight to fulfill an ancient prediction. According to that prediction, Igitur must complete this act to negate chance and thus ensure the memory of his family; in symbolic terms, we can see this as the poet's attempt to ensure the memory of his poetry. Igitur knows that negating chance is necessary but insane, an impossibility; how could one possibly negate chance by rolling the dice—an act that exemplifies chance, that brings chance into existence each time the gesture is repeated. It is a "Folie utile," and Igitur finally realizes that this act is useless: "car il y a et n'y a pas de hasard" (Mallarmé, *Œuvres* 442). The tale ends ironically with Igitur, the anachronism, completely alone, lying atop his ancestors' ashes after having consumed the last drop of nothingness. Although the formal aspects of "Igitur" have nothing in common with *Un coup de dés*, the two poems share several key themes—most obviously, the notion of a roll of the dice linked to chance and the principal character as representative of the poet.

READING *DANS TOUS LES SENS*

To read words on the page, one must first be able to see. The page, the words, and the script are the most elementary ingredients of reading. However, after a lifetime of reading, we become unaware of these elements. Letters and text surround us, permeate our lives, give order and meaning to most of our actions. However, because the letters that encircle us generally signify something other than their specific signifiers, because they are always subjugated to the primacy of their meaning, we forget to see them. We constantly read them and no longer just look at them. Although graphic arts sometimes make use of the aesthetic qualities of letters, their effect often works on an unconscious level, and we generally try to understand the meaning of the words at the expense of truly seeing their shapes.

Ironically, given that literature classes are concerned primarily with reading, students first must cease reading when confronted with *Un coup de dés*. They need to look at the text, to see its spaces, its fonts, the shapes that the words and sentences constitute on the page. The students should let their eyes run across the page in order to attend to the links between type fonts and sizes, to see the tectonic structures created by the different lengths and spaces of the lines, and to let the metonymic and structural similarities between the words play out. Just as it helps to first read poems written in a conventional way out loud, so it helps to first see Mallarmé's poem as a visual object. Although the forms that the words and sentences of *Un coup de dés* take are not immediately recognizable, I have found that providing my students with examples of Guillaume Apollinaire's calligrams helps them envision types of poems beyond fixed forms and free verse. "Il pleut" or a simpler calligram, such as "Un cigare" from "Paysage," works well (64, 27). Through the use of simple pictopoems, students practice seeing the poem before reading it.

Space is the most important component of *Un Coup de dés*. It constitutes most of the poem and is the first poetic element we see. But space on the page is also easily ignored. We are so accustomed to seeing white space surrounding poems that even when space is far more than a simple frame, we overlook it. In *The Dynamics of Space: Mallarmé's* Un Coup de dés jamais n'abolira le hasard, Virginia A. La Charité highlights the blank areas in the poem. She writes, "To come to grips with Mallarmé as poet and *Un Coup de dés* as his maximum poetic sign is to understand space as poetic substance" (37). Space is as integral to *Un coup de dés* as form or rhyme scheme is to a Shakespearean sonnet. Focusing on space allows La Charité to bring to light the printing history of *Un coup de dés* and to remind us that few teachers have actually seen what Mallarmé intended to show his readers. Although Mallarmé specialists generally use the out-of-print 1914 Nouvelle Revue Française edition when discussing *Un coup de dés,* teachers often use the Gallimard editions of the poem.[2] In contrast to the octavo Pléiade edition, Mallarmé originally planned the poem as a folio, and the 1914 edition re-creates this format; each single page measures an expansive nine by thirteen inches and is awash in the open space Mallarmé envisioned. The words seem to float across the page and swim and swirl much more actively than the words on the cramped leaves of the Pléiade edition. In her analysis of the page proofs, La Charité argues that since Mallarmé's corrections concerning the placement of the words outnumber those concerning fonts or word choice, the spacial disposition of the words is more important than the different font sizes: "Placement on the page is disciplined, . . . ordered assembly is a skillful construction. . . . *Un Coup de dés* has such an imposed, immutable order which cannot be changed, anymore than a spectator can change the order of the stars in the sky" (43). Her conclusion is ultimately true, for Mallarmé's poetry, as for all poetry; however, I have found it pedagogically useful to encourage students to forget the spatial word order for a time and to have them pay attention to the fonts, which provide an organizing principle for the poem.

READING IN THE CLASSROOM

Students come to class in a panic after reading *Un coup de dés* at home. I show them the calligrams by Apollinaire, and then we look at Mallarmé's poem. I draw their attention to the patterns that the words on the page create. What do they look like? No page of *Un coup de dés* is as figuratively representational as the calligrams, but each page does evoke images in students' minds. In a controlled Rorschachian exercise, I encourage students to let their minds wander, to associate the shapes they see with ideas or feelings but within certain subject areas—the shipwreck and the dice. Students see the movement of the tumbling dice (akin to early chronophotography or Marcel Duchamp's multilayered *Nu descendant un escalier* from 1912), waves, coral, peaks and valleys, the sinking ship, boulders on the ocean floor (this was one of my favorite comments concerning the page that shows nothing but "N'ABOLIRA" low in the left corner [465], as though the boulder will not abolish the ship). The page that begins "LE MAÎTRE" (462) looks like a spout of water, not unlike Apollinaire's "le jet d'eau" (Apollinaire 74) while the self-referential "*plume solitaire éperdue*" (468) resembles a bit of foam floating on the ocean surface.

Next we move onto the sense of the poem. The space and word order of *Un coup de dés* are critical, but Mallarmé insists that we also read the poem through the syntax of font, not of words. After all, the title of the poem, *Un coup de dés jamais n'abolira le hasard,* is constituted through typeface, not through linear placement on one page. To teach *Un coup de dés,* we have to coax the students out of the habit of reading left to right, but this way of reading cannot be disregarded. To understand the poem, students must use different modes of reading: from left to right, in small bunches of words, through text associated by font, across the break between pages. Throughout, of course, they must continue to see. Several exercises can help them focus on these various ways of reading. To encourage reading by font, I divide the class into three groups and give them each two different typefaces that they track throughout the text. I ask them to read the words out loud in linear fashion, essentially translating the difficult font syntax into our more customary word syntax. La Charité notes that there are seven type sizes and three typefaces (48). However, for the uses of this exercise, I exclude the title font and collapse a couple of the harder to distinguish fonts into one category. This leaves six fonts—out of which two compose most of the poem (see app.). After the students read their fonts, they can uncover the specific images and types of words that Mallarmé uses. For example, they should notice that there is a great variety of extremely active verbs in the poem; "étaler," "planer," "enfouir," "surgir," "envahir," "hurler," "bifurquer," "sursauter" are only a few, and they all reflect in turn the vigorous movement of the words up and down the page.

A second exercise I use to encourage the students to break the habit of reading left to right involves giving each group a certain number of pages from which they must construct a rational story by reading, literally, "dans tous les sens." I explicitly tell them that they do not have to honor the word order—which is disordered in Mallarméan fashion. For example, after reading the four pages beginning with "LE MAÎTRE" (462–65), the students might tell a story of a captain who slowly drowns in the water after his ship has already gone down in the storm. We see him "surgit" and then "jeter dans la tempête"; he hesitates and then "la partie[,] au nom des flots[,] envahit le chef"; his beard floats in the water. The narration continues: with the death of the captain vanishes an ancestral secret (shades of "Igitur"). The italicized pages (466–72), which begin with the parenthetical "*COMME SI,*" might transcribe the delirious inner thoughts of the captain, thoughts that touch on the profound: life, "*le mystère,*" poetry, "*plume solitaire,*" infinity, and the profane: the velvet cap and his "*petite raison virile.*"

Finally, to understand this text, students must free-associate, which reading Mallarmé demands of us all. "[*A*]*igrette*" is a heron or a feather crest (*Œuvres* 470), which in Mallarmé's ideolect is the plume or pen. This instrument of poetry also represents the ultimate impossibility of creation—a feather is so light it almost does not exist—and is reminiscent of the poetic sterility that cannot be broken. The quintet of capitalized, simple past verbs, "EXISTÂT-IL," "COMMENÇÂT-IL," "CESSÂT-IL," "SE CHIFFRÂT-IL," and "ILLUMINÂT-IL" (473), highlight the circumflex. When associated with the preceding clause, "*C'ÉTAIT LE NOMBRE*" (472–73), which spans two pages, we remember that the circumflex marks a missing element; the "s" used to appear in the words but has now disappeared, just as the number existed but no longer does. The number was, yet no longer is, just like the "s," just like the captain-master-poet. But these words also highlight the importance of verse, the hermetic and spiritual qualities of the master's poetry. He existed; was born; died; disguised himself (from "chiffrer," meaning to *code* or *cipher*); and, finally, he was illuminated. The poet and his poetry are one. These exercises facilitate a polyphonic mode of reading—where the students integrate seeing and reading in every direction. To begin to access *Un coup de dés,* they must use their associative, more irrational skills of perception and comprehension combined with the synthetic, more logical and syntactical clues that Mallarmé hides throughout the text and his oeuvre.

But what about the roll of the dice, the chance this act represents, which stands at the core of the text? Not only does the tumbling movement of the words across the page evoke the dice rolling along the game table, but the title is not about a shipwreck; rather, it refers to the dice themselves. *Un coup de dés jamais n'abolira le hasard* is a tautology. Etymologically, the word "hasard" derives from the name of an archaic Syrian game of dice, from the Arabic *az-zahr,* meaning "one die." Thus Mallarmé's etymological play turns his title into a pleonasm—"le hasard jamais n'abolira le hasard"—which leads us to understand the final phrase of the poem, "Toute Pensée émet un Coup de Dés," as "all thought radiates chance." By erecting chance—the core of the nineteenth-century prince of poets' masterpiece—as the all-important poetic element, Mallarmé calls into question the whole idea of poetic genius. The Romantic idea of the genius who creates universes, whose genius is a gift from God and who is a spiritual emissary (e.g., Lamartine), is at last laid to rest by Mallarmé. In the work of Balzac, Baudelaire, and Zola, this idea was slowly being eroded through those writers' association of genius with insanity and addiction.[3] Finally, with the publication of *Un coup de dés* in 1897, Mallarmé showed that genius is nothing but chance, a roll of the dice, "le hasard." Although human beings have endeavored to gain immortality through myriad ways, whether they explore new lands and seas, attempt to master nature, or write texts intended to last through eternity, they are destined to fail. Nothing will live on but chance. But perhaps the only way to understand *Un coup de dés* is to let chance play itself out, allow the students' interpretations to run wild, permit an orchestration of readings that come together to create a new totality each time we teach this text.[4]

Students reading *Un coup de dés* experience the cooperative act that takes place between the poet and the reader; they realize the importance of the reader's role at the heart of the poetic act, a realization that can lead to a model students can follow every time they read poetry. Within the context of nineteenth-century French art and literature, *Un coup de dés* furnishes a lesson in how to read symbolist and decadent texts and can serve as an entryway into modernism. Modernist writers and artists have taught us that the reader's role in the work of art is crucial, that our analytical response and even our unconscious understanding are key to the success or failure of the creator's work of art. *Un coup de dés* requires that we create a polyphonic mode of reading, that we read "dans tous les sens" as a powerful mise-en-scène of the importance of the creator and the viewer-reader's cooperation in understanding the modernist text.

Reading Mallarmé in this way paves the way for understanding other modernist texts deemed difficult. I tell students that to best enjoy Proust, one must read as though watching a dream. The author of *A la recherche du temps perdu* transforms the customary linear, textual associations between scenes into the metonymic and metaphoric links that occur so often in our daydreams. Other modernist masters, Céline, Joyce, even Eliot, demand a similar kind of flexible, playful, open reading. Mallarmé's work stands as the perfect portal between the nineteenth and twentieth centuries. His earlier poems and sonnets, although always imbued with his trademark hermeticism, at times evoke Baudelaire, while his later work, *Un coup de dés* in particular, thrusts us firmly into the graphism and self-referentiality of twentieth-century modernism and postmodernism.

APPENDIX

The following texts consist of the different type sizes and fonts grouped together by linear word order. I include em dashes to signal new pages, and treat both the recto and verso sides as one page, ignoring the break between facing pages.

Group 1: QUAND BIEN MÊME LANCÉ DANS DES CIRCONSTANCES ÉTERNELLES DU FOND D'UN NAUFRAGE—SOIT—LE MAÎTRE—EXISTÂT-IL COMMENÇÂT-IL ET CESSÂT-IL SE CHIFFRÂT-IL ILLUMINÂT-IL—RIEN—N'AURA EU LIEU QUE LE LIEU—EXCEPTÉ PEUT-ÊTRE UNE CONSTELLATION

Group 2: que l'Abîme blanchi étale furieux sous une inclinaison plane désespérément d'aile la sienne par avance retombée d'un mal à dresser le vol et couvrant les jaillissements coupant au ras les bonds très à l'intérieur résume l'ombre enfouie dans la profondeur par cette voile alternative jusqu'adapter à l'envergure sa béante profondeur en tant que la coque d'un bâtiment penché de l'un ou l'autre bord—hors d'anciens calculs où la manœuvre avec l'âge oubliée surgi inférant jadis il empoignait la barre de cette conflagration à ses pieds de l'horizon unanime que se prépare s'agite et mêle au poing qui l'étreindrait comme on ménace un destin et les vents l'unique Nombre qui ne peut pas être un autre Esprit pour le jeter dans la tempête en reployer la division et passe fier hésite cadavre par le bras écarté du secret qu'il détient plutôt que de jouer en maniaque chenu la partie au nom des flots un envahit le chef coule en barbe soumise naufrage cela direct de l'homme sans nef n'importe où vaine—ancestralement à n'ouvrir pas la main crispée par-delà l'inutile tête legs en la disparition à quelqu'un ambigu l'ultérieur démon immémorial ayant de contrées nulles induit le vieillard vers cette conjonction suprême avec la probabilité celui son ombre puérile caressée et polie et rendue et lavée assouplie par la vague et soustraite aux durs os perdus entre les ais né d'un ébat la mer par l'aïeul tentant ou l'aïeul contre la mer une chance oiseuse Fiançailles dont le voile d'illusion rejailli leur hantise ainsi que le fantôme d'un geste chancellera s'affolera folie—de la mémorable crise ou se fût l'événement accompli en vue de tout résultat nul humain une élévation ordinaire verse l'absence inférieur clapotis quelconque comme pour disperser l'acte vide abruptement qui sinon par son mensonge eût fondé la perdition dans ces parages du vague en quoi toute réalité se dissout—à l'altitude aussi loin qu'un endroit fusionne avec au-delà hors l'intérêt quant à lui signalé en général selon telle obliquité par telle déclivité de feux vers ce doit être le Septentrion aussi Nord froide d'oubli et de désuétude pas tant qu'elle n'énumère sur quelque surface vacante et supérieure le heurt successif sidéralement d'un compte total en formation veillant doutant roulant brillant et méditant avant de s'arrêter à quelque point dernier qui le sacre Toute Pensée émet un Coup de Dés

Group 3: *COMME SI COMME SI—SI—C'ÉTAIT LE NOMBRE CE SERAIT*

Group 4: *Une insinuation simple au silence enroulée avec ironie ou le mystère précipité hurlé dans quelque proche tourbillon d'hilarité et d'horreur voltige autour du gouffre sans le joncher ni fuir et en berce le vierge indice—plume solitaire éperdue sauf que la rencontre ou l'effleure une toque de minuit et immobilise au velours chiffonné par un esclaffement sombre cette blancheur rigide dérisoire en opposition au ciel trop pour ne pas marquer exigüment quiconque prince amer de l'écueil s'en coiffe comme de l'héroïque irrésistible mais contenu par sa petite raison virile en foudre—soucieux expiatoire et pubère muet rire que La lucide et seigneuriale aigrette de vertige au front invisible scintille puis ombrage une stature mignonne ténébreuse debout en sa torsion de sirène le temps de souffleter par d'impatientes squalmes ultimes bifurquées un roc faux manoir tout de suite évaporé en brumes qui imposa une borne à l'infini—Choit la plume rythmique suspens du sinistre s'ensevelir aux écumes originelles naguères d'où sursauta son délire jusqu'à une cime flétrie par la neutralité identique du gouffre*

Group 5: *issu stellaire pire non davantage ni moins indifféremment mais autant*

Group 6: autrement qu'hallucination éparse d'agonie sourdant que nié et clos quand apparu enfin par quelque profusion répandue en rareté évidence de la somme pour peu qu'une

NOTES

1. The first chapter of Gardner Davies's *Vers une explication rationnelle du* Coup de dés provides a thorough history of the generation and creation of the poem. Although it is perhaps too detailed for the teacher preparing a lecture on *Un coup de dés*, it is nonetheless a fascinating study.
2. La Charité mentions one other folio reproduction of the poem, edited by Mitsou Ronat (1980), which is also out of print.
3. See especially Frenhofer in Balzac's *Le chef-d'œuvre inconnu*, Baudelaire's prose poem "Enivrez-vous," and Claude Lantier in *L'œuvre* by Zola.
4. Another entry into this complex poem can be offered by music. Scholars such as Kate van Orden have linked *Un coup de dés* to "pure" music (166). The composers, Pierre Boulez and John Cage were highly influenced by Mallarmé's work on chance, and certain of their pieces might be used as a segue into a classroom presentation of the poem. See van Orden for the specific musical pieces one could use.

Laurence M. Porter,
Anita Alkhas,
and
Larry Kuiper

Fostering Creativity in Literary Study

Ideally, students will bear their education away when they graduate, not discard it along with their old term papers and bluebooks. If education flows from personal discovery and self-expression, it can become part of students. We empower their creativity when we inspire them with faith in their originality. Authorities—teachers, textbooks, critics—stifle their imagination. Can we maintain control of our class yet still set students free? We must first meet them on a ground of common experience—not what we teachers know, but what students and teachers both have lived.

How can we foster creativity in our classes? Providing broader contexts gives students' imaginations greater scope, but students have little time for extra work. Even when we are limited to teaching the text itself, however, inspiration can spring from the interaction of familiarity with the text, time to reflect on it, and defamiliarization tactics that free students from the routine ways they have been taught to read. Rereading is essential. A second reading may involve only five to ten percent of a text, but rereading makes each detail interact in the student's mind with all the details he or she encountered in the first reading. Potential associations of ideas increase exponentially.

To familiarize students with the assigned texts as early as possible in the term, front-load the syllabus. For example, if students have Racine's *Phèdre* in mind for six weeks instead of three, they double their chances of finding affinities and contrasts between the play and their readings in other courses, current events, and the personal and vicarious experiences of everyday life. Thus a front-loaded schedule increases a teacher's chances to show instead of tell the "relevance" of literature and, above all, to elicit observations from students.

Besides providing the broader view of intra- and intertextual links, a second reading offers a deeper view that recognizes implications, including the comic and ironic effects that mark sophisticated literary, linguistic, and cultural communication. Finally, situating each part of a work within the whole will allow students to develop critical judgment by contrasting their sets of associations with those selected by various theories. For some critics, a cigar is just a cigar; for others, a phallic symbol; for still others, a mark of self-absorption, a farcical element, or an environmental pollutant. Critics' theoretical hubris often makes them overlook how meager their contextualizations are compared with those created by authors, whose breadth of context is one reason we enjoy reading literature more than literary criticism. In Gustave Flaubert's *Madame Bovary*, for example, the act of smoking first characterizes Bovary père's chronic depression; then, Charles's inexperience and ineptitude; next, Rodolphe's indifference to Emma as a person; and, finally, Emma's growing insensitivity to social opinion.

The typical course syllabus militates against imaginative flexibility by proposing elaborate, rule-governed rituals. But teachers can exploit this difficulty by playfully foregrounding it for the students. To be creative, one must know the rules and approach them as enticing challenges rather than as daunting barriers to originality. Breaking a rule through ignorance is one thing; breaking it for effect, quite another. Most artists and writers work primarily within the constraints of their medium, only occasionally bending or flouting rules, reserving such free play for moments when it can achieve maximum effect.

To succeed in literature classes, a student must master two different yet not unrelated sets of rules: the conventions of literary and critical texts, which we all presumably study explicitly, and the conventions of a particular literature class, that is to say, the course requirements, which we misguidedly tend to gloss over. After all, from our course title, description, and syllabus, it is clear that students will be required to read, think, discuss, and write. To motivate them to comply, we choose works we find exciting and develop writing assignments that appeal to and stimulate students. In addition, we may rely on various pedagogical techniques such as consistent modeling, process-approach writing, or small-group work. But we often shy away from addressing the immediate, practical concerns of students—how do they get the course work done?—fearing that by focusing on requirements, we will only increase the intimidation they may already feel with regard to literature and the course topic. Why not, instead, begin our courses with an explicit discussion of schoolwork, to relate what is required of a student to what is required of anyone who creates? Yes, there are requirements and rules for this course as there are for all endeavors, we can explain, but rules are productive if you approach them creatively.

By giving rules playful twists, such as those suggested below, we acknowledge the conventionality required by academic endeavors and help students develop their insights into creativity, which they can then apply to their study of literary works.

Rule 1: Students must read the required texts.

Read this work in a place where you have never read anything before. Bring a description of the place and your reason for choosing it to the next class meeting.

Reread this text in five different locations. Bring a list of where and when you read it.

Complete this reading assignment in its entirety before class begins, but procrastinate as much as possible before you begin reading it. Be prepared to discuss how you accomplished this.

Reserve several times in your schedule to read this text, but read it only if you feel inclined to read it. Do not miss class. If you have not read it before class, you may read it in the hallway while the class meets; we will set aside time at the end of class for you to share your impressions of it.

Rule 2: Students must think about and discuss the required readings.

Insert comments or questions into the text on self-stick notes. Choose five of these comments or questions and transfer them to a separate sheet of paper. (Choose five that you feel are either closely or not at all related to one another.) You will use them as the basis for discussion next class period (the instructor will not speak during this discussion; students will ensure that everyone else speaks and that the discussion continues until the end of class).

Bring in an object you have found in your daily life that relates to one of the topics we have studied and explain how it relates. (Possibilities include but are not limited to a handmade or manufactured object, a photo, a song, part of a conversation you overheard, an advertisement.)

Do not hand in the drafts of your writing assignments on class days. They are due on nonclass days so that you can spend class time discussing them instead of printing them out at the last moment.

Rule 3: Students must write about the required readings.

Keep a reading log in which you reflect on the texts we have read. Submit entries (of any length) by e-mail or on paper as you write them, for a total of at least ten entries, half of them to be submitted before midterm. Do not write two entries in a row on the same work.[1]

The final version of this paper should be exactly five hundred words.

No written assignments will be accepted late unless you hand in another assignment early by the same amount of time that the other assignment was late.

Write in class for a set amount of time and on a topic to be determined. At home, double the amount that you have written by expanding your statement at any point, but without deleting or editing what you have already written in class. Use a word processor and two fonts to distinguish your original text from your additions.[2]

But simply stating a goal and giving students the assignments that demonstrate their ability to approach it omits important preliminary steps. The assignments calling for creative interpretation include the last steps in a process. Before reaching the final product, we must ask which preconceptions (about art, literature, creativity, and so forth) our students have. How do they view literature? How do they perceive the act of reading? How much reading have they done? Why do they read (or not read)? Answers vary from student to student, course to course. A questionnaire passed out on the first day may help answer some of these questions. For other questions, the instructor can anticipate certain responses and plan lessons accordingly. The ideal course syllabus conforms not to the rhythm of the teacher's exposition but to the rhythms of the students' development.

The initial tasks of introductory courses in literature should focus on personal development: empowering students, sensitizing them, and bridging the gaps between their experience and the chosen imaginary worlds of art. An introductory literature course should help students become confident that, although they are inexperienced, they still can be creative and original—that they can be players. On the first day of class, a definition exercise can dramatically reveal to students the potential for originality that they already possess. Propose consideration of a key concept such as love, death, honor, disgrace, comedy, tragedy, hope, or despair. Ask the class members to take a few minutes to think of a definition that they would be willing to share. Then have several students share theirs. Each definition will be different: if two are alike, the teacher can ask the students who proposed them to define a second key term within their definitions. At this moment, act as a cheerleader, praise the students for having been original, independent thinkers, telling them that they will be refining this ability for the remainder of the course.

After the definition exercise and before actual reading of the texts, the instructor can use the title of the first assigned reading for a free-association exercise that leads to hypothesizing, the essence of active reading. The greatest hindrance to a literary education is the widespread preconception that reading (or watching movies, viewing paintings, etc.) is passive, that the reader need only receive and enjoy. Remedial activities can show students the active role that readers play. For example, before they read Jean Anouilh's play *Le bal des voleurs*, students can work in groups to brainstorm anything they associate with the word *bal* and then with *voleur*. Next they can compare their group's two lists with others. Then they may examine the words appearing on both their *bal* and *voleur* lists (some possibilities: mask, deception, riches, disguise, being light-footed) and speculate on character relationships in a play with such a title. They can discuss whether the play might be a comedy or tragedy and what tragic or comic elements they are likely to find. Thus students will have compiled an inventory of hypotheses about the play's content after having read only its title. The instructor can point out how actively the students have read just two title words and how such hypothesizing is a constant activity for any reader. Further prereading activities can reinforce the notion that reading is active and participatory. For instance, students can formulate hypotheses from the play's character list or scene descriptions before they have read one line of dialogue.

Students should monitor their hypothesizing during reading. At the end of a scene, chapter, or verse, students may be asked to write down which of their hypotheses seem correct and which ones need modifying. The events they read about will either fit or contradict their own life experiences and thus their hypotheses.[3] Similarly, students will encounter forms in texts that are either familiar or new to them based on their experiences. Students may be surprised, delighted, or disturbed by certain words, phrases, structures, or concepts and how the author links them to events described. They should monitor and log these reactions as well. Journal writing creates a record to which students can refer later when writing a more thorough critical account. Without this record, a student's critical view may be pure hindsight and students may, therefore, see the text as static while ignoring its catalytic dynamism during reading. Too often in literature courses, the act of reading becomes artificially separated from writing. The unfortunate consequence is that attention is diverted from the processes of engaged reading that are the essence of criticism.

The moment when the first text in a course has been completely read provides a timely opportunity to introduce the linguistic concept of the marked choice. It is well to begin by reminding students that a literary work is not expressed but made: every aspect of it—settings, situations, and outcomes, as well as words and figures of speech—reflects the author's choices. Not only style in the ordinary sense of a characteristic way of writing but all the elements of a text are traces or residues left by the author's past choices. When student-readers expect linguistic or other textual characteristics to appear, students can identify them as unmarked or default choices made by the author. Marked choices, however, may entail startling extremes. To take an example from everyday life, if you wish to ask information of a stranger on the street, you initially have two goals: to attract his or her attention and to apologize for your intrusion. An unmarked choice for attracting attention might be to say "Excuse me." To say "Hey, you!" instead also attracts attention but fails to apologize. This choice is marked by rudeness. But if you say "I beg your pardon," your choice is marked by excessive politeness. Such excessive politeness will probably make your interlocutor think uneasily that you must be eccentric or a foreigner or difficult to deal with. Conformity enables social intercourse but deadens literature.

The concept of marked choice proves fruitful for stimulating classroom discussion and for relating the virtual experience of literary works to students' lives. For example, to discuss fictional time, you might propose that a virtual present is unmarked, whereas the past or the future is marked. At the end of one class, you could ask students when in their daily experience they dwell on the past or on the future. Allowing time for reflection, you might ask for answers at the beginning of the next class. For the following class, you could ask which kinds of literary works themselves dwell on the past (fairy tales, pastoral, confessions) or on the future (prophecies, utopias, science fiction). Finally, you could ask how the particular work under discussion treats time. A discussion might eventually conclude, for instance, that Emma Bovary resembles many romantic heroes insofar as an idealized past makes her and them dissatisfied with the present but that Emma differs sharply from romantic heroes because she is so enterprising: she tirelessly tries to realize the idealized past in her present and future. She finds such illusions easiest to create in an environment she can control—within the confines of a single room. In this way, she resembles Huysmans's decadent modern materialist, Des Esseintes, more than she does Musset's "enfant du siècle" or Chateaubriand's René. Lacking Des Esseintes's wealth, however, Emma cannot literally rebuild an environment; she can only simulate one with an overlay of fetishized commodities such as rugs, draperies, scarves, and knickknacks.

For most of us, the unmarked experience of space alternates between private (home) and public (work), indoors and outdoors (gardening, walks, commuting, errands, trips). Inner compulsion or external constraint generates marked forms that lack alternatives: either confinement (prison, illness, oppressive work, the study, the love nest, the refuge, the drug den) or wandering (exile, quest, loitering). In literature, neither confinement nor wandering has a predetermined value: either condition may sometimes seem desirable (Des Esseintes's voluntary retreat in *A rebours*, the prison of Stendhal's Fabrice in *La chartreuse de Parme*) and sometimes undesirable (Poe's prisoner in "The Pit and the Pendulum," the seminary in Stendhal's *Le rouge et le noir*).

In interpersonal relations, the unmarked choice is equality. Marked relational styles may emphasize flight (the other seems stronger and hostile; see Hugo's "*Mors*" in *Les contemplations*) or fight (the other seems weaker and hostile; see Hugo's "Réponse à un acte d'accusation," also in *Contemplations*), compliance (the other seems stronger and friendly, like Baudelaire's "La géante," or hostile but unavoidable, like Cupid in Baudelaire's "L'amour et le crâne") or nurturance (the other seems weaker and friendly; see Baudelaire's "L'invitation au voyage"; all Baudelaire examples are in *Les fleurs du mal*), or a mixture of these, because the lyric self can be either giver or receiver. Crude schemes such as the static four-part binary grid sketched above or a dynamic three-part dialectic, as in Aimé Césaire's *Cahier d'un retour au pays natal*, are valuable and thought-provoking pedagogical devices. Once exposed, the ambivalent quality of fictional compliance suggested above—that fiction doesn't fit into a single box—can lead the class to consider the issue of the actual compliance of literary works that are at odds with their society and that strive to evade censorship while still sending a subversive message. By disingenuously using diagrams such as binary grids, the teacher demonstrates the virtues of a constraining intellectual system: it confronts one with the complexities of a truth that eludes it.

Consider, for example, the rigid traditional dichotomy of sanity and madness. In time, psychologists recognized a gray area between its two poles; they bridged the gap with the concept of neurosis. This additional concept exposed a newly obvious gap between neurosis and madness, which had to be filled with the concept of the personality disorder; and, finally, the now-apparent gap between the personality disorder and madness had to be filled with the concept of the borderline personality disorder.

Deconstructing binaries releases students into the open intellectual space of independent evaluation. An ideal classroom approach to this second stage of sophistication is a move from thinking about the subject (or topic) to thinking about the theme of a work. A definition may not embody a theme. A theme is not just a situation (childhood, love, ambition, death) but also an evaluation, an axiological reaction. Does a situation seem good, bad, or indifferent? Ask students to reflect on the definitions they formulated at the beginning of the term and to pass judgment on the situations these definitions described. One can prime them with sample evaluations: for instance, death may be variously interpreted as torment, release, atonement, vindication, defeat, triumph, humiliation, or Pyrrhic victory. Students can be asked to prepare friendly debates that explore why evaluations of the same fact of life (such as love or death) may differ.

When a discussion of whether death is good, bad, or indifferent concludes with the view that it depends, one can introduce to students the notion of a thesis. A literary theme, like a thesis in an essay, refers to the message, to what the writer is trying to prove. As critics, students will decide what they want to prove, but then, unlike fictional authors, they must support their ideas with real examples from the imaginary situations of literature. Authors typically select a theme and then invent evidence to support it. Literally and figuratively, the characters are framed by the plot they inhabit: it passes judgment on them. Whereas literary authors rely primarily on fabulation, with the aid of literary devices such as metonyms (chains of events in stories, of which character development is both the cause and the effect), metaphors (transformations in lyric poetry—e.g., "a girl is a rose" or "death is sleep"), and antitheses (conflicts in drama), critics rely primarily on deduction (hypotheses developed through logical structures) or on induction (amassing observations that coalesce into evidence).

After discussing theme, teachers should introduce the concepts of artistic elaboration and authorial self-consciousness. Authors usually minimize or conceal their self-awareness behind the screen of literary convention; some critics, therefore, are tempted to portray authors as the helpless pawns of their repressed emotions. But nearly every text shows traces of calculated authorial intervention and self-criticism in the form of typographic self-consciousness (such as part and chapter divisions, playful font choice, and expressive arrangements of words on the page); interpretive self-consciousness (forewords and epilogues, notes, interjections, parenthetical remarks, maxims and other generalizations); dialogic self-consciousness (addresses to or virtual interactions with a personified readership); and authorial self-consciousness (self-communing; comments on the sources, creation, and success of the work in progress; or meditations on its destiny).

A participatory exercise on voicing helps reveal the interpretive, dialogic, and authorial forms of artistic self-consciousness. Voicing risks being overlooked in the often unmarked polyphony of fiction. To a bright class, one may introduce the phrases "signs of the narrated" and "signs of the narration." While showing a page of the text being studied on the overhead projector and on a handout, the instructor can ask students to indicate where the author implicitly or explicitly identifies the literary work as his or her creation. Then, they can be asked to mark such places in various corresponding colors: for example, numbering and typographical divisions, interpreting, connecting to the audience, and self-evaluation. Record their best suggestions on the transparency. Soon the image on the screen will look like a Christmas tree.

Next, have the students pretend for a moment that they contain two faces of the same, self-conscious person, simultaneously an author and a self-critic. Recall to them some familiar definitions of the topic they discussed earlier to learn the distinction between subject and theme—let's say, love—and ask how they feel about those definitions. "Love is a many-splendored thing"; "love is the contact of two epidermises"; "love is the redemption of the world through Our Lord Jesus Christ"; "love is never having to say you're sorry." Now they are no longer evaluating the experience of love itself (the story) but the class's provisional definition of that experience (a possible theme).

In a class discussion where students share their initial reactions to a completed reading, one may use a gradated series of exercises to involve them in the creative process by getting them to elaborate on the text. First, students give their opinion on the plot. They describe how, if they were composing a literary work, they might voice their approval or disapproval of or their indifference to the attitudes expressed in the themes they created earlier in the course by defining key words. They might borrow the voice of one character in a dialogue. They might comment as a narrator and report a definition as part of a character's thoughts. They might depict either a character or a narrator engaged in an internal debate between two or more possible, opposing reactions. And they might write an exemplum or an impersonal maxim. Time permitting, the instructor can assign a brief written voicing exercise of this kind to be turned in one or two classes later; the best can be shared.

Second, students can try to see the text more vividly by inventing stage directions. The instructor tells them to imagine a story or poem as a play. What props could be used? What sets and lighting? What do the characters look like and how are they dressed? Where, when, and how do characters (including the lyric selves of poetry and the impersonal narrators of fiction) enter and leave the stage? What gestures do they make? What postures do they assume? Where are they located in relation to one another? What are their facial expressions and tones of voice? A text posted on the class Web site can be glossed in italics initialed by each contributing student, printed out, and shared. Once students have finished an assignment, they can be asked to fill in the thoughts of characters in various scenes when these characters are mute or when they seem to be saying one thing but thinking another. Finally, when students have finished a work, they can compose brief spin-offs that involve individual characters: scenarios for prequels, parallel stories, or sequels. Such expansion is a staple of artistic elaboration. Many familiar examples from popular culture can be mentioned.

Ideally, the instructor will initially limit his or her role to text marking, alerting students to what they may look for while leaving to them the work of interpretation. From Flaubert's "Un cœur simple," for example, one can mention certain tag names and their homonyms (Félicité; Mme Aubain/Aubaine; Bourais/bourré; Paul et Virginie, who take their names from the title characters from Bernardin de Saint-Pierre's novel; Victor the cabin boy). How are the traits suggested by each tag name confirmed or ironically refuted by the narrative? Such discussions should be postponed until students know the entire work.

Overarching patterns to which students could be alerted in Flaubert's tale might include progressive privation. Félicité loses, one by one, everybody whom she loves, but she is compensated by the blooming of illusion in the form of the parrot that acquires an ever-more grandiose spiritual power in her imagination, even as in reality it becomes increasingly unsubstantial (first alive; then dead; then worm-eaten; and, finally, given away). Universals reflected in Flaubert's story could include a loving person who is exploited by others, is comforted by religion, and then faces death. Cultural topics could include surrogate parenting, the master-servant relationship, and the Catholic faith of which Félicité may be one of the last true believers. Does Flaubert suggest that her death symbolizes the death of idealism?

The context initially invoked, then, is synchronic rather than diachronic. This strategy does not limit us to narrow, sterile aestheticism. Literature is a special form of language, but language is a special form of culture. Before students acquire the resources to historicize, they can "culturalize" by virtue of their experience as human beings. Often introduced too early, historical approaches—notoriously, literary history—force students to compare before they fully realize what they are comparing.

What cultural issues are raised by or implied in students' interpretations? (Should political leaders be chosen by heredity, single combat, group combat, or election? Should personal fortunes be protected or redistributed? Should deviants be assimilated or expelled?) To help students discover how literature problematizes accepted values, point to situations where two things that should occur together have been separated: marriage and love, honesty and success, genius and esteem, kindness and gratitude, courage and triumph.

We advocate the pedagogical ideal of fostering creativity. But teachers will have trouble doing so unless they continually challenge their own creativity. As teachers, we often slide into stodgy routines while spellbound by the paradigm shifts of the fashionable approaches of the day: cultural studies, deconstruction, feminism, and postcolonial studies. As teachers of undergraduate courses, we should be concerned less with triturating the text in the mortar of a new theory than with the student's growth. The finest children's literature and the strongest essays on teaching creative writing (ideally, with examples) are more appropriate models than critical theory for the processes we hope to see unfolding in our classes. As Martin Luther King's famous "I Have a Dream" speech showed, hopes, daydreams, and fantasies can exert powerful leverage on external reality. We need to celebrate our own imagination. The bibliography below suggests some inspirational reading. We instructors too require renewal.

Teachers make a tragic error when they try to clone themselves. If we could succeed in so doing, we would be bored and dissatisfied with the results, and the future would be limited to the range and possibilities of our present vision. In many colleges and universities, only ten percent of those enrolled in introductory courses on literature will major in that subject, and only ten percent of those who earn a PhD in literature will eventually surface as noted scholars. But seeing that our task is humble can embolden us. The primary pragmatic goal of literature courses should be to teach students to read and write: richly to understand verbal messages from others and effectively to express themselves. Such skills prove valuable in any career and are essential for either teamwork or leadership—which ideally means motivating, guiding, and facilitating teamwork. But skills should always remain leavened with creativity. We need to encourage the spontaneity that combines understanding and selecting from among others' examples with the unpredictable freedom of self-expression.

NOTES

With thanks to Ross Chambers, Lucia Flórido, the late Michael Issacharoff, Armisted Leigh, Lelia Madrid, Marjorie R. Porter, Mark Statman, and Rosanne Stead.

1. This apparently simple, unstructured assignment has proved quite effective in inducing students to synthesize their thoughts on a number of the texts studied and to keep all the texts in mind throughout the semester.
2. We had our students write a microessay entitled "Procrastination and Me" and then add to it on two occasions, using different fonts to show each successive expansion. We then made an analogue to the three successive stages of Montaigne's essays.
3. For a provocative example of how such a tactic may be applied to teaching, see Shattuck.

A SELECT BIBLIOGRAPHY ON CREATIVITY AND TEACHING

Aymé, Marcel. *The Wonderful Farm.* Illus. Maurice Sendak. New York: Harper, 1995.

Bayles, David, and Ted Orland. *Art and Fear: Observations on the Perils (and Rewards) of Artmaking.* San Bernardino: Borgo, 1994.

Cameron, Julia. *The Artist's Way: A Spiritual Path to Higher Creativity.* New York: Putnam, 1992.

Carroll, Lewis. Alice's Adventures in Wonderland *and* Through the Looking Glass. Illus. John Tenniel. New York: Penguin, 1998.

Chambers, Ross. "The Classroom versus Poetry; or, Teaching Transportation." *Approaches to Teaching Baudelaire's* Flowers of Evil. Ed. Laurence M. Porter. New York: MLA, 2000. 170–82.

Crews, Frederick. *The Pooh Perplex: A Freshman Casebook.* New York: Dutton, 1965.

Juster, Norton. *The Phantom Toll Booth.* Illus. Jules Feiffer. New York: Random, 1993.

Koch, Kenneth. *Rose, Where Did You Get That Red? Teaching Great Poetry to Children.* New York: Vintage, 1990.

———. *Wishes, Lies, and Dreams: Teaching Children to Write Poetry.* New York: Harper, 2000.

Kohl, Herbert. *I Won't Learn from You*. New York: New P, 1994.
May, Rollo. *The Courage to Create*. 1975. New York: Norton, 1994.
Pennac, Daniel. *Comme un roman*. 1992. Paris: Gallimard, 1995. Trans. as *Reads Like a Novel*. Trans. David Gunn. London: Quartet, 1994.
Pinkwater, Daniel M. *The Big Orange Splot*. New York: Scholastic, 1993.
Rodari, Gianni. *The Grammar of Fantasy: An Introduction to the Art of Writing Stories*. New York: Teachers and Writers Collaborative, 1996.
Root-Bernstein, Robert Scott, and Michele Root-Bernstein. *Sparks of Genius: The Thirteen Thinking Tools of the World's Most Creative People*. New York: Houghton, 2000.
Statman, Mark. *Listener in the Snow: The Practice and Teaching of Poetry*. New York: Teachers and Writers Collaborative, 2000.
Willis, Meredith Sue. *Deep Revision*. New York: Teachers and Writers Collaborative, 1993.

PART TWO

Exploring the Cultural: Pedagogical Devices

Anne E. McCall

Culturally Uncompromising

The commitment among practitioners of cultural studies to extending the concepts of texts, representations, and discourse and to engaging in ideologically focused, rhetorical studies across disciplinary boundaries constitutes a serious attack on century-old hierarchies and has generated intense debates since the early 1990s among scholars working in history, philosophy, sociology, and law. In language and literature departments, however, where the mission of teaching texts traditionally brought faculty members together, disagreement has sometimes centered less on research methodologies than on the implications that cultural studies have for the content of instruction.[1] The relative speed with which programs and courses appeared on college campuses—in cultural studies, French cultural studies, French studies, European cultural studies, and even French and European studies—has made it possible to assess the effects of some of the changes that have occurred, both at a programmatic level and within the boundaries of standard core courses. In this essay, I propose to review briefly how a relatively traditional program (in the department of French and Italian at Tulane University) has included cultural studies in the undergraduate curriculum. I then consider the challenges and opportunities that this model poses for the structure of a required French civilization course. After considering some of the innovations undertaken at other schools, I explain the premises of the Tulane revisions and some directions I have pursued to move the course toward a more effective pedagogical practice of teaching cultural studies.

PARALYZING INNOVATIONS AND DUBIOUS REVOLUTIONS: FROM PROGRAMS TO CORE COURSES

Programmatic innovations have predictably received the most attention, and many universities organize graduate-level training in cultural studies and in French through variously organized, independent, or coordinate programs and tracks. After a struggle over philosophy, content, and names in the 1980s (Yaari and Mark), Penn State University instituted a track and then a doctoral program in civilization. Columbia University, among others, offers an MA in French cultural studies. Some institutions, like Princeton University, where French majors can earn recognition for work in European cultural studies, grant undergraduate as well as graduate certificates. In departments including the University of Virginia, which have long-standing undergraduate tracks in literature, language, and civilization, the debates of the 1980s provided new justifications for these tracks; elsewhere, such as at Harvard University, students choose between concentrations in French and francophone literature and French and francophone studies.

Less visible but potentially more revolutionary are the changes within French programs that have rejected the principle of separate tracks. The 2001 University of Pennsylvania Web page advertised "an integrated program" ("Major and Minor Program"), and in 2004 it still touts the "double aim" of promoting "linguistic fluency in French" and "cultural literacy in the fascinating and complex francophone world" ("French Studies"). Universities usually strive to meet this goal by increasing the types, number, and sources of elective courses that count toward the major. Thus at least one and up to four of a Georgetown University French major's six upper-division electives come from a list of culture and civilization courses. Whether traditional or iconoclastic, goals for cultural literacy similarly justify the recognition of required or optional courses in English for foreign language majors: students at the University of Illinois, Urbana, must take six to eight credits of Western civilization, those at Yale University may count up to five courses in English, and Tulane University French majors can use one such course. This allowance widens the range of inquiry possible for students whose inadequate mastery of French would make a similar class in the target language either intellectually simplistic or linguistically daunting, but the trend can also signal a surrender to intellectual laziness and linguistic incompetence (Bell, "Disciplining" 128).

The recognition of courses in English and the existence of diverse electives work together to put new pressure on the remaining required courses to ensure that mid-level students have minimal linguistic fluency and acquire a bank of common, culturally focused, historical knowledge. The more central position of the standard French civilization or culture class within the core curriculum can, somewhat paradoxically, stymie attempts to rethink a content that is not systematically taught elsewhere. With greater constraints but apparently smaller stakes than its graduate-level counterparts, the overhaul of the traditional and traditionally scorned core civilization and culture course at the undergraduate level has attracted less vehement critical attention. The learning experiences of our students can improve greatly if we insist on consciously working with and through the tensions under which this course continues to function in many institutions.

My commitment to the civilization and culture course in all its paradoxes is grounded as firmly in personal experience as in intellectual analysis. Having spent an inordinate amount of energy as a student avoiding a course consisting, to the best of my understanding, of the same shallow, chronological, disparate summaries of cultural movements, current events, and wine regions that Laurence Wylie decried for years (4), I was dismayed to learn, as a junior faculty member, that such courses still existed and that I might be asked to teach one. Luckily, my arrival at Tulane University coincided almost perfectly with a collective reform of the major, including the transformation of the "French civ" course into French Society and Institutions.[2] I have taught the new French 325 course regularly and enthusiastically, yet I remain concerned about the position it occupies in our curriculum and in that of many institutions, a position where the converging and conflicting goals of many French programs meet.

AMBITIOUS INTENTIONS: CULTURAL STUDIES IN SURVEY CULTURE CLASSES

A comparison of the current and past catalog descriptions of Tulane University's required culture course for undergraduate majors, French 325, indicates the difficulty of using cultural studies to define a course that retained its traditional responsibilities. The pre-1995 course French Civilization embraced a chronological perspective in an onomastically overdetermined national history "from the Gauls to de Gaulle" and a collective identity based on a chorus of approved celebrities, "sacred heroes and arch villains" (*Undergraduate Catalog*). The 1993–94 description suggested the course's ability to satisfy the fantasies of students who would further their "Frenchification" by learning what French students do "from kindergarten to *Baccalauréat.*" The main innovation of the post-1995 course, French Society and Institutions, was to shift focus from individual toward group agency: collectively authored under the influence of cultural studies, the description advertises "[a]n introduction to French society and the institutions that shaped it."

It can be argued, however, albeit somewhat perversely, that the outdated description left a space for cultural criticism that is only implicit in the new description. The old description presented France's key historical figures as "sacred heroes and arch villains" and mentioned the role of the school system in perpetuating identities. The new description treats "French society" as a passive vessel "shaped" by conceptually and materially autonomous "institutions" acting on it with the same unilateral force of the apotheosized individuals in historical versions now considered obsolete. The list of historical periods is heteroclite, and the only specific topics included in the description—monuments and provinces—appear as disparate, isolated elements. Because their status as institutional forces and creations is unclear, the description may even leave the impression that the course promotes institutional enforcement and dissemination of a narrative that many of us had intended to question. Although this impression of the approach offered by the four professors who share responsibility for this course may be inaccurate, that this interpretation is even possible suggests that despite the "notion of history as a central interlocutor for French culture and civilization studies" (Yaari, "Toward," 36), the integration of the objects, topics, and methodologies of cultural studies into a historically cast national-culture survey course was more delicate than we realized. If the evolution of the description of Tulane University's French culture course underscores the real risk of critical paralysis entailed in "the absorption of cultural studies with established programs" (Ousselin 98), teaching in and through its contradictions represents an equally real opportunity for introducing students to interdisciplinary and cross-disciplinary work through research-based, problem-solving pedagogies.[3]

Given the conceptual indeterminacy of French 325's description, it is hardly surprising that faculty members teaching the class may find themselves overwhelmed with potential topics as well as the number and variety of reading materials that should arguably be included in the syllabus. Yet the impossibility of achieving any sort of completion in a class with such historical breadth and range is a liberating realization, and the same goes for my understanding of the course's ability to fulfill, at least directly, the criteria for culture classes as articulated either by Lawrence Kritzman (11–15) or, for the graduate level, by Monique Yaari ("Toward" 35–36). Insofar as most of the students come into the class with little knowledge of France today, its history, or cultural studies, the real challenge is to spark their curiosity in the face of what can easily appear a combination of excessive material and inadequate coherence—a challenge not that dissimilar, ironically, to those previously voiced against traditional civilization classes. Responding to the historical mandate for the class, I center my syllabus on Kritzman's "memorialist" function (13–15) and use topics that engage semiotic, socioepistemic, and ethnocultural analyses as tools for bolstering students' understanding of memorialism while inhibiting the development of the "highly aestheticized model of the nation" that Kritzman associates with pre-1980s French culture classes and that remains a real risk in the newer ones (7).

The goal of simultaneously developing cultural literacy and its critique presents a set of hard choices in a one-semester, chronological survey. As critical thinkers and content experts, professors may not see a fundamental obstacle in the concomitant project of teaching and unteaching, as it were. For inexperienced students, the situation is more complicated: they wonder if they should focus their energy on the facts that could, alone, occupy their time; on the power structures that dictate and contest the transmission of those facts; or on the human factors that make us care. Resolving this tension would entail reverting to event history or effectively abandoning any goal of factual acquisition. I try to honor students' wondering by remaining between these positions, alternating historical and textual sources with academic analyses and more speculative texts and addressing the competing disciplinary and institutional demands, as Charles Stivale writes of doing at the graduate level ("A la recherche" 257).

Readings from the first week are both crucial for setting up this three-pronged reflection and exemplary of the work that continues throughout this semester. In 2003, for example, I began the semester by having students read the three-page conclusion to Pierre Birnbaum's *La France imaginée,* a text in which Birnbaum muses over the declining relevance of criteria previously used to define France's national identity, then abruptly avoids the logical conclusion by resurrecting what looks like old-fashioned national character-trait analysis. Students recognize his critical pirouette, are intrigued with it, and eagerly debate both the existence of a contentless identity and the ways in which such a reality can be used. The next assignment throws students off guard because, although it does not negate the national domain, it embraces a more profound realm. Michel Serres's "Erres dans les cimetières" can be read as a justification of our imminent excursion into cultural foundations; more advanced students react to Serres's reflection on our attempts to distance ourselves from death. Finally, I spend a day on prehistory and the birth of the field in the context of nineteenth-century nationalism and conflicts between religion and science. I use the topic to introduce students to reading for both the past and the present. The French government's Internet presentation of recent discoveries of prehistoric sites is spectacular and includes texts explaining their value for young citizens (Ministère). Beginning students can learn about early Homo sapiens culture on French soil and use these documents to reflect on the way that France's packaging of its past reinforces its autoidentification with culture.[4] Even though the class reads less theory than professors such as Gayle Levy include in their classes ("Teaching" 109–10), the students have, by the end of the first week, spent time considering important areas of inquiry in cultural studies; have focused, although not exclusively, on its memorialist dimension; and are ready for innovative assignments.

BALANCING THE BOOKS: PLEASURES, PRICES, AND PROFITS

Students often remain somewhat confused until the class arrives at the nineteenth century. The cross-temporal presentations that are standard fare in French culture classes are, in this regard, as problematic as they are alluring. The study of contemporary commemorations, which has the advantage of teaching students about a historical event and about the practice of recycling and transforming the meanings of such commemorations, gives students a chance to see the twentieth century before we officially get there, but it can, as Yaari has pointed out, be logically perilous ("Culture Studies" 25). Juxtapositions such as the 1996 commemoration of Clovis's fifth-century baptism and coronation to Gregory of Tours's contemporaneous account of those events in *Histoire des Francs* and to François Guizot's nineteenth-century translation of the *Histoire* render the material more compelling to students and may help in conveniently proving the wisdom of the professor in choosing the topic. But, problematically, such juxtapositions suggesting the existence of an eternal French identity may fail because the ideological contexts of the comparison are too complex and unfamiliar to students. For instance, I enjoy using examples of technological advances of the Middle Ages to engage students in questioning our confidence in technology as a necessarily liberating factor of daily life. Régine Pernoud's classic explanation of the role that a few key inventions played in dramatically improving the lives of medieval women can be read alongside Kristin Ross's work on the role that time-saving products and appliances served in enforcing gendered restrictions during the post-World War II and Algerian War periods. Since most students are unfamiliar with both medieval inventions and Fourth Republic society, the time spent establishing comprehension inhibited rather than encouraged reflection.[5]

In more recent renditions of the course, I have tried harder to balance my pleasure, as Stivale advises, with that of the students, because I need both for the course to be successful. Since students in a core undergraduate course tend to have limited historical knowledge, linguistic mastery, and critical experience, learning content is challenging enough for them; the structure of the course should not further complicate matters. For this reason, I also moved away from syllabus structures centered on five topics and reverted to chronological order. Circularity introduced through the inclusion of juxtaposed or recycled events initially confuses students, but the overarching chronological order facilitates acquisition of historical information and gives students time for the mechanics and technique of temporal layering to become more meaningful. The danger of losing students who never make the intellectual leap that the class asks of them is considerable, primarily because the very aspects of culture and cultural studies courses that tend to confuse and frustrate students are elements that make these classes attractive to faculty members. We must, therefore, show care in considering the question of pleasure that Sally Sieloff Magnan and François V. Tochon (1093–95) have also emphasized for language and culture learning—whose, how much, and at what cost—for the class to serve as a breakthrough for students.

The use of *la petite histoire* poignantly illustrates this issue, since it often binds cultural studies practitioners and students together but exacts a high price in a survey course. Indeed, notwithstanding Christopher Prendergast's reservations concerning the use of analogy ("Circulating Representations" 100–03), teachers of cultural studies value the ways in which elements previously relegated to *la petite histoire* speak eloquently for broad movements (Kelly 115–16), and students often find such elements more memorable in encapsulating cultural shifts than the traditionally enshrined, public acts of France's *grands hommes*. For example, the political innocuousness of bell ringing in the United States renders the church bell controversies studied by Alain Corbin either curious or bizarre to students. Their suspicion can serve as a springboard for understanding the ambitions of and resistances to revolutionary reforms and repressions, enriched by students' knowledge of a particular intersection of daily life and local space with high-profile political debates. The topic can lead to a discussion of the ideological function of artistic representations, since bell ringing occupies pictorial and fictional space in the nineteenth century. Finally, this class session can draw students into a broader dialogue concerning the recycling of entrenched practices associated with a regime no longer in place and the importance of daily life practices. If the course contains a creative writing assignment, students can imagine a future revolution and the controversy that could arise from the banning of a widespread public or private practice in the United States. The main drawback of this strategy is, of course, the time that it takes to implement.

Since as many as half the students in the class do not know the century during which the French Revolution took place, it is fair to wonder if they might benefit more from studying one exemplary and illustrious sociohistorical episode or from learning in less depth about numerous areas of change during this largely cultural revolution. Given the importance of developing analytical thinking in undergraduate education, the loss of coverage is easier for me to rationalize than the choice of the episode on which to focus. Since I remain convinced of the value both of using *la petite histoire* and of learning about well-known events, I compromise, alternating from one to the other throughout the semester, hoping that, if nothing else, students are more aware of the types of material missing from discussions of each period.

This compromise raises the question of using English-language publications in a course conducted in French and intended to improve the students' command of French. Debates on this topic often do not do justice to the serious consequences of using English-language materials and degenerate into caricatured opposition. Assuming, however, that core undergraduate survey courses in culture or civilization must accomplish this basic training, the integration of cultural studies, in which many exciting texts are in English, might lead to reduced expectations in the development of skills in the target language. My enthusiasm for particular topics led me at first to underestimate this issue and to include many readings in English, albeit most often in tandem with a French text. Experience has since taught me two things: these texts in English are valuable not just for the information they provide but because they add a sense of urgency to the topics, proving through their own discursive authority the importance of our work. Second, whenever students are assigned a reading both in English and in French, they focus on the one in English, make fewer efforts in language acquisition, and begin turning in sloppy work in French. My current rule of thumb is to include at least one but not more than two assignments in English, an arrangement that transforms these assignments into treats.

COLLABORATIVE RESEARCH IN A SURVEY COURSE

The underlying question motivating the above analysis is the effect of a class teaching both culture and cultural criticism on our students' formation as beginning French majors. Although none of the challenges and concessions outlined above might appear definitively compromising in isolation, the readings and course topics leave open the basic question: do these characteristics, considered together, represent the alleged disciplinary or scholarly capitulation to popular culture, history light, and American culture that Alain Finkielkraut and others lament in contemporary Western thought? However one responds, written assignments that require both focused inquiry and broad-based, critical reflection are important for obtaining the optimal result from students. Incorporating this staged research experience carefully into the class allows students, as Yaari reminds us, to have it both ways ("Culture" 53), to have French culture while reading, writing, and analyzing it.

Having experimented with several formats and writing assignments for French Society and Institutions, I have found the most important element to be the inclusion of at least one required, formal, interdisciplinary group research paper. My most successful assignments have involved the simple transformation of the traditional explication de texte into either a semester-long or shorter collaboratively framed document analysis. Whether the document under consideration is a published text or a handwritten manuscript, the central requirements for the project's success are that students have access to pertinent research but that the text has not been the object of too much critical attention. In addition, a sufficient portion of the semester's grade and of class periods—three to five, depending on the document—must make the students' mastery of the document both materially probable and strategically worthwhile. Manuscript documents, however, most easily ignite student interest and are worth the supplementary class period required to assist students in the initial decryption of foreign handwriting. Several structures work well; in some classes, I have introduced the text early in the semester and come back to it periodically until the class catches up with the era in which the document was written. At other times, I have used short response papers on a variety of topics to prepare students for the types of inquiry that they will undertake later in the semester, in a more thorough fashion.[6]

Group-centered case studies and document analyses form the glue that brings different traditions within cultural studies together in the service of student development.[7] Working in a group with others who come to specialize in different aspects of the text or in different forms of analysis leads each student to think through the document or issue from a new point of comparison. In other words, the students participate, at least metaphorically and occasionally more concretely, in the cartographic project that Tom Conley identifies as fundamental to French culture ("French Studies" 26–27). These case studies combat intellectual or personal alienation in almost any classroom and create a literal as well as a critical space within which students work toward the seemingly paradoxical goals of the semester: competency in cultural literacy, cultural criticism, and language skills. Because they secure the overall success of the French class in which these goals are featured, these assignments are now the signature element of a pedagogy that allows students to understand for themselves just how uncompromising culture can be.

Although cultural studies may be "seen variously as an area, a field, a program, a discipline, or a conspiracy" (Appadurai 28) and hence may take on contradictory, even amoebic, traits (Guerlac 53–60; Debouzy 3), the course has brought cultural studies into the curricular mainstream. This structural naturalization of cultural studies and the positive attitude of professors who are happy with the theoretical luster that cultural studies scholarship has added to culture classes cannot, or at least should not, avoid the serious curricular issues and challenges that the subject matter and methodology pose to professors and students alike. If cultural studies involves teaching "against the grain," whatever that may be at a particular moment (Le Hir, "Transatlantic Solidarity" 241), then it is also by embracing rather than glossing over these difficulties that professors can make the class a prime vehicle for reaching the disciplinary-specific goals of a French major and fulfilling the broader mission of undergraduate education.

NOTES

1. Scholars expressed reservations of different kinds. Some consider that the noncanonical topics cynically play to student interest (Ingram 1152; Fourny and Schehr 3; Petrey, "Literature" 16) or trivialize the academy's mission (Compagnon, "Why French"). More bemoan the displacement of French thinkers from contemporary theorization in the *sciences humaines*. In this view, cultural studies constitutes the academic version of an all too American globalization movement; ineffectively disperses the focus of literature programs; and is redundant, since foreign language programs had long embraced culture as central to their literary mission (Petrey, "Literature" 12, 22; David F. Bell, "Disciplining" 128; Schwartz, "Everyman" 132).
2. Our department revised our entire major at the time. Department members came to meetings with drafts of new descriptions, and we edited them as a group. We do not, however, use a common syllabus. The class currently rotates among a medievalist, a Renaissance specialist, and two of us who work in the nineteenth and twentieth centuries.
3. See the culture objective developed at the University of Iowa (Hope 466).
4. France's Ministry of Culture and Communication Web site contains beautiful material on the caves themselves, including Chauvet-Pont d'Arc (Ministère). The accompanying documentation and discussion of the site as part of France's heritage, much like Georges Bataille's essay on Lascaux, implicitly promote France as a land predestined for cultural primacy by the existence on its territory of early, consummate examples of art.
5. I do still include one session like this each semester, mostly as a teaser for more quizzical or advanced students, but I make sure to surround that day with more standard assignments, and my goals for the day are modest.
6. Space limitations prevent a detailed description of a full case study.
7. These traditions are as varied as the Birmingham school in England and the contestation of the premises of traditional French schooling (see La Capra 170, 175–77; Klein 7–9; Yaari, "Culture" 39–42; Conley, "Afterword" 274).

Adrianna M. Paliyenko

Collaboration Matters: Sparking a Connection between French Literary and Cultural Studies

In the article "Learning a Foreign Language in a Monolingual World," Sander Gilman suggestively asserts that "the study of languages can have any meaning, based on where you stand" (1032). This view of learning languages, which draws on a social constructivist or new historicist account of knowledge, invites us to reconsider how we approach teaching a foreign language in a multicultural and yet essentially monolingual world. What, then, does it mean to teach French language, literature, and culture at a time when our enrollments are threatened by various factors, among them the perception that learning French has little cultural value in a technological and postliterary age? Advocating languages across the curriculum, "teaching the complexities of the cultures in which [a] language is used" (1034), Gilman pushes beyond the pedagogical model of linguistic acquisition to refocus the study of French through a sociocultural literate lens.[1] If we adopt in principle the integration of language and culture, albeit outside the parameters of a program of language study across the curriculum, how do we adapt curricular contents to accommodate various levels of linguistic proficiency and cultural competence? How, moreover, can we reach the current generation of students and enable them to make connections between nineteenth-century France and the twenty–first century? It may be that, by discovering anew the cultural relevancy of the past, students will rethink the place of French studies in the century that has dawned. In this essay, I consider a small liberal arts college's attempts to invigorate the curriculum at the intersection of past and present cultural issues.

The vexing issue of declining enrollments prompted the creation of a double track in French literature and French studies at Colby College in 1995.[2] This curricular development succeeded in drawing many majors but inadvertently jeopardized the future of literary studies in our department. Eighty-nine percent of our students elected the cultural track to complement a primary interest in international studies. Moreover, course selections at Colby and in programs of study abroad suggested that our French studies majors did not readily recognize the fundamental role that literature still plays in the development of cultural literacy. In the wake of this trend, in the fall of 2000, I devised an upper-level course entitled The Cultural Legacy of Nineteenth-Century France, with the aim of enrolling both tracks of majors. French studies majors are anxious about their ability to read literary texts critically and with aesthetic sensitivity, whereas students majoring in French literature question their ability to approach visual culture with the discernment of an art historian. Through my attempt to reconcile the curricular imbalance between literary and cultural studies, I discovered a provocative alliance between literary and cultural competence. The use of graphic presentations, which served to launch and frame discussion, introduced an element of surprise that powerfully engaged my class in the cultural production of meaning and sparked productive connections between the art of reading disparate texts and of visualizing their contexts.

A RETROSPECTIVE STANCE

A primary concern with enrollments, then, determined both the retrospective bent from the vantage point of today's student that framed my course and the methodological turn to PowerPoint presentations aimed at illuminating richly textured connections between the literary and visual culture of nineteenth-century France.[3] These graphic presentations, which juxtaposed the literary and the visual without explicitly connecting them, put into play a collaborative element that would bridge gaps in linguistic, literary, and cultural competence between majors following ostensibly distinct tracks. The first day of class I asked students to look back at the twentieth century and represent the past through salient moments. In response to their revision of the

American past, I reproduced a visual retrospective of important figures of twentieth-century French culture published in the January 2000 issue of *Journal français*; among them, Marguerite Yourcenar, Jacques Cousteau, Jean-Paul Sartre, Charles de Gaulle, Edith Piaf, Paul Bocuse, and Yannick Noah. This exercise framed the objective of the course raised in the form of two queries: What does the nineteenth century represent in the history of French culture? How did nineteenth-century French creative artists, including writers and painters, remember or represent their century?

My students would soon see that any looking back at the past involves a process of "re-vision," in Adrienne Rich's feminist elaboration, "the act . . . of seeing with fresh eyes" (*On Lies* 35). Any revision or representation is inflected with sociopolitical preoccupations—and one's own subject position. As citizens of the twentieth and the twenty-first century, my students had to consider at all times the distance between themselves and the minds of the nineteenth century to avoid filtering literary and visual representations of nineteenth-century culture through the lens of the modern world. As they gained knowledge of a past century and the creative minds it produced, they began to understand the role that artistic expression plays in the production of culture and cultural meaning. By representing the nineteenth century visually, through photogravures, paintings, and photographs, to capture salient historical and political moments or sociocultural developments in literature or art, I refocused my students' cultural competence. Students learned to grasp the ideological complexity of nineteenth-century poetic and prose texts as a form of creative visualization and to view turning points in nineteenth-century France as moments that words and images mutually illuminated.

FRAMEWORK

The syllabus (see *Web Support*) makes apparent the chronological framework of the course, organized by decades. Historic moments, significant developments, and discoveries form the backdrop against which I positioned our readings of literary and visual representations of public and private life in nineteenth-century France. A series of thematic pairings and oppositions, including personal-public, domestic-commercial, sacred-profane, and French-foreign, loosely guided my eclectic selection of course materials, including poetry, essays, short stories, novels, paintings, drawings, and photographs. I aimed for my students not only to gain an overall sense of the century in its temporal development but also to filter the texture of its unfolding through the context and creativity that produced the cultural legacy of nineteenth-century France.

Paintings and Images of Women

To set the stage for a collaborative reconstruction of the cultural legacy of nineteenth-century France—from the *mal du siècle* to the fin de siècle in fourteen weeks—I chose *Le consulat et l'empire*, a modern filmic representation of the historical moment and sociopolitical scene opening the century. In the shadow of Napoleon's ascent to military power and ideological rule, we considered women's revolutionary rise and postrevolutionary fall, first visually and then in literary representations. Creative tension filled the room as I apprehensively launched my first PowerPoint presentation, not knowing whether I would overcome my uneasy relationship with computer-assisted learning or what the images I had chosen would show my students about a world far removed from their own. Through the course of the semester, my students and I learned that the element of surprise invariably provided a fresh perspective from which to consider the texts in question with poetic sensibility à la Baudelaire, "au fond de l'inconnu pour trouver du nouveau" ("to the depths of the unknown to find the new" [*Œuvres* 127]).

The painter and lithographer Louis Boilly produced visual accounts of women circulating freely in public, and thus politicized, spaces, notably *Triomphe de Marat* and *Club de la femme patriote* (1792), representations of ostensibly liberated women that did not strike my modern viewers as particularly revolutionary. Eustache Le Sueur's *Divorce* (1793), however, which we read through the lens of early nineteenth-century French women writers who advocated in various ways for women's rights, such as Olympe de Gouges, Constance de Salm, and Adelaïde Dufrénoy, struck a modern chord and prompted a lively discussion. Majors in art history focused on the cultural significance of women's positions in the various tableaux (deftly brought back into critical view with a mere click of the mouse), whereas literature specialists underscored the cultural import of women's literary representations of their private and public lives.

De Gouges's boldly feminist revision of the 1789 "Déclaration des droits de l'homme et du citoyen" made clear what was at stake, both socially and politically, for liberal women at the turn of the nineteenth century: "Toute femme naît et demeure libre et égale à l'homme en droits; les distinctions sexuelles ne peuvent être fondées que sur l'utilité commune" ([1791] 52; "All women are born and remain free and equal to men in rights; sexual distinctions can be based only on the common good" [my trans.]).[4] De Salm thus represented the dawning of the nineteenth century as a propitious moment for women: "O femmes, c'est pour vous que j'accorde ma lyre; / . . . Un siècle de justice à nos yeux vient de naître / Femmes, soyez aussi ce que vous devez être" ("O women, it is for you that I tune my lyre; / . . . A just era has dawned / Women, also be what you are supposed to be") (Planté 4). See also "Sur les femmes politiques" (Planté 7–8). Legislation permitting divorce, which met feminists' demands, passed in 1792. Women's public lives, however, did not always mirror their private thoughts. Dufrénoy's poem "Le divorce, une romance," composed the day the divorce decree was issued (10 Aug. 1792), expressly opposed a law that put asunder a union consecrated before God (in Planté 29).

Raising the subject of women during the revolution at the outset of the semester prepares the groundwork for later discussion of women's shifting status. Students followed this line of thinking from Germaine de Staël's "Des femmes qui cultivent des lettres" to the early feminist movement in the 1830s elaborated in the writings of Claire Démar. From mid-century through the fin de siècle, students discovered competing portraits of woman represented alternately as a degenerative femme fatale (Maupassant, Baudelaire, Zola) and as a devout maternal figure (Desbordes-Valmore, Sand, Morissot, Cassatt). Intermittent literary and visual treatments of hysteria (Edmond de Goncourt and Jules de Goncourt, *Germinie Lacerteux*, and, along with Bouillet's *Une leçon clinique à la Salpêtrière*, drawings by Vièrge and Régnard of the wards and therapy sessions at the Salpêtrière) complicated for the class the early trajectory of women's sociopolitical movement. Whereas one student presented nineteenth-century women in their sartorial splendor, another student's final PowerPoint presentation masterfully fleshed out the nineteenth-century woman in full sociohistorical and political context (Student presentations are available through my syllabus online at *Web Support*; select Exposés).

Napoleon and the Mal du Siècle

Through the course of our collaborative thinking about nineteenth-century France, Napoleon emerged as a major figure, whose complex legacy haunted the cultural imagination of the nineteenth century with telling ambivalence. From the work of classical and Romantic artists, such as Jacques-Louis David (*Bonaparte franchissant les Alpes*), François Gérard (*Bataille d'Austerlitz*), Antoine Gros (*La bataille d'Eylau*), and Théodore Géricault (*Officier de chasseurs à cheval de la garde impériale*), students gleaned representations of Napoleon (and the imperial army) displaying the heroic feats of a military genius. Other creative minds of Napoleon's day, however, remembered him as a profane tyrant (Lamartine, "Bonaparte," *Secondes méditations*) and as the seminal force of the *mal du siècle*, poignantly evoked by Vicomte François-Auguste René de Chateaubriand's *René* and Alfred de Musset's *Confession d'un enfant du siècle*.

Visual accounts of Napoleon's military campaigns fail to capture the private lives and discontents of French citizens. As Musset recalls in *La confession d'un enfant du siècle*, "pendant les guerres de l'Empire, tandis que les maris et les frères étaient en Allemagne, les mères inquiètes avaient mis au monde une génération ardente, pâle, nerveuse" (65; "during the wars of the empire, while husbands and brothers were away in Germany, anxious mothers had given birth to a passionate, pallid, and nervous generation"). Under Napoleonic rule, French culture was radically transformed, since "Napoléon avait tout ébranlé en passant sur le monde" (Musset, *La confession* 70; "Napoleon had disturbed everything in his wake"). Such literary representations of the psychopathology of everyday life in nineteenth-century France enabled students to contextualize the visual culture of the early nineteenth century as representing, or rather idealizing, Napoleon at the height of his glory. In the light of the Romantic representations of Napoleon's rise and fall, his specter came into sharper focus in the troubled Restoration society that emerged in his shadow (see Balzac, *Le Colonel Chabert*). In final PowerPoint projects, one student developed the question of Napoleon's legacy in literary representations, as in *Le rouge et le noir*, and another studied his place in military history. As we remapped France in the wake of Napoleon's sweeping expeditions, we also considered the role played by other worlds in the cultural imagination of nineteenth-century France (see one student's PowerPoint presentations on Delacroix by going to *Web Support*).

REMAPPING WORLD VIEWS

For students learning French at the beginning of the twenty-first century, where diversity and difference form an integral part of their core curriculum and social sensibility, issues of race, class, and identity are clearly of significant interest. The scope of France's colonial expansion in the nineteenth century provided my students with a historical framework in which to consider shifts in France's stance on slavery throughout the century. Claire de Duras's *Ourika* (1823) and Prosper Merimée's *Tamango* (1829) gave rise to social and political debates about France's colonial enterprise that gathered force before the abolition of slavery in 1848. These literary texts by nineteenth-century thinkers with abolitionist leanings reconstructed the cruel realities of the Atlantic slave trade and its cultural consequences for France and its conquests.[5] Students considered such abolitionist ideas, first, as imagined from the standpoint of a Senegalese girl raised by an aristocratic French family during the French Revolution who wears, in Frantz Fanon's theoretical terms, a "white mask" and, second, from that of a slave trader with "black skin." PowerPoint presentations that I prepared enabled students to picture the manner in which slaves were transported and to envision other focal points of the slave trade. A student's presentation about Gorée Island at the semester's end made vividly and poignantly manifest the point of no return for the African slaves, many of whom were sent to the French Antilles.

To situate Anaïs Ségalas's *Récits des Antilles: Le Bois de la Soufrière* (1885), which treats with a troubling bias the power struggle between the civilized French creoles and the uncultured former slaves, I visually evoked for my students, again with a PowerPoint presentation, the rich vegetation of Guadeloupe. Students were fascinated by Ségalas's literary representation of a place that the author had never visited and yet had compellingly recreated in its topographical richness and cultural complexity, albeit with apparent prejudice. Thus students questioned a surprising nostalgic turn to a conservative ideology and the forces driving Ségalas's subjective position that gives voice to a former female slave advocating a return to the days of slavery: "Aujourd'hui que les pauvres nègres ne sont plus esclaves, il faut bien que de bonnes blanches comme Mme de Beaumanguier viennent les secourir, quand ils ne peuvent plus travailler. Ah! Monsieur, où est-il, le bon temps de l'esclavage?" (129; "These days, because the poor negroes are no longer slaves, it is necessary that good white folks like Madame de Beaumanguier help them when they can no longer work. Alas! Sir, where have the good old days of slavery gone?").

It is in similarly melancholic terms that nineteenth-century visual and literary artists considered the advent of modernity as paradoxically grounded in loss and symptomatic of degeneration.

Photographs depicting Georges-Eugène Haussmann's reconstruction of Paris at various stages and myriad scenes of private and public life in Paris in the latter decades of the century, drawn from the realist school (Courbet, Manet, Degas), framed and evoked the world depicted in Charles Baudelaire's *Tableaux parisiens*. Baudelaire's poetic haunts were both linguistically and conceptually difficult for many students in the class, some of whom had only a passing familiarity with French poetry. By this point in the semester, they knew what it meant to read texts, whether visual or literary, in context, but the life of Baudelaire's mind nevertheless was far removed from their own on many levels. Paintings and photographs capturing diverse scenes of nineteenth-century life enabled students to grapple with some of the effects of the Industrial Revolution and its attendant social movement. Among the scenes we viewed were women working in factories and in mines (a link to my PowerPoint presentation is on the online course syllabus; see *Web Support*); patrons sitting at cafés; and streets, where passersby encounter the dizzying movement of a modern city and their own anonymity.[6] By teasing out the associative, cultural networks of Baudelaire's emblematic tableau, students considered how a nineteenth-century dweller may have experienced and remembered the modernization of Paris in "Le Cygne": "Le vieux Paris n'est plus (la forme d'une ville / Change plus vite, hélas! que le cœur d'un mortel)" (*Œuvres* 81; "The old Paris is gone [a city's shape / Changes more quickly, alas, than a mortal's heart]"). Looking back at Gustave Courbet (*Les baigneuses* and *Le sommeil*) and Edouard Manet (*Le déjeuner sur l'herbe* and *Olympia*) through the constructed lens of a nineteenth-century viewer, students grasped the complex relation of modernity and decadence and the cultural shifts that prepared the fin de siècle. Marie Krysinska's *vers libres*, the symbolist expression that closed the century—and our semester of collaboration—provided a perfect opening for a final student project that allowed us to dwell on the possible connections and meanings of music, art, and poetry in a world that we had attempted to see in a nineteenth-century light.[7]

TOWARD A CREATIVE END

One way to respond creatively to visual and literary texts is to use language poetically to call into existence what was not there before, to make a connection that is essential to the production of meaning. My experiment with PowerPoint presentations as a way to make the past, specifically the nineteenth century, come alive and into critical focus for the current generation of students demanded a leap of surrealist faith in the ability of juxtaposed and disparate elements to form such a connection. The interdisciplinary nature of the course was instrumental in setting the stage for the social and intellectual engagement that I hoped to develop with my students, who would come to rethink where they stood in relation to nineteenth-century French culture on the basis of our critical examination of the past. Thus, at the semester's end, student presentations modeled collaborative investigations that integrated critical and creative thinking about visual and literary texts that brought nineteenth-century French culture and twenty-first-century minds into conversation with each other.

Collaborative learning has indeed come of age at a time when counteracting "larger societal trends of fragmentation, lack of civic involvement, and undercurrents of alienation" truly matters (Smith and MacGregor 9).[8] By pushing the envelope of conventional pedagogies and joining creative forces with our students to foster engaged reading, writing, and thinking, we may recast what teaching a foreign language means for literature. Cultural studies may shed new light on literature if we collaborate with our students in thinking about what the study of visual and literary texts in context can reveal about creative expression and the nature of knowledge. Through the study of a foreign language in its cultural context, students may learn that they themselves are carriers of cultural attitudes that play a significant role in how they see what they read and read what they see. As teachers working in concert with students to look back at the past with fresh eyes, our role productively shifts to a form of collaboration that challenges students to make sense of foreign subject matter and to discover that their own relation to the cultural production of meaning indeed depends on where they stand.

NOTES

1. From the standpoint of language acquisition, Heidi Byrnes addresses "foundational concerns that pertain to the existing configuration for language and literary-cultural studies in collegiate foreign language departments" to consider how "the cultural turn in foreign language teaching" complicates the relation between culture and language (115).
2. In 2001, the two tracks were merged in a restructuring of the major in French studies at Colby College that explicitly links literary and cultural studies.
3. Mark Ingram highlights the technical and pedagogical use of PowerPoint in the following note: "PowerPoint is a software program allowing one to create multimedia presentations composed of visual 'slides' along with music and other sound accompaniment. The options allow one to create slides with written bulleted headings summarizing the main points of the presentation, or to use all of a slide for an

image (either taken from a website, scanned from a book or photograph, or copied from an existing electronic file). The finished product is projected much like a slide show and can be a very creative component of an individual's or a group's oral presentation" (1161n5).

4. Compare the first article of the "Déclaration des droits de l'homme et du citoyen": "Les hommes naissent et demeurent libres et égaux en droits. Les distinctions sociales ne peuvent être fondées que sur l'utilité commune" ("Men are born and remain free and equal in rights. Social distinctions can be based only on the common good").
5. A final PowerPoint presentation by a student with familial ties to Cambodia provided a unique perspective on the legacy of France's colonial project.
6. Duby and Perrot's volume offers a rich selection of visual texts and was a principal source for presentations of nineteenth-century women's private and public lives in my course. The volume includes photographs of women working in various conditions, among them, "Femme travaillant dans la mine à Wigan" (322; "Women Working in the Mine at Wigan"); "Ouvrières d'une fabrique d'allumettes" (247; "Women Workers in a Match Factory"); and "Ouvrières travaillant à la fabrication de boîtes métalliques" (349; "Women Working in the Manufacture of Metal Cans"). In the context of the Industrial Revolution, moreover, a double major in French and economics focused on the evolving role of the French café as a space where the imbrication of the personal and the public, the domestic and the commercial, cut across boundaries of social class and gender.
7. This undergraduate student's presentation exemplified the intellectual fruits of interdisciplinary labor, treating intersections between artists and writers, including Eugène Delacroix, Frédéric (François) Chopin, Frédéric (Étienne) Barbier, Albert Roussel, Claude Debussy, and Stéphane Mallarmé.
8. Barbara Leigh Smith and Jean T. MacGregor persuasively argue, "[T]he academy mirrors larger societal trends of fragmentation, lack of civic involvement, and undercurrents of alienation. Collaborative learning, with its emphasis on social and intellectual engagement and mutual responsibility, aims to counteract many of these educational and societal trends" (9). In a pertinent article, Jerome McGann raises important questions about how we teach the nineteenth century. McGann's probing analysis of the claim that "the artifice of centuries is only useful as a foil against which to pose searching queries about poetry, cultural expression, textual practice, etc., all of which have to cross those boundaries, [and] have to bring new considerations and old works back to the fore for real and very substantive reasons" has rich implications for collaborative learning (1415).

Kathryn M. Grossman

Teaching *Notre-Dame de Paris*: A Classic Case

As one of the world's most celebrated but least-read texts, Victor Hugo's early masterpiece *Notre-Dame de Paris* (1831) presents special challenges in the classroom. On the one hand, this Romantic reworking of Mme Leprince de Beaumont's *La belle et la bête* (1757) has become a permanent feature in our mythical landscape. Thanks to the popularization of its basic story line not only through numerous abridgments and *bandes dessinées* in a range of languages but also through a succession of theatrical and cinematic renditions, the novel has been in the global public eye almost since its publication. Disney's *The Hunchback of Notre Dame* and the rock opera by Luc Plamandon and Richard Cocciante, *Notre-Dame de Paris*, are two examples of how the novel has been transformed into popular entertainment.[1]

On the other hand, the original *texte intégral* remains largely unread today. Hugo's five-hundred-page opus is long and difficult. The opening moves slowly and seems strangely static; the French medieval setting strikes many American students as remote and irrelevant rather than charming and exotic; the constant intrusion of historical, geographic, philosophical, and aesthetic digressions, especially in the first half of the story, distracts, annoys, and finally discourages first-time readers; and the vocabulary is demanding in any language, while translation fails to capture the wordplay, auditory effects, and metaphoric resonances of Hugo's poetic prose.

Given the many opportunities and constraints that surround the work, I have developed an array of successful strategies for teaching it at different academic levels. At Penn State, I regularly include an unabridged English translation of *Notre-Dame de Paris* (Oxford UP ed.) in general education courses aimed at freshmen and sophomores; excerpts from the French text (Classiques Larousse or Garnier-Flammarion ed.) in introductory literature courses for French majors and minors; and the *texte intégral* (Garnier-Flammarion ed.) in graduate seminars on French Romanticism or the nineteenth-century novel. Many of the course materials that I have devised can be aimed at more than one kind of audience, and, since I am fortunate enough to teach in wired classrooms, I can use videos, CD-ROMs, and the Web to enrich the study of the text. In this essay, I discuss the ways in which I approach Hugo's novel.

READING *NOTRE-DAME DE PARIS*

Although the last half of *Notre-Dame de Paris* contains some of the most moving, spectacular, audacious, and spellbinding scenes in literary history, the leisurely opening presents a formidable obstacle to engaging undergraduates. The situation sets up a sad and frustrating dichotomy: students who make it to the end of the novel often declare it one of the best books they have ever read; those who get bogged down in the initial scene—or in the many seemingly irrelevant digressions that pile up in the first two hundred pages—may display behavior ranging from boredom during class discussions to discouragement with their own reading prowess to resentment over the amount of time (a minimum of two weeks) devoted to the work. Still, putting it on the syllabus is a risk that, if well managed, can lead to ample rewards. After all, as Richard Maxwell has shown, *Notre-Dame de Paris* was one of the most important works of the nineteenth century, influencing a wide assortment of writers—Charles Dickens, Robert Louis Stevenson, and Eugène Sue, among others. In my view, students deserve the opportunity to discover the magic of its "urban mysteries" for themselves (Maxwell ix).

To underscore the literary significance and contribution of *Notre-Dame de Paris* while mitigating the demands that reading it entails, I employ a number of simple strategies:

Context First, I never begin the semester with such a lengthy and complex text. Rather, in general education courses where we read the entire novel in translation, I place it in the context of thematically related works that are much shorter in length. For a freshman seminar titled Images of *la Femme Fatale* in French Fiction, for instance, students read Abbé Prévost's *Manon*

Lescaut, Chateaubriand's *Atala* and *René*, and Claire de Duras's *Ourika* before undertaking *Notre-Dame de Paris*. As a result, they are intellectually prepared to deal with issues like male-female relations, parents and children, racial prejudice, nature versus culture, exotic otherness, religious orthodoxy versus spirituality, utopianism, and Romanticism versus neoclassicism; they have developed a historical perspective and some skills in textual analysis and interpretation; and they have acquired confidence in their abilities to understand and appreciate thematic patterns, character development, and imagery and tropes.

By the same token, in my intermediate-level literature class for students of French, we read excerpts from the novel only after completing a unit on Romantic poetry from Alphonse de Lamartine to Hugo.[2] At this point, the class has some grasp of Hugo's control of epic, lyric, and satirical voices, as well as of his predilection for mixing genres. This background proves helpful in promoting appreciation for the appearance of all three poetic voices in the text, along with conventions derived from melodrama (especially the numerous trial and recognition scenes and the use of antithesis, as in the juxtaposition of the sublime and the grotesque) and the Gothic novel (the medieval setting; a lustful, villainous monk; dark fantasies; violence, murder, and horror; gloomy crypts; and so forth). After completing our study of *Notre-Dame de Paris*, we look at works by Prosper Mérimée (*Carmen*), Honoré de Balzac (*Facino Cane*), Théophile Gautier (*La morte amoureuse*), and George Sand (*La mare au diable*) that likewise interweave realism and idealism in depicting different forms of courtship and obsessive love.

Motivation As much as we might want to dive immediately into a great text or to elaborate on its historical, political, and cultural issues, it is important to remember that our students long for good stories—one of which can be a quick overview of the author's life. Far from constituting biographical criticism, such details enable students to empathize with a writer and so to take a personal interest in his or her work. Hugo's biography is valuable because students learn that the novelist, contrary to many of the familiar, official portraits, was once young like them; that his childhood, informed by his parents' troubled marriage and frequent separation, was difficult; that he felt a special literary calling during his adolescence that earned him considerable glory before the age of thirty; that his childhood sweetheart, whom he had wooed and married in his early twenties, was no longer sleeping with him by the time he began *Notre-Dame de Paris*; and that he had procrastinated so long on drafting the novel that he had to use the July Revolution as an excuse to get an extension from his editor. The resemblances between the darkly beautiful Adèle Hugo and Esmeralda or between the young author and the sexually frustrated Frollo—whether purposeful or coincidental—bring Hugo's cast of characters immediately to life.[3]

Assignments To help students make a good start in the novel and eventually reach the end, I do not insist that they read carefully all the introductory, digressive, or more difficult passages. A good rule of thumb, I tell them, is that they should speed up their reading when they start to lose interest and slow down to savor the parts that really interest them. Though my advice is counterintuitive—students are used to stopping when bored and to flying without too much reflection through the most thrilling scenes—it has proven extremely beneficial. The most mature readers, of course, take in every word. (Some have already covered the novel in high school and are ready to explore the sections they missed the first time around.) But the others have the pleasure not just of progressing rapidly through the parts that do not capture their attention but of dwelling on the most memorable scenes in the book. Better yet, Hugo's construction of affinities, analogies, and metaphoric equivalencies throughout the text ties together digressions and action scenes in ways that enable virtually all the students to contribute to class discussions, regardless of what they have skimmed and what they have read in depth.

Permission to skim functions particularly well for the opening section (bk. 1, chs. 1–4), as well as for books 3 and 5. There are, however, several passages in "Ceci tuera cela" (bk. 5, ch. 2) that I ask everyone to read, notably the first four paragraphs (Oxford UP 192–93; Classiques Larousse 40–41) and Hugo's summary of his views on the printing press (Oxford UP 199–200; Classiques Larousse 50–51). These descriptions are essential for developing reflections on the connections between the historical artifact (the cathedral) and Hugo's historical novel (which bears the same name). They also introduce notions of dethroning, oedipal conflict, and revolution that link Quasimodo's rivalry with his adopted father, Claude Frollo, to the people's struggle for freedom from the French monarchy.

Guides Finally, to enhance my students' ability to grasp the main features of the text as they read along—and thus to stimulate both their interest in the work and their ability to participate in discussions—I provide questions (in English for the literature in translation course, in French for the intermediate-level literature course and for graduate seminars) that serve as reading guides. I include queries about books 1, 3, and 5 in the hope that they will encourage students to attempt the more difficult sections instead of just skimming them (or—dare I suggest?—skipping them altogether). The examples that I have prepared (in French and in English [see *Web Support*]) are based on my own interpretation of *Notre-Dame de Paris* (see *Early Novels* 150–208) and are by no means intended to be comprehensive or prescriptive.

DISCUSSION STRATEGIES

The possible subjects for exchanges centered on *Notre-Dame de Paris* are so plentiful that any pretensions to coverage must be considered illusory. I prefer to convey certain core notions about the text through interaction with and among the class members rather than through lecture alone. Above all, I strive to get students to trust their personal reactions and to think creatively about the many ways in which the text plays with *them*. As students make progress through the novel, they not only gain increasing confidence in their reading skills and accomplishments but also learn to analyze and to articulate their responses to Hugo's work.

Setting As noted above, a brief overview of Hugo's life and times can pique students' interest in the text even before they begin reading it. In conjunction with providing such information, one can facilitate the entry into the medieval setting in a number of ways. Certainly, the historical context becomes less intimidating when viewed in the light of Hugo's efforts to preserve the "ugly" ruins of an era neglected, despised, and misunderstood—first by succeeding centuries that had embraced the neoclassical ideal and then by a postrevolutionary culture that associated Gothic architecture with the deposed French monarchy.

When I first began teaching, my classes were populated mainly by first-generation college students who had ventured little outside Pennsylvania. Today, many young people enter college having already lived, traveled, or studied abroad. It is an easy matter to ask those who have done so to share their impressions of Notre Dame, to reflect on other Gothic edifices (churches, abbeys, castles) that have been restored, and to recall the huge number of ruins in France still awaiting repair. Pertinent questions might be, What do the government signs posted at restoration sites indicate about the costs involved? Why are the French willing to pay higher taxes to save old buildings like these? When did national commitment to such projects evolve and under what circumstances? What is the significance of the title of Hugo's novel? What role might the text have played in conserving Notre Dame Cathedral for future generations?

At this point, I like to introduce the historical novel as a genre and to ask what other works in this genre students have read. With any luck, the undergraduates will have heard of Sir Walter Scott, and the graduate students will be familiar with at least one of his works. The concept of local color may be new to many (though readers of *Atala* will recognize it here as well), but it is critical to an appreciation of the Romantics' contribution to postrevolutionary literature. In courses that include realist texts, enabling students to see that the techniques applied to past history by the Romantics are also used by the realists to dissect present history is an important step in giving them a global understanding of literary history. By discussing at the beginning of the course how depictions of the past might obliquely refer to current events by eulogizing or satirizing them, students become better prepared to recognize the social criticism in *Notre-Dame de Paris*. Most of them have seen various *Star Trek* episodes, for example, and many have read popular works of science fiction. Once they understand that the utopian and dystopian aspects of future history that gesture toward present-day reality correspond to what Hugo was undertaking in his portrayal of the French past, they are more willing to consider historical fiction as a daring, provocative—and potentially revolutionary—genre.[4]

The setting of *Notre-Dame de Paris* in 1482—the date serves as the novel's subtitle—is likewise worth a few minutes of class time. Why did Hugo choose this particular time frame? What was happening in the world during the late Middle Ages? What new era was about to be born, and what further changes did it bring? After exploring such questions, one can ask students to look for characters in the text who embody traits of France's past or its future and for themes, events, or scenes, not only in the plot but also in the digressions, that might allude to the period in which the author lived. By now, students should be oriented to read for meaning as well as for pleasure, without being overwhelmed by excessive lecturing and analysis before they even open the book.

Study Questions The questions that students take home act as guides for their reading and for discussion. A word of caution: Nothing is more inimical to curiosity and learning than giving students the impression that the instructor has only one answer in mind for apparently open-ended questions. The questions must therefore help them feel that they are gaining mastery over a complex text that lends itself to a shower of personal readings. To this end, I am careful to stress that my objective is to assist them in finding repeating patterns (words, themes, scenes, images, metaphors, etc.) in the text, since these are nearly always significant, and I urge them to think freely and to develop their own explanations and interpretations for any patterns they discover.

Over the years, I have tried several approaches to integrating the questions into class sessions. Sometimes I ask everyone to talk about the salient features of each book in the novel; sometimes we focus only on the questions with which students had difficulty or, conversely, on the ones that especially interested them; sometimes I ask for volunteers to lead the discussion on a given book in the next session (they themselves choose the questions for which they are responsible); sometimes I break the class into small groups where students compare answers, impressions, and interpretations for one or two books, after which one person reports the comparisons to the class. The approach depends on class size, the students' level of sophistication, and the formats used to discuss previous works. Since I distribute lists of questions (or of important themes, features, and structures to look for) in all my courses for most of the texts we read, I try to vary the discussion format from day to day to incorporate a number of learning styles and maintain freshness and spontaneity in classroom interactions.

Hugo's Humor Whether read in the original or in translation, Hugo's work does not immediately reveal its sense of humor and dazzling wordplay. The deadpan delivery, erudite digressions, and tragic resonances seem far removed from anything that might be considered funny. And yet it is essential to strip away the appearance of *Notre-Dame de Paris* as a stodgy old masterpiece if students are to perceive its novelty and audacity. One way to do so is to highlight the many kinds of comedy that permeate the text.

One useful starting point is to have students review the classic characteristics of comedy (see, e.g., Frye 163–86), an exercise that reinforces the recognition of Hugo's daring *mélange des genres*. To be sure, the denouement plays ironically on the convention of the happy ending, first with the "Mariage de Phœbus" (bk. 11, ch. 3), then with the "Mariage de Quasimodo" (bk. 11, ch. 4). But with prodding, students should also be able to see the humor in the opening scene of the novel (a spoof of the notions of opening night and the sensitive poet [bk. 1]); in the self-referential "H" of the cathedral façade (graphic humor [bk. 3, ch. 1]); in Gringoire's startling encounter in the Cour des Miracles with the blind people who can see and the lame people who can walk (social satire [bk. 2, ch. 6]); in the "dialogue de sourds" ("dialogue of the deaf") embodied by Quasimodo's encounter with the deaf judge (a dramatic play on words [bk. 6, ch. 1]); in the hunchback's displaced sexual frenzy as he rides the bell with the huge clapper (a visual pun [bk. 4, ch. 3]); in the travesty of justice at Esmeralda's trial (black humor [bk. 8, chs. 1–3]); and in the *truands'* attempt to penetrate "Our Lady of Paris" by ramming the door (another visual pun [bk. 10, ch. 4]). Such an exchange leads naturally to an overview of the differences between high and low comedy, both of which run throughout Hugo's novel.

Oral Presentations Thanks to its multifaceted presence in the media, *Notre-Dame de Paris* lends itself to lively oral reports by students (individually or in pairs, depending on class size), who enjoy the creative latitude that such resources allow.[5] When each student becomes a teacher, the rest of the class can be quick to respond in the follow-up discussions, especially if the instructor stays in the back of the room and allows the questions and reactions to flow. Again, presenters concentrate on some aspect of the text that appeals, intrigues, or puzzles them, tying it to their research on the topic and, as appropriate, to other works in the course. Courtship rituals, race relations, *coups de foudre*, Gothic elements, melodramatic conventions, social satire, images of harmony and discord, recurring metaphors, relations between plot and digressions—students are eager to explore such dimensions of Hugo's novel, debate their significance, and compare them with those in texts they have already read.

TEACHING WITH MULTIMEDIA

Having grown up, like my students, with television, I am all too aware of the power of visual stimuli. Some of my colleagues consider them distracting, but I have found them invaluable in focusing student attention on specific points. Since I was not to technology born, I have attempted to learn one new skill each year in order to develop an arsenal of strategies from which to draw as I prepare each day's session. For the past few years, I have held all of my undergraduate classes in wired classrooms equipped with computers, Zip and CD drives, Internet connections, VCRs, DVD players, and large screens. These resources allow for many kinds of instructional support:

PowerPoint So many students are learning PowerPoint in high school that I can now require that oral presentations include that format. Students understand that integrating text and image enables them to practice skills they will need in the professional world. In seeking appropriate illustrations for their talks, they devote much time to Web research on subjects such as Hugo's career, medieval and nineteenth-century Paris, Gothic architecture and Notre Dame Cathedral, and popular renditions of Hugo's novel. The imaginative use of image, color, graphics, and motion, combined with projected outlines, enlivens their analyses of the text and, judging by the quantity and quality of subsequent comments and questions, engages the rest of the class far more than do traditional presentations.

CD-ROMs Several years ago, I purchased an outstanding CD on Hugo's life, times, works, and contemporaries (writers, artists, musicians, scientists, politicians)—*Le XIXe siècle: Le siècle de Victor Hugo* (Soussigne)—that provides the portraits, biographies, chronologies, and textual excerpts for many intermediate- and upper-level literature classes, including the ones devoted to *Notre-Dame de Paris*. Thus the images of young Victor, his spouse, and his children illustrate my summary of the writer's literary beginnings, humanizing and rejuvenating him for a new generation of readers. Sometimes I leave one picture displayed behind me for the rest of the session, a tactic that directs students' attention toward the front of the class and that seems to stimulate both left-brained and right-brained, logical and creative, activity. It is also possible to project some of the key passages from the novel (in French) for reading aloud in groups (which brings out the poetic, euphonic qualities of the text) and for general discussion and analysis.

Zip Disk My home library is replete with illustrated editions of Hugo's novels, reproductions of his striking watercolors and drawings, biographies, and scholarly books with photographs, political cartoons, reproductions of his work as a journalist and politician, and so forth. In the past, I would dutifully lug my volumes to school and pass them around in class for the students to enjoy. Today I can scan at home any materials that I want to use, transporting them to class on a Zip disk. Besides relieving me of physical labor, this approach allows all the students to look at the same image at the same time, thus fostering questions, comments, and discussion rather than solitary, asynchronous viewing.

World Wide Web As I do with CDs or Zip disks, I turn to the Web only to galvanize and supplement class discussions centered on the text. Since sites pertinent to both Hugo and *Notre-Dame de Paris* change regularly, using a metaindex like *Les saucissons chauds* or *HAPAX: French Resources on the Web* can be helpful. To emphasize Hugo's current interest to collectors and the value they place on different editions of the novel in English and French, I like to show the numerous entries under his name on eBay, some with illustrations, on any given day. When referring in general education courses to the enduring place of *Notre-Dame de Paris* in popular culture, I go to the Disney story Web site (http://disney.store.go.com) and type in "Hunchback" for a look at Disney's spinoffs of the novel. Very often, the crass commercialization of Hugo's work (which does not even bear his name here) provokes powerful responses from the students in defense of the original.

Videos Though my department has a large inventory of videos that instructors can borrow, I have amassed a personal collection of cinematic versions of Hugo's novels that I can use in different combinations in the undergraduate classroom to supplement what my students come up with for their own presentations. In the famous scene on the pillory, for example, Hugo illustrates his aesthetic of the sublime (Esmeralda) and the grotesque (Quasimodo). Showing clips from one or two films—the 1923 silent *Hunchback of Notre Dame,* a 1939 rendition, and a 1997 made-for-television movie—promotes fruitful reflections on the dramatic elements of the scene, the various interpretations of the principal roles, the ways in which the episodes are framed, and the cinematic prompts for the sublime. The 1996 portrayal of Esmeralda by Disney works well for exchanges about how freely a classic text may be interpreted or about the perceived need to appeal to a postfeminist audience. Frollo's role in some movies as a priest, in others as a judge, can be explored as a possible function of social climate or aesthetic choice. And, although Frollo is thrown from the cathedral in every adaptation, there is a wide range of endings pertaining to Esmeralda. She dies hanged, as in Hugo's work, in a 1956 motion picture of *The Hunchback of Notre Dame* but ends up with Phoebus in the 1923 and Disney versions and with Gringoire in the 1939 and made-for-TV movies. Making such comparisons provides provocative angles from which to consider the substitution of comedy for tragedy and the risks involved in closing with a scene where sympathetic characters crumble into dust.[6]

Rock Opera To date, I have hesitated to integrate the contemporary rock opera of *Notre-Dame de Paris* into the classroom. The musical has yet to achieve the recognition of *Les Miz* by American audiences, and I find playing an unfamiliar song and asking students to compare it with the text to be a chancier and more time-consuming activity than looking at an image or watching and reacting to a film clip. However, in keeping with my intention of trying something new every year, I am currently experimenting with threaded discussions, a technology that may prove valuable for considering the rock opera. Next year, I will introduce one of the arias in my advanced oral communication course and ask the students to post their responses outside class. If they are able to express substantive opinions about the song without having read Hugo's novel, I will deem the experiment a success and will use the same means to continue to broaden the appeal of *Notre-Dame de Paris* in future classes.

I make no extravagant claims for the results of these strategies. The evidence that they work includes not only lively class interactions and substantive research papers but also the numbers of students who go on to major in French or who take upper-division literature courses or who elect to take another course with me. But nothing replaces the anonymous comments in the end-of-semester student evaluations that say, quite consistently, "*Notre-Dame de Paris* was the best work we read in the course."

NOTES

1. See Grossman on Hugo as a popular phenomenon in both the nineteenth and twentieth centuries in "From Classic to Pop Icon."
2. I no longer teach in a purely chronological manner, interspersing poetry, theater, and fiction according to dates of publication, as I did early in my career. That approach makes it much harder for undergraduates to learn the terminology and the conventions for particular genres and to compare works within each tradition.
3. See Décaux; Maurois; and Robb for particularly insightful—and occasionally riveting—accounts of the young poet's childhood and his rapid rise to head the French Romantic movement.
4. For an inspired explanation of the historical and political dimensions of *Notre-Dame de Paris*, see Laurence Porter (*Victor Hugo* 20–23; 25–26).
5. Students sign up on the first day of class for the date and topic on the syllabus on which they wish to give a formal presentation. This exercise is limited to undergraduate courses where the number of students is no more than double the number of sessions. If we devote two or three weeks to *Notre-Dame de Paris*, talks on different aspects of the text can, in principle, be scheduled for each day it is covered. At the graduate level, students developing a research paper on the novel report on their findings for a bibliographic essay that surveys the critical literature.
6. For the relation of *Notre-Dame de Paris* to the cinema, see Grossman, "From Classic to Pop Icon" (486–89); Laster (372–73); and Laurence Porter (*Victor Hugo* 30; 154).

Véronique Flambard-Weisbart

Potential Reader, Potential Writer: Global Simulations in the French Literature Classroom

Globalization owes much to the flourishing technology of the Internet, which has largely contributed to transforming all the rules of communication. E-mail, chat rooms, news groups—all are informal tools of communication that break barriers. However, the interactive potential of this technology has not often been applied to the French literature classroom. In this essay, I consider the legacy of virtual interaction that French writers developed before the age of cyberspace, examine how virtual reality has reached the French literature classroom, and describe how we might pursue virtual interactive capabilities to reach students beyond the traditional classroom framework.

SURF'S UP: FROM POETIC PLAY TO ROLE-PLAYING GAMES AND SIMULATIONS

Literary fiction has brought ideas, dreams, imagination, and feelings into readers' lives and has helped readers think about and experience the human condition through the intermediary of an often omniscient narrator. In this way, it has opened windows on the subconscious and satisfied readers' desire for otherness. Readers have gained access to imaginary worlds by identifying both with characters and with situations created by authors and have thus lived experiences foreign to their daily routines. In 1950s France, the authors of the *nouveau roman* (New Novel) began to challenge the role of literary fiction by rejecting the conventions of the traditional realist novel as well as the politically committed philosophical novel. French literary-fiction practices would be changed forever by the new practices these writers introduced: temporal discontinuity; fragmented characters; shifting points of view; multiple, contradictory meanings; intertextuality; reflexivity; and the use of ludic textual structures.

In the 1960s, members of a group known as Oulipo challenged the traditional role of literary fiction in their own way. By focusing their narratives on role play and interactive language games, they downplayed the role of the narrator in literary fiction. They also illustrated their belief in literature for the sake of literature by stepping away from the dogma of authorship and style. Instead, they articulated the potentiality of every reader as a writer. Marcel Bénabou and Jacques Roubaud, two members of Oulipo (Wolipo),[1] described their group as follows:

> WOLIPO? What is this? What is that? What is WO? What is LI? What is PO? WO is WORKSHOP, a workroom. To create what? some LI.
>
> LI is what you read and delete. What kind of LI? The LIPO.
>
> PO means potential. Literature in unlimited quantity, potentially producible until the end of time, in enormous quantities, useless for any practical end. . . . What do WOLIPIANS do, the members of WOLIPO . . . ? They work. Certainly, but for WHAT? for LIPO to progress.
>
> Certainly, but HOW? By inventing constraints. New and old constraints, difficult and less diiffficult and too diiffiicuuult ones. Wolipian literature is a LITERATURE UNDER CONSTRAINTS. (my trans.)[2]

The authors of Oulipo simultaneously describe and deconstruct the structures of exchange and representation of the era's consumer society while creating original literary forms. In their works, Georges Perec, Raymond Queneau, François Le Lionnais, Jacques Roubaud, among others, playfully adapted traditional poetic constraints and invented new ones. They pledged absolute obedience to these virtual constraints. The poetic act no longer was the result of the imagination or individual style of authors but was generated by authors' deliberate and playful application of a geometric or mathematical formula. When Queneau, for example, in *Exercices de style*, followed one such formula to the extreme, he and writers like him literally became instruments for allowing the text to self-generate, a fact that is demonstrated in Marcel

Bénabou's *Pourquoi je n'ai écrit aucun de mes livres* ("Why I Did Not Write Any of My Books").

In the spirit of Oulipo, virtual reality became extremely popular in the late 1970s and early 1980s; role-play games, such as Dungeons and Dragons, invented by playful mathematicians and scientists, made a massive appearance on the market. The games consisted in the creation—or the simulation—of imaginary worlds, realistic or not, in which all players had to work together by taking on assumed roles at the same time and in the same imaginary world. Role play was particularly relevant to the game because the game relied on virtual constraints that were determined by the roll of statistical dice. The rules of the game were based on these virtual constraints, which, as in real-life situations, could not be foreseen before the roll of the dice. In role-play games, rolling the dice replaced the author's role in fiction and multiplied the potentiality of characters and situations by a calculated percentage. Role play was but another little step toward cyberspace and thus toward access to virtual reality; the rest is history.[3]

GLOBAL SIMULATIONS: FROM THE STREET TO THE CLASSROOM

With the advent of global communication, today more than ever before we can do the impossible. In the age of cyberspace, although easily accessible information is still the commodity of technologically sophisticated countries, global communication mitigates elitism. Any life situation can be simulated in cyberspace, and anyone can function in a virtual reality and reinvent oneself with only a computer as intermediary. As global communication creates a virtual global village, the traditional role of literary fiction as a window on the subconscious may seem obsolete.

To instructors in French studies, this predicament may sound eerie. Indeed, to students who from a young age are adept at experiencing the global potential of virtual reality and its technology, specializing in French studies may sound dull and limited, and French is therefore less frequently studied.

In today's context of global communication, our extensive use of interactive technology and our systematic tapping into virtual reality bring us a step closer to imagining and experiencing the world from the perspectives of others, to becoming other on demand, without the intermediary of an author or a narrator. From this perspective, an increasing new role imparted to instructors in French studies is to make virtual reality and literary fiction coexist harmoniously. Hence, we instructors in French studies need not attempt to defeat the wave of virtual reality (Charrière and Magnin 54). Rather, we must simply learn to surf this wave to the shore of French literary fiction. Of course, efficient pedagogical tools for surfing are necessary to reach this shore painlessly. One tool that smoothes the obstacles along the ride without compromising the essence of literary fiction is global simulation, which, far from replacing the poetic act, participates in the "construction" and the "animation" of an invented universe (Bourgignon 1). Such simulation consists in the creation of a virtual environment, which has the potential to enact participants' desire.

Patrick Charrière and Michèle Magnin explain how global simulations penetrated the 1970s French pedagogical context and why such simulations need to be considered a valid pedagogical tool to teach French as a foreign language in the current surge of virtual reality:

> The nature of learning audiences has undergone an upheaval without precedents over the last twenty years. In fact, the generations born from the 1960s onward have been absorbed in an omnipresent audiovisual environment, which did not exist before. We are not yet certain of the consequences of this surge of images and of the interactions they impose on the modes of cultural acquisition. Yet, it is certain that to propose a simulation experience in a pedagogical framework is to speak a familiar language to these "irreducible players who fell into the pot of interactive games when they were little."
>
> (54; my trans.)[4]

Indeed, the objective of global simulations, whether on paper or in cyberspace, is the same: to invent imaginary worlds, realistic or not, and to simulate together and at the same time in the classroom. Since students have been fed interactive and role-play games from birth, they could feel right at home.

Francis Debyser demonstrates how global simulation is a visionary tool that can pedagogically exploit the surge of virtual reality. In *L'immeuble*, an original global simulation that he developed, the role-play game, just like any other game, is based on rules or constraints. An animator of virtual reality (the instructor) is responsible for ensuring that the players (the students) respect the rules. No game is worth playing if it does not have rules or constraints, and a global simulation is no exception to this dictum. The pedagogy of *L'immeuble* is, in fact, strongly influenced by the structure and development of narrative techniques in Perec's *La vie mode d'emploi*. These techniques consist of planting a virtual character in a virtual site (the building) and making the character evolve through written extensions and digressions. Each participant must not only display linguistic ability in the French language but also help the simulation progress toward the larger goal set for the classroom. Furthermore, to maintain coherence in the simulation at the level of the classroom, participants need to ensure that their interests coincide beyond the personal. In the simulation, nothing is ever taken for granted. Each participant is constantly engaged in negotiations, debates, and questioning to resolve problems for the benefit of the goal each specific simulation is set to reach.

POTENTIAL APPLICATIONS FOR THE LITERATURE CLASSROOM

At a time when French literary fiction is reinventing its role in the face of global communication, this new role needs to be reflected in French literature classrooms. Although French literary fiction is not an endangered species, instructors in French studies have had to update their pedagogy to impede the drop in student enrollments and to attract students to their classes. Course descriptions lure students to French classes with such key words as *virtual reality* or *role play*, which is a promise to have fun. I wish to relate how my understanding of the simulation approach works in the literature classroom. Starting in the mid–1990s, I used global simulations in my course titled French Stylistics and Composition, which out of concern for accuracy I renamed Writing Workshop in French. My students have the goal of developing their written skills semester after semester and have therefore benefited from creating virtual buildings or villages located in the French-speaking world and virtual French-speaking characters to inhabit them. Using information found on the Internet, they made these virtual worlds coherent and realistic. The enactment of a virtual French reality during class time succeeded in breaking down linguistic and cultural barriers where more traditional pedagogical approaches had failed before.

I have learned, therefore, that there is plenty of room to exploit further the potential benefits of global-simulation pedagogy. Indeed, though the use of this pedagogy, which is communicative and interactive, has been extensively implemented in French language classes and considerable work has been done on text-based virtual reality,[5] global-simulation pedagogy remains disconcertingly rare in the French literature classroom. I therefore resolved to extend this pedagogical approach. Encouraged by the results obtained in Writing Workshop in French, I have adapted global-simulation pedagogy to the French literature classroom to enhance students' experiences and understanding of French literary fiction. In a collaborative effort with Magnin, I developed two potential course scenarios to teach French literary fiction with global simulations (Flambard-Weisbart and Magnin). Both aim at entertaining and instructing the student without compromising the requirements established in French studies programs.

The first scenario uses a simulation with a survey approach, which can be applied in a French literature and culture course—for example, in a course on postrevolutionary French literature. The second scenario proposes a simulation with a selected-topic approach, which can be used in a French literature course with a narrower focus, on a time period or a social, political, artistic, philosophical, or literary movement—for example, in a course on French fiction and globalization. Whether the course is a survey of postrevolutionary French literature or it just focuses on French fiction and globalization, its syllabus relies on the principle of role play and requires students to reinvent themselves in a virtual space and time created in a broad array of narrative cultural parameters introduced by the instructor.

A simulation may look like reality but it does not replace reality and does not stand for a poetic act. Rather, a simulation requires an understanding of reality, because it uses reality as a basis for role play. Simulation imitates literary fiction's reality. It is ruled by constraints, which must be respected. Students create virtual characters and develop them through negotiations in and extensions of a virtual reality.

This outcome can be achieved only with careful preparation. More than ever, a detailed syllabus is necessary. Besides a reference bibliography (e.g., anthologies, novels, critical essays), the syllabus must provide a detailed outline of the simulation's rules and specify the proper space for both individual and collaborative work, either in groups or by the whole class. The simulation's context must be made explicit: where, when, and how does it start, progress, and end? Of course, each syllabus will have to be adapted to the specific needs of each simulation. It should also offer a reference list of basic

Internet sites providing appropriate context for the simulation, which students may consult for the simulation to progress in the proper direction.[6] In a simulation, where instructors become virtual-reality animators and students become players, success depends on the animator's ability to direct the players on the proper path. To ensure that students do not lose sight of the original goal of the simulation while playing, the instructor must prepare them for unknown factors that they may encounter on the path toward success. Finally, a simulation needs to end because of real-time constraints.

SCENARIO 1: THE SURVEY APPROACH

The first scenario relies on a chronological approach that encompasses an entire course—in this example, a survey of French literature and culture from the Enlightenment to the present period. This course is structured around a global simulation in which each student becomes a contemporary time traveler, an explorer, by adopting a borrowed identity and assuming expertise (e.g., as a historian, a physician, an architect, a sociologist, a philosopher, a writer, a scientist, or the archivist that each group must include). With a team of fellow explorers, each student moves through space (in France) and time (from the French Enlightenment to the present) using a time machine. Every stop of the time machine sets the context for selected texts studied in class and allows teams of explorers to gather information on the era the text was written in and that it's about. Interaction takes place both in class through oral reports or group work and at home through a cyber travelogue, the extensive writing component of the course. The log is an account kept by each explorer that details his or her virtual environment, while traveling in time. To create the log, students first share with one another, in class, their diverse virtual encounters with real historical characters or fictitious literary characters; that is, they share their informed participation in historical events. Then, at home, students write the log; it is always written in the first person and sent to all participants in the simulation. Through this individual and collective work, each student advances the simulation and thereby contributes to a diverse yet detailed chronological fresco of France's postrevolutionary culture—and this results in a collective written work that represents the intensive writing component of the course and that elaborates on the teamwork started at midterm.

A possible way of starting a simulation with the survey approach is to show students *Les visiteurs*, a French comedy. Since the film relies on the concept of time travel, it is used to introduce virtual reality. Students can appreciate the comic effects produced by anachronisms and by comparing social systems (feudal versus capitalist) and cultural differences from one century to the next. Above all, the film serves the purpose of an antimodel. Students are made aware of the easy traps that they need to avoid during the simulation, such as clichés, commonplaces, and gratuitous anecdotes. The playful element is essential in a simulation, but playfulness can only result from skillfully applying and questioning the rules of the game.

In the survey approach, it is important to end the simulation coherently, in a way that encompasses society, philosophy, and science. Student-explorers who have invested themselves in the simulation throughout the term cannot simply leave the simulation by walking out the classroom door; more than ever, they need real closure. This is where the collaborative cumulative project started at midterm comes into play. The last few weeks of class are dedicated to synthesizing all the information gathered by student-explorers—and saved by each group's archivist—during the term and to constructing a chronological fresco of France's postrevolutionary culture. At midterm, each student is assigned the responsibility of writing one chapter of the fresco. Each student must contribute his or her own research to the project yet ensure the coherence of the whole project. Furthermore, the global-simulation experience transforms the classroom dynamic for the better, because students feel responsible not only to the instructor but also to their peers; indeed, no one wants to be the weakest link in the simulation. Finally, in contrast to more traditional course endings, students get a copy of the chronological fresco their individual and collaborative efforts have produced. More than notes in a folder that they may never look at again, more than an individual research paper written at the last minute, the students' final project is a short manuscript developed over time that is theirs to take home. This is a useful and accurate reference document that they are proud not only to have produced but also to show to their peers outside the classroom. Above all, students take home an experience that stays with them forever.

SCENARIO 2: THE SELECTED-TOPIC APPROACH

The second scenario is a French literature course that adopts a specific focus, such as French Fiction and Globalization. It uses the same assessment tools as the survey scenario—extensive and intensive writing, oral reports, teamwork, individual work, and the collaborative cumulative project for the whole class (the pastiche)—but this time the students' virtual journey takes place in novels. Students begin the simulation by breaking into as many small teams as necessary to represent the different novels selected for the course by the instructor. Each student borrows the identity of a character from the novel chosen by his or her team and is responsible for developing this character in the simulation beyond the frame of the novel. Each virtual character must evolve in the social and historical context of the specific novel yet interact with the characters of other novels in the simulation. Class time is divided between formal analysis of the novels and interaction that takes place during the simulation and through oral reports. The reports are delivered by individual virtual characters in the novels or by teams representing specific novels and offer insights into the mechanisms that make the characters in the novels function or into the diverse historical, social, artistic, and philosophical contexts of the novels. Interaction also takes place outside class as each student elaborates on his or her character through extensive writing, in the form of either a cyberjournal or a travelogue written from the first-person perspective of the character, in which the character gives details about surroundings and context; the cyberjournal or travelogue must always be sent to the whole class. The intensive writing component of the class is also met both outside and inside the classroom, in the form of individual short essays that develop the material presented in the oral reports and through the pastiche, a narrative written collectively online and after midterm that parallels the novel's narrative.

To present a simulation with a selected-topic approach, students choose a novel to read and analyze that opens the gate to whatever topic the course covers. The novel must provide a narrative system that students can emulate in the simulation; it must also reflect the effects of global communication on French fiction yet demonstrate the diversity of French authors facing these effects and dialoguing with them. There is a wide variety of texts to choose from.

One example is *Zones*, by the Parisian novelist-journalist Jean Rolin, which makes a convincing demonstration of our senseless need to communicate. His experimental writing about visiting Paris is neither picturesque journalism nor cheap sociology. Using a travelogue format, Rolin offers his impressions of Paris and its immediate periphery. He alternates between tidy descriptions and personal observations, diverse anecdotes and incidents taken from the real and the imaginary, and literary quotations. The French icons that Rolin scatters in his descriptions of Paris reinforce the image of a metropolis touched by the effects of global communication and its technology. Rolin also decries that things previously mute now have the urge to communicate, such as the electronic billboards in the metro that welcome anonymous passengers and send commonplace messages into the void. Because of the novel's explicit intertextuality and a style that feels impersonal, *Zones* appears to be Rolin's senseless communication into the void, but his desire for literary enactment stands forth and succeeds in communicating. In a novel that could implicitly have been inspired by the *nouveau roman* or Oulipo's techniques, Rolin bases his narrative on virtual systematic constraints that create an original and self-reflective literary work. By reading and analyzing a novel such as Rolin's, students grasp a particular French historical and social context and are exposed to French diversity in the arts, politics, literature, and other cultural phenomena. To begin the simulation, students should outline the targeted cultural context. Students can emulate Rolin's narrative techniques and use other novels to simulate a journey. By selecting novels and using their setting and literary context as the basis for a global-simulation exercise, students are given the tools and setting for stretching their imagination beyond what would normally be possible in the classroom.

Again, students end the simulation by producing a cumulative project. It is possible to construct this collaborative literary pastiche, a short narrative written in the style of an author, beginning at midterm. Echoing the playful narrative constructions of Oulipo, such as those in Perec's *Espèces d'espaces* that describe the street, students might write their collective narrative about one novel they select while respecting the constraints of its context. In some ways, students' pastiches constitute a portrait of French culture in a global context, and students may even use other authors read during the term to challenge the selected author's point of view. Furthermore, to produce a successful literary pastiche, with or without a satirical intent, students do not merely imitate the previous work of an author; they also demonstrate their deeper understanding of both the narrative techniques and the cultural context that animated the original work. Students do not leave the classroom empty-handed, since each student creates a portfolio, which includes a selection of revised entries from the individual cyberjournal or travelogue, a revision of the short individual essays, and a copy of the collective pastiche.

Above all, students bring home their real expertise on French culture in a specific context, one they could acquire only during their experience in the global simulation.

I encourage teachers to try an experiment with students by asking them to simulate a randomly chosen virtual world. I predict that they will stare at you blankly, unable to understand what you are suggesting, much less to release their creative potential. To imagine a virtual world, we need the constraints of a cultural context, especially in the pedagogical situation of the French literature and culture classroom. Global simulation offers a tool to unleash students' imagination by using technology with which they have long been familiar for ends that support the pedagogical goals of French studies. As long as its parameters are clearly defined, understood, and respected by all participants from beginning to end, global simulation offers unlimited potential for reaching students beyond the traditional classroom framework.

NOTES

1. For this particular passage to make sense, I translated Oulipo into Wolipo. However, for the rest of the essay, I use Oulipo.
2. "OULIPO? Qu'est ceci? Qu'est cela? Qu'est-ce que OU? Qu'est-ce que LI? Qu'est-ce que PO? OU c'est OUVROIR, un atelier. Pour fabriquer quoi? De la LI.

   LI c'est la littérature, ce qu'on lit et ce qu'on rature.

   Quelle sorte de LI? La LIPO

   PO signifie potentiel. De la littérature en quantité illimitée, potentiellement productible jusqu' à la fin des temps, en quantités énormes, infinies pour toutes fins pratiques. . . . Que font les OULIPIENS, les membres de l'OULIPO . . . ? Ils travaillent. Certes, mais à QUOI? A faire avancer la LIPO.

   Certes, mais COMMENT? En inventant des contraintes. Des contraintes nouvelles et anciennes, difficiles et moins diifficiles et trop diiffiiciiiles. La littérature Oulipienne est une LITTERATURE SOUS CONTRAINTES. . . ." (Bénabou and Roubaud)
3. See, for example, the work of Marie-Laure Ryan, *Narrative*, in which she describes narrative as virtual reality.
4. "La nature des publics d'apprenants a subi ces vingt dernières années un bouleversement sans précédent. En effet les générations nées à partir des années 1960 ont baigné dans un environnement audio-visuel omniprésent qui n'existait pas auparavant. On ne connaît pas encore très bien les conséquences de ce déferlement d'images et des interactions qu'elles induisent sur les modes d'acquisition de la culture. En revanche, il est certain que proposer, dans un cadre pédagogique, une expérience de simulation, parle un langage familier à ces 'irréductibles joueurs qui sont tombés dans la marmite des jeux interactifs quand ils étaient petits.' " The context of the citation by Charrière and Magnin is the preface of Debyser's *L'immeuble* (1).
5. See, e.g., David Bell, *Introduction*; Haynes and Holmevik; David Porter; Marie-Laure Ryan (*Cyberspace*; *Narrative*); Schneider and von der Emde; Sudweeks, McLaughlin,

and Rafaeli. All these authors represent the considerable work done on text-based virtual reality, especially using MOO's, for pedagogical purposes.

6. For example, the Web site established by Magnin, which she frequently updates and which features numerous pages and links on global simulations in the pedagogical section.

John Anzalone

Teaching in the Margins of the Nineteenth Century

How does one teach the French fin de siècle at the undergraduate level? In describing a course on this period, I work from a premise so simple that it may seem as if I'm breaking down open doors. Still, I hope my premise provides insight on this volume's focus on cultural studies' possible influence on our teaching. The premise can be summed up in the words of that canny old pol from my once-upon-a-time congressional district, former Speaker of the House Tip O'Neill, who was fond of saying, "All politics is local." I will be thinking locally here: for me, teaching noncanonical writers of the fin de siècle period—*la pédagogie en marge du dix-neuvième siècle*—at Skidmore College involves conditions I might not encounter were I teaching the same material elsewhere, without the specific curriculum we have put in place.

Thinking locally is another way of thinking about pragmatic imperatives. It's the obverse of a coin we have all flipped on many occasions in designing our courses. In deciding what to emphasize, given the basic objectives we have for the class, we routinely ask ourselves what problems are inherent in the writers, periods, and texts we teach; we frequently work out strategies that can help us manage the difficulties we anticipate our students will encounter. The writers I came to love as a student and to write about as a scholar possess certain features that I must acknowledge to teach their works effectively. Authors of the fin de siècle period, like Joris-Karl Huysmans, Auguste Villiers de l'Isle-Adam, Léon Bloy, and Octave Mirbeau, to name but a few, are difficult for a host of reasons: they are linguistically challenging—indeed, increasingly so—and in the undergraduate curriculum they're chronically noncanonic, that is, they suffer from an underexposure that makes their unfamiliarity a signifier of impenetrability.[1] For the student who does have the opportunity to approach them closely, their ideologies often seem a baffling mix of visionary modernity on the one hand and reactionary recklessness on the other. It is routine for us to consider how to handle such factors when preparing to teach; indeed, just these paradoxes that make the period exciting to teach.

It is just as important that we consider who our students are, how much background they have in what we're teaching them, and how the material fits into a curriculum. Established over time by groups of colleagues, curriculum develops through a consensus that usually emerges only when exhaustion makes compromise preferable to continued fighting. Curriculum is a key matter of local politics; in some respects, it is even harder to manage than students and their backgrounds, because negotiations with colleagues are distant from the actual classroom transaction. Yet when we delve further into how our courses fit both our students and our institutions' major or minor programs, we occasionally discover approaches or strategies we might not have used otherwise, at least not as readily or as soon.

THE SETTING

Skidmore College is a *smallliberalartscollege* (four words always spoken as if they were one) of some two thousand students, situated in Saratoga Springs, New York. We have a language requirement that was restored to the core curriculum during a period of sweeping change in the early eighties and that brought an interdisciplinary emphasis through the program we call Liberal Studies. My arrival at the college in 1985, as a first-year associate professor, coincided exactly with this new requirement system. Students were called on to demonstrate intermediate-level competency in a foreign language. Liberal Studies introduced incoming students to interdisciplinarity through a sequence of four courses, one team-taught, the other three designed and delivered by individual faculty members.[2] In practical terms, this organization meant for me, as a teacher, taking up obligations that were also, to be sure, opportunities to rethink the curriculum in French. The revised curriculum, itself a work in progress at the time, prompted me to adopt a cultural studies angle for some of my courses.

Each of the new requirements imposed conditions. The analogies between interdisciplinarity as a key component of course design and cultural studies—in a fairly broad acceptance of that term—are easy to discern: each promotes cross-fertilization through a diminished emphasis on the canon; each seeks to see things first through a wide-angle lens before zooming into narrower areas of focus; each downplays mastery as its intended purpose, shifting the emphasis instead to inquiry and process. The most immediate consequence for me of the Liberal Studies curriculum was the design of a course on French cinema called The New Wave: From Criticism to Creation, whose objectives, according to the guidelines, had to involve inquiry into an artistic form in the specific context of critical or theoretical discourse. I offer two observations about that class, which I still teach: first, the serious questions it raises about canon formation in the cinema lead students to passionate inquiry into the sociological, economic, and historical conditions of the new wave's genesis in the culture of postwar Paris; second, it is taught in English.

This last, bald fact of life about our otherwise exciting interdisciplinary curriculum evokes one of Sandy Petrey's most telling objections to the field of cultural studies: its decided monolingualism ("French Studies").[3] At Skidmore, that monolingualism led me back to the language requirement, which created a different set of issues, just as telling about the limitations of the revised course design as Petrey's objections. I decided to teach the new-wave film course in French. It was a simple matter to teach it for majors as a special-topics course, since most of the secondary materials I used were originally in French, as were the films themselves. But my experience teaching the revised Liberal Studies curriculum got me thinking about ways to modify the French curriculum, which had not changed much since before my arrival. Given my research, I was especially anxious to work with the fin de siècle period, and I began creating a course that would satisfy my interests and the curriculum, which I saw from the start as complementary.

But first I had to acknowledge a whole new area of local difficulty. Our intermediate-level requirement is based on oral proficiency, on the acquisition of practical language skills by students whose high school training was not strong enough for them to satisfy the requirement by placement examination.

The intensity of oral practice and the strengthening of conversational abilities in class have not been matched by a parallel insistence on the acquisition of the skills needed to read literature critically and in its historical contexts. When, for example, was the last time those of us with responsibilities for language teaching at the earlier levels of a proficiency-based curriculum actually taught students—systematically—the *passé simple*; any of the exotic subjunctives; or, despite proficiency's oral emphasis, the astonishingly varied, vital colloquial styles of spoken French that one readily encounters outside a classroom or textbook?

Unless our students already possess a strong enough background in French so that they come directly into the advanced curriculum or unless they quit the language because they've met the requirement (is there a worse unintended consequence of a language requirement?), most arrive at the specialist level underequipped to process critical texts in the target language—and it doesn't matter one whit whether we're dealing with canonical literary or journalistic or marginal texts. The gap is there, it is wide, and we all work at varying levels of frustration to cope with it. Now this will be true to some degree for any and every course that we teach, from the advanced-intermediate level and up. My colleagues in seventeenth-century studies confront the problem no less drastically when trying to teach Molière or Pascal as I do *du côté des décadents*. I therefore felt it crucial to the content of a course on the fin de siècle to foreground struggle with the language as a given and to do so in such a way as to denaturalize the struggle. I wanted to render it an artifact, itself worthy of self-conscious scrutiny.[4] If you sniff a remedial agenda somewhere in this strategy, I won't play innocent.

THE COURSE

These were some of the reflections that led to my conceptualizing a course in which students already encouraged to approach their learning from an interdisciplinary perspective could confront the fin de siècle fruitfully, despite the evident linguistic challenges posed by the work I had decided to highlight. The late nineteenth century in France exhibited upheaval in many spheres: social, artistic, scientific, psychological. In important ways, the period ushered in changes and conflicts that remain contemporary, at the same time as it presented new tools for the analysis and understanding of those changes. In keeping with the thrust of the Liberal Studies curriculum, I was not aiming for mastery of the issues involved, nor was I interested in topical parallels between that fin de siècle and the late 1990s. Instead, I opted to have students examine the mentalities that collided one hundred years ago through a close study of a single novel that stages those collisions in a peculiarly compelling way: *L'Eve future* (*Eve of the Future Eden*) by Villiers de l'Isle-Adam.

Defiantly unconventional despite his deep-seated traditionalism, Villiers produced a body of writing that went unrecognized in the canon for almost a hundred years. Villiers's survival depended for a time on a cult audience: his major works, passed along by previous initiates in whatever out-of-print editions could be had, continued to find a small core of happy few. But Villiers has begun creeping onto university reading lists in the last ten years, finding a new audience that has in a sense caught up with him. Emergent critical and theoretical practices that challenged the canon by their focus on oppositional discourse or marginality—the deconstruction of hegemonies central to cultural studies—have made new readers receptive to Villiers's voice.[5] As the focus of recent criticism was brought to bear on disturbing aspects of his works that earlier inquiry elided entirely, *L'Eve future* achieved a special prominence.[6] The story of the creation by a scientist, a lover, and state-of-the-art technology of an android woman in the name of impenitent idealism, this prescient work confronts with breathtaking focus central taboos of the fin de siècle, a decadent period that we still find pressing today. For example, in *L'Eve future* a woman who resembles a work of art but is deemed spiritually deficient by her lover is replaced—thanks to the visionary genius of a scientist-inventor—by an artificial device that resembles a woman but is spiritually more satisfying. This replacement raises questions about the power and limits of machines and science over the human capacity to think and experience the real and about sexuality, desire, and gender for the express purpose of shattering comfortable categories.

The extended foray into the uncanny in the novel depends on an intimate identification between art and technology that achieves the new woman. It is this nexus that I decided to work at untangling with students in the seminar. The dominant ideologies—Villiers's favorite satirical targets—of the nineteenth century in France, when subsumed by the frequent technological marvels of the age, result in *L'Eve future*'s remapping of the feminine. Although not extremely long, the novel is difficult to read. Villiers's composite style merges several Romantic and Parnassian strains, in what has been called an "écriture artiste" tending to a "dynamic phenomenalism emphasizing objectivity, impersonality and the neglect of causality" (Arnold 875). It is challenging even to those more fluent in French than my usual audience, many of whom had only satisfied our language requirement a few years earlier. It was thus important to pinpoint ahead of time some of the features of the novel and the prose that the class would be thinking about. This pre-established context could simplify the reading.

However, the language of the novel has much to tell us about how Villiers and other writers of his time developed an ideology of impenetrability that contributed to a self-imposed marginality that marked a rejection of their society and its values. Needless to say, this impenetrability goes to the core of problems of canonicity, of literary milieus and markets, and of societal constructs that I wanted the students to confront. In keeping with the spirit of the age under consideration, I opted for paradox: translation seemed to me the best way to achieve self-conscious foregrounding, in which struggling with their linguistic deficiencies would enable the students to comprehend how the opacity of the language embeds the novel in the particular conditions of its time. Note that I first encountered Villiers through his short story "Les brigands" (in *Contes cruels*) as a college freshman, thought it the hardest thing I'd ever read (and not understood), and vowed I'd never read anything by him again.

I placed the two extant and excellent English translations of the novel, by Marilyn Gaddis Rose and by Robert M. Adams, on library reserve for the class. Rose's volume ends with a pithy afterword in which she discusses her strategies for translating the novel from the perspective of translation theory, a valuable addendum for my purposes. I asked students to compare specific passages in the two translations and to produce their own as well, justifying their choice of passages in terms not only of the lexical or structural features of the text in question but also of the cultural scenario in play. It so happens that *L'Eve future* is for the most part a series of conversations—scientific, philosophical, artistic, spiritual—between its protagonists, Thomas Edison, the scientist-inventor, and Lord Ewald, the suffering lover, concerning the conduct, meaning, and effect of their experiment that creates a robot woman. Each shift in emphasis in each conversation calls into play a different network of allusions that students can analyze both linguistically and in terms of the prevailing ideologies of the period through secondary readings. Part of the novel's considerable power comes from its status as a work of revolt, but a revolt doomed to a catastrophic failure that, once again, brings the mentality of the fin de siècle into sharper focus. The purpose of the characters is to escape the networks in which they are embedded; the bitter ironies of the novel detail how the characters remain bound to their illusions.

Critics have long understood that the fascination with science and technology is a fundamental aspect of Villiers's particular genius. As Marie Lathers has shown so clearly (see *Aesthetics* and "The Decadent Goddess"), in *L'Eve future*, science and art share ways of imaging woman that bind, petrify, and render Eve inert for the experimenters' ministrations. The experimenters' tools are identified as photosculpture, three-dimensional sculptural modeling, photography, and cinema—all relatively new technologies of the age. Moreover, the language of the android's user's manual in Villiers's novel can be found in then-nascent medical discourses (Hustvedt) and writings on hysteria and psychoanalysis. Modernity's ways of imaging woman call on the new means of mechanical reproduction that promote the artificial at the expense of the real. The novel's central metaphor of the statue of the Venus de Milo as the representation of the perfect woman allows the class to explore the powerful implications inherent in the similarities between the model's pose in the sculptor's atelier and the hysteric's positioning in the clinical demonstrations of Jean-Martin Charcot.

By mirroring significant nineteenth-century artistic and technological developments, *L'Eve future* invites cross-disciplinary discussion that helps students situate and decipher its ideological discourse on the feminine. To further flesh out these issues, two additional works appear on the syllabus. In Charles Baudelaire's *Le peintre de la vie moderne* and Bram Dijkstra's *Idols of Perversity*, we look to art criticism to help us unravel some of the ideologies at work in Edison and Ewald's fantasy. Finally, I enlist the support of colleagues from other departments for presentations on such relevant issues as the birth of psychoanalysis and the status and evolution of science and technology in the period.

However challenging *L'Eve future* might be for nonspecialists, especially undergraduates, it seems tailor-made for interdisciplinary study of the type I have briefly sketched out here. The novel brings the marginal into perspective by revealing the constructed nature of the canon. A hybrid, boundary-crossing work, it encourages discussion of its imbrication in the sociocultural circumstances of its time. The novel's manifest content puts gender and male-female relationships into play in ways that, once again, point to constructs. And the opacity of *L'Eve future*'s language not only reminds students of a critical factor in marginality but also provides opportunity for exercises in translation and stylistics that allow practice in idiom, which the proficiency-oriented curriculum has not encouraged adequately. Such emphases make the novel and its time accessible to an audience that might have difficulty managing the novel in a more conventionally designed course. Students have found the book extremely compelling. To be able to read and comprehend something this difficult provides motivation for students to do more.

It will be obvious that a fundamental eclecticism prevailed in the shaping of the course. I do not address here the considerable dangers for French and French studies of a hard cultural studies approach to curriculum that Petrey uncovers and articulates so cogently (see "French Studies"), although I surely remain mindful of them. I seek instead to be exclusively descriptive, not prescriptive, in keeping with my local-politics premise. What has worked for me has a great deal to do with understanding my institution, its curriculum, and the kind of language training most prevalent among its students. That is not to say that my approach cannot be adapted elsewhere. I am considering a similarly designed course using several texts by Huysmans, Bloy, and Villiers to approach one of the lost yet most controversial subjects of the fin de siècle: religion. *La suite*, as Honoré de Balzac said, *prochainement* ("to be continued").

Shortly after my arrival at Skidmore, I had a conversation with a dean whom I admire. We were discussing new curricular initiatives for summer school and for our Paris program. There were the inevitable wrinkles, and someone at the meeting wondered aloud how hard it would be to defend the proposals to the curriculum committee. The dean promptly dismissed the likelihood of resistance by saying, "Exigent circumstance drives curriculum." At the time I was mildly surprised; the remark seemed close to a cynicism I had not suspected of him. Over the years, however, I have recalled the remark repeatedly; it has revealed itself to be, quite simply, pragmatic. In his way, he was reminding us of the need to think and act locally. Circumstances can—indeed often do—change many of the givens that we have come to rely on, and sometimes to accept without questioning, by pushing us to reshape creatively our strategies for teaching.

NOTES

1. It is not just undergraduates who are affected. In an exquisite example of the importance of timing that dramatically underscores the chronic noncanonicity of these writers, papers on them as well as other aspects of the fin de siècle were

scheduled head to head in the very last sessions at the Nineteenth Century French Studies Colloquium over a period of several years in the mid-1990s. This effectively guaranteed minimal audiences in a forum where one might have expected greater awareness of (and sensitivity to) marginality.

2. What was known for several years as the new curriculum involved other requirements, and in the intervening years it has been revised several times. My focus here is exclusively on the nexus between language and interdisciplinarity. At bottom, the new curriculum ordained new approaches, and, as in cultural studies, the debate about their worth was not only about differences between the partisans and the skeptics but also about how an individual participant could end up feeling like both a partisan and a skeptic.
3. Petrey urges that we realize the extent to which monolingualism is a threat to the study of foreign languages and cultures. That I agree with his assessment will be clear in what follows, though my local approach has as its focus only what I tried discretely to do in order to address the problem in designing Mentalités Fin de Siècle.
4. I approach the problem in much the same way as the late Michel Benamou did for the learning of basic French in his textbook *Mise en train*, to my way of thinking still one of the most original and effective pedagogical approaches to second language acquisition I have ever used.
5. Such a decentering also provides "an invaluable corrective to the sclerosis of certain parts of humanistic education in the United States" (Petrey, "French Studies" 389).
6. See Alan Raitt's preface to John Anzalone's *Jeering Dreamers* for a brief history of the fate of the novel over the last century and especially on why its fortunes have risen.

Michael Garval

Teaching Tours de France

My Eureka! moment came not in the tub but at the kitchen sink. In February 1999, I was washing the dishes, listening to the radio, and thinking about the Advanced French Conversation: Contemporary French Cultures course I was supposed to teach in the fall. Book orders were due soon. Faced with the usual, depressing assortment of readers, with their earnest, dull selections on ecology, feminism, Jacques Cousteau, and the TGV, I still hadn't chosen a text. But I was in the middle of reading a great schoolbook, a century-old one: *Le tour de la France par deux enfants* (Bruno; The Tour of France by Two Children). That summer in Paris, out of simple curiosity, I had picked up a copy of the 1998 reprint edition. Before dinner, stealing a few moments from my hectic schedule, I read the chapters on Savoy, Mont Blanc, and avalanches (38–40). Seven o'clock p.m. brought a news headline: "Avalanche in the French Alps, near Chamonix." That's it, I thought, struck by this fortuitous juxtaposition of past and present. Why not recast Advanced French Conversation as Tours de France, organizing it around *Le tour*, paired with current-day materials? How exactly to do this was unclear at first, yet I knew intuitively that the idea had potential.

Over the past several years and six class sections of Tours de France, I have designed a course that engages past and present in the kind of rich, complex, and fruitful dialogue that I imagined from the outset—amid piles of dirty dishes and visions of avalanches. More to my surprise, this design also mitigates some of the most nagging pedagogical problems we face today in French studies and, more broadly, in the humanities: how to choose and use innovative primary materials; foster critical thinking; teach to different levels; frame a pedagogy at once flexible, rigorous, and compelling; use instructional technology effectively; bridge gaps between lower- and upper-level course work; meet individual student needs while accomplishing broader disciplinary and curricular goals; and do all this so efficiently that there is still time left over not only to wash dishes but also to indulge in the kind of aimless reading that can turn out to be profitable. For, as the epigraph to chapter 7 reminds us, "Quand on apprend quelque chose, on ne sait jamais tout le profit qu'on en pourra retirer un jour" (17; "When you learn something, you never know how useful it may be one day").

DESCRIPTION

The course undertakes simultaneous tours of France, using *Le tour* as the main text, complemented by *Découvrir la France* (Discovering France), a French guidebook; Web sites; and video material. On this journey, as students discover and discuss so much about the history, geography, economy, and cultural heritage of modern France, they develop greater oral fluency, acquire a broad knowledge base (Where is Auvergne? What is a *poulet de Bresse*? Who were the *bourgeois de Calais*?), and begin to discern significant patterns of change and continuity.

Le tour was published in 1877 as a daily reader for the *cours moyen* (fifth grade). A revised, expanded edition appeared in 1906. Although published under the pseudonym "G. Bruno," it was actually the brainchild of the pedagogue and children's author Mme Alfred Fouillée, as Jacques Ozouf and Mona Ozouf point out, in their excellent article on *Le tour* (277). Conceived soon after the debacle of the Franco-Prussian War, in the tenuous, early years of the Third Republic, *Le tour* follows André and Julien, young orphaned brothers from Lorraine, on a journey across France in search of their uncle and their "mother"—France itself (277). Crammed with adventure (fires, crashes, storms, shipwrecks), information (on everything from butter making to railroads, Vercingétorix to Daguerre, *les puys d'Auvergne* to *l'École Polytechnique*), and high-minded lessons (about education, industriousness, progress, patriotism, fraternity),[1] *Le tour* was a tremendously successful and influential textbook. In all, eight and a half million copies were published, although, as Ozouf and Ozouf note, it doubtless reached an audience many times this number

(277–78). *Le tour* guided generations of French schoolchildren toward the interdependent republican ideals of achieving literacy, discovering their own country, and assimilating the Republic's values and principles. As the preface contends, "La connaissance de la patrie est le fondement de toute véritable *instruction civique*" (4; "knowing about your fatherland is the foundation of all true *civic education*"). Modeling André and Julien's studiousness, intellectual curiosity, patriotism, and virtue, young readers would become model citizens and perfect the great Republic extolled in their schoolbook. Although modern American college students clearly have no part in this process, *Le tour* does offer them, along with so much else, an education in the ideology and ideological heritage of the Third Republic.

The syllabus for Tours de France follows *Le tour* from cover to cover. On average, students read and prepare five chapters per class session, or ten per week. They also select passages in *Découvrir la France* and search for Web sites that match up with the people, places, or things André and Julien encounter along the way. In addition to reading and Web surfing, students keep a logbook or *journal de bord* of their vicarious travels, handed in and graded at semester's end. This logbook includes the following sections, to be completed for each session:

summary of André and Julien's adventures
a similar personal experience
an idea in *Le tour,* to defend or refute
readings in *Découvrir la France*
Web sites visited
comparison between France then and now
new vocabulary items and idiomatic expressions

Like the logbook, class meetings are designed to integrate the historical and the contemporary, the academic and the personal, with sessions held, alternately, in a conventional classroom and in a computer classroom.[2] The topics of conversation range widely, particularly in the computer classroom, where students work through batteries of questions, prompts, and themes projected onto a large screen with a visualizer and related to experiences, concerns, and problems raised as well as to moral, ethical, and ideological positions espoused in *Le tour.* André and Julien's first visit to a big city (" 'Oh! . . . quelle grande ville que ce Lyon!' s'écria le petit Julien" [146; "Oh! What a big city Lyon is!"]) might give rise to discussion of students' experiences with and attitudes toward life in cities, suburbs, small towns, and rural areas; the advantages and disadvantages of such different settings; and broader societal issues of urbanization, development, or demographics and how these issues intersect with individual values and aspirations. A brief passage on the great surgeon Guillaume Dupuytren's career (130) might prompt an exchange of views on premedical and medical studies, doctors, and health care, as well as more general questions about ambition, education, success, and altruism. Likewise, the sententious lessons at the head of each chapter provide rich fodder for discussion of subjects from study habits to Good Samaritan laws, family ties to business ethics, progress to pollution.

During students' discussion, the instructor monitors these conversation exercises from a central console. Although students know that the instructor could be listening to their group, they do not know when, unless the instructor chooses to intervene by offering gentle reminders using the system's intercom function, to keep them on task and in the target language and to help with vocabulary, grammar, or pronunciation. Here, as the technology may heighten the perceived intrusiveness of the instructor's intervention, a delicate balance must be struck: facilitating conversation without disrupting it.

Student work for the course includes:

extensive class participation
the logbook of observations, reactions, and reflections
one ten-minute oral presentation (five minutes for the presentation, five for questions) on a topic of particular interest to the student, related to the material read for that day
a midterm (half oral, half written)
a cumulative final (half oral, half written)

Grades are calculated as follows:

⅓ = class participation (quantity + quality)
⅓ = independent work (oral presentation + logbook)
⅓ = exams (midterm + final)[3]

RATIONALE

Why teach with these materials and in this way? How, in particular, can real historical and cultural documents be integrated into course work, when students may be ill equipped to deal with such unfamiliar and potentially challenging material? Tours de France engages students with genuine French language and culture, past, present, and would-be eternal (a particularly important category of time for the French, as students soon learn). Yet the nature of the materials and the way they are integrated into the course make them understandable for students at the undergraduate level.

To begin with, while *Le tour* offers all the richness and authenticity of a first-rate primary source, it remains at least as accessible as otherwise uninspiring contemporary readers for students of French today. Chapters are short; preceded by descriptive titles, recapitulative headings, and thematic epigraphs; and accompanied by numerous, copiously captioned illustrations. At the end of the book, a comprehensive table of contents and a map of France detailing the boys' itinerary provide further support. Throughout, precious little is taken for granted about the reader's knowledge of French history, culture, or geography.

In addition, *Le tour* is episodic, like the successful language-learning programs *French in Action* or *Destinos*, and its narrative structure is reinforced by the spatial orientation of the tour itself. Moreover, like Robert and Mireille's saga in *French in Action* (thankfully, minus his haircut and her wardrobe), *Le tour* is skillfully structured enough to keep students intrigued, yet endearingly corny and melodramatic enough (at least from our twenty-first-century perspective) to stimulate discussion through irony and parody of the story.

The contemporary print and online materials I pair with *Le tour* are similarly authentic yet accessible. Much like André and Julien's eventful journey, the students' guidebook explorations and virtual peregrinations bring all sorts of discoveries, delights, disappointments, and surprises. Likewise, the materials aid comprehension: in the guidebook, these include maps, alphabetical ordering and color coding of regions, and extensive indexing; on the Web, search engines, site maps, and links that home the reader in on specific information; and, in both, concise blocks of text accompanied by abundant headings, illustrations, and graphics. These overlapping sources (*Le tour*, *Découvrir la France*, and Web sites) provide clarity because they cover the same ground in different yet mutually illuminating ways.

The Tours de France course materials thus become not only more understandable but also richer through their juxtaposition. For example, when *Le tour* reaches Salins in the Franche-Comté (76), and students try to locate the town in *Découvrir la France*, they discover that it is now called Salins-les-Bains (91)—a name change richly emblematic not just of the town's shifting identity, with its traditional saltworks supplanted by thermal spas, but also, more broadly, of the rise of tourism and of the change from a production- to a service-based economy. Along similar lines, a student who is intrigued by the engraving "Le sabotier des Vosges" (14; "The Clog Maker of the Vosges") and who searches the Web for more information about it under the keyword *sabotier* ("clog maker"), can find sites dedicated to vanished trades and crafts that display wonderful late-nineteenth-century postcards of traditional clog makers at work (e.g., www.carte-postale.com/bretagne/sabotiersenbretagne .htm). The keyword *sabot* ("clog"), however, can lead to a French fetishist's site (www.chez.com/clogfan/), exhibiting photos of the fetishist's twin obsessions: clogs and braces (i.e., "appareils dentaires"). Once again, the contrast between then and now is suggestive, to say the least.

That overlapping materials also provide divergent perspectives addresses the larger issue of how to foster critical thinking through students' interaction with primary texts alone, if students are not ready, linguistically or conceptually, for more-abstract or more-theoretical secondary texts. Shuttling constantly between past and present—between Salins and Salins-les-Bains, clog makers and clog fetishists—students in Tours de France not only expand their linguistic horizons and enhance their knowledge of things French but also develop a historical bifocal vision that encompasses continuity and change. They see that the Roman amphitheater in Nîmes still stands proud, whereas Le Creusot, the site of Europe's largest factory one hundred years ago, now boasts an "écomusée" (museum of ecology). In the light of World Wars I and II, students feel the poignancy of the Franco-Prussian War called "la dernière guerre avec la Prusse" (9; "the last war with Prussia"). *Dernière,* in context, suggests the last war in an ongoing series. Or students may feel the poignancy of André and Julien, who, just having arrived on French soil, "marchaient joyeusement sur une route française, marquant le pas comme de jeunes conscrits" (25; "walked gleefully down a French road, marking time like young draftees") or of Vichy, which is noteworthy only as "le plus grand établissement d'eaux minérales du monde entier" (119; "the largest mineral-water spa in the whole world").

Students thus begin to develop a profounder sense of history, so often lacking in the United States yet indispensable for understanding France, which is obsessed with its past, its *patrimoine* ("cultural heritage"); its *lieux de mémoire* ("realms of memory"). The students begin to develop critical perspectives on the events of history and on their ideological underpinnings. While their awareness occurs independently, as students interact with the material, it can also be useful for the instructor to offer information, guidance, or contextualization. As students note the repeated connections made in *Le tour* between cleanliness and virtue, the instructor might comment briefly on nineteenth-century discourses on hygiene, perhaps giving as an example Alexandre Parent-Duchâtelet's parallel interests in sewers and streetwalkers. When, however, students encounter the outrageous engraving "Les quatre races d'hommes" ("The Four Races of Man"), which has a long caption beginning, "La race blanche, la plus parfaite des races humaines . . ." (184; "The white race, the most perfect of human races"), more-extensive comment is in order. This may include an overview of French colonialism, decolonization, and immigration; a discussion of racism, anti-Semitism, xenophobia, and nationalism in France, past and present; and an examination and discussion of Web sites—*SOS Racisme, le Front National*—that offer perspectives lacking in our contemporary guidebook and that students might not find on their own. The point of this intervention is to help students place this part of *Le tour* in its proper historical, cultural, and ideological context and to convey that one can appreciate the book's many charms while not endorsing its less-appealing aspects.

Clearly, a one-size-fits-all approach does not work in dealing with different ideological issues or in dealing with different students. This problem raises the broader question of how to teach to divergent levels of ability, preparation, and motivation. Tours de France was designed to offer substantial flexibility, in part because of the specific institutional context in which it was developed. North Carolina State University, located in the state capital of Raleigh, is a land-grant, research I-extensive university with over 29,000 students, which has a strong emphasis on science, engineering, and technology. Traditionally, the Department of Foreign Languages and Literatures has offered only undergraduate programs, although a master's program in French and Spanish will begin in August 2004. A handful of students major in French each year; a modest number pursue minors. Those who do major or minor often combine their studies in French with concentrations in very different disciplines, from management to textiles, zoology to electrical engineering. Because of the university's urban setting and location in the Research Triangle area of North Carolina, advanced language courses may attract international students, retirees, and advanced local high school students. The advanced conversation course in particular seems to attract these populations. To wit, one recent section included students from France, Haiti, and Ethiopia; heritage speakers from Québec and Haiti; an Austrian doctoral student in textiles; two retired engineers; and two high school students. Ostensibly more typical classmates ranged from first-year students taking their first advanced French course to a senior French major just back from a year in Lille and engaged to a Frenchwoman. Such diversity suggests that those who teach the advanced-conversation course face a daunting range of interests, abilities, preparation, motivation, and life experience. Further complicating matters is that the course is a hybrid (as its catalog name indicates) because it is supposed to serve as both an advanced-skills course and as a civilization and culture offering.

Although some of these conditions may be particular to North Carolina State University, the broader trends that have produced them are not. Enrollment in French dropped precipitously nationwide between 1990 and 1998, leveling off in recent years (Welles, table 5). As fewer yet more varied students fill ever fewer course sections, a greater range of students ends up in each classroom, and course offerings may be streamlined and consolidated. The challenges are many. How can we teach, at once, to the weakest and strongest students? Majors and nonmajors? Humanists and scientists? Young and old? Such challenges demand flexibility both in the materials chosen and in the approaches taken to them.

The course materials for Tours de France offer a wealth of possibilities for the class to explore—narrative; information; vocabulary and idioms; and moral, ethical, and ideological stances. Likewise, the ways in which students work with and are evaluated on these materials are student-centered. Students are thus allowed to go in different directions, pursue their own interests, and perform at their own level through the logbooks, lab-conversation exercises and oral exams, written exams that offer them a choice of items to answer, and independent oral presentations for which they choose their own topics. One engineering student, for instance, was intrigued by something to which I had not paid much attention before, the engraving of a submarine in the epilogue to the 1906 edition, thus captioned:

> SOUS-MARINS. Les bateaux sous-marins, inventés en France, sont mus par l'électricité. Ils voyagent sous l'eau et peuvent lancer des torpilles pour faire sauter des navires ennemis. (309)
>
> SUBMARINES. Submarine vessels, invented in France, are powered by electricity. They travel underwater and can launch torpedoes to blow up enemy ships.

The student's oral presentation on the history of submarine design and the role the French played in it was fascinating, especially for the historical connections he helped us make. We became aware that by World War I the Germans had eclipsed the French in military submarine technology and that this advance had lasting ramifications. More broadly, we learned about the repeated pattern of the French investing heavily in an earlier, inferior version of a technology, resulting in their slowness to adopt the later, superior versions (such as the electric-powered versus diesel-powered submarines, the optical versus electric telegraph, and the Minitel versus the Internet). This student's presentation is just one example of how the course enables so many different yet parallel tours.

"Different yet parallel" suggests that such salutary flexibility can coexist with the clarity, coherence, and sense of purpose that frame a rigorous and intellectually compelling course but are often in short supply in many standard offerings in the French studies curriculum. Language courses may serve up a tenuous hodgepodge of grammar, structures, vocabulary, and themes. Traditional literature or civilization surveys, with their chronological straitjackets, can impose a false sense of order. More recently developed literature and culture offerings tend toward looser clusters of issues and ideas, sometimes privileging critical complexity over coherence. In Tours de France, however, the students follow the adventures and itinerary of André and Julien, which not only provide a wealth of discussion topics and ample opportunity to develop storytelling, summarizing, and critical and analytic skills but also create a strong sense of thematic coherence and shared experience of continuity and community. With the course anchored in *Le tour*, everything—from the complementary materials to class discussions and student presentations—seems to mesh organically.

On another level, Tours de France addresses broader concerns about curricular coherence, about how to bridge gaps between the acquisition of language skills and the study of literature and culture. It should be obvious by now that the course makes abundant connections between language and culture, but what about literature? Advanced Conversation: Contemporary French Cultures is often the first 300-level course taken by students completing or placing out of North Carolina State University's four-semester beginning- and intermediate-language sequence. As a de facto fifth-semester course, it needs to ready students for more-advanced offerings, including those in literature. Arguably the greatest challenges in French literature courses today are students' difficulty in reading and their limited experience with literature. In this respect, *Le tour* provides a valuable apprenticeship, helping students build skills, knowledge, and confidence through regular practice reading a French text that, although perhaps not literary, is at least highly literate. *Le tour* offers quaintly elevated diction; devices like foreshadowing, suspense, and symbolism; and emulation of elements from such genres as the picaresque, the bildungsroman, and the adventure novel à la Jules Verne. Class discussion familiarizes students with useful literary terms in French (*personnage, intrigue, narration, peripetiea, denouement*, etc.), and with common literary structures and themes.

Specific elements in the text also help prepare students for further literary study. Experiencing the maximlike epigraphs to each chapter or the narrative's epistolary chapters (87–88) can make students more receptive readers of François de la Rochefoucauld and Choderlos de Laclos. An epigraph such as the one at the head of the chapter on Mont Blanc and avalanches (ch. 38), "Les beautés de la nature doivent élever notre pensée" (84; "Natural beauty should elevate our thoughts"), gives students a remedial education in nineteenth-century received ideas that will enable them to better appreciate how those ideas are expressed in literature, as in the scene in *Madame Bovary* in which Emma and Léon exchange romantic commonplaces about the sublime in nature. By considering nineteenth-century discourse on hygiene and notions about cleanliness and virtue in particular, students come to Émile Zola's *L'assommoir* ("The Dram Shop") better able to make sense of Gervaise and Coupeau's sensuous embrace amid piles of soiled laundry. More surprisingly, perhaps, reflecting on the skillfully integrated illustrations in *Le tour* can prepare students to think critically about André Breton's slippery use of ostensibly documentary images in *Nadja*.

Such examples may give the impression that this course requires endless class preparation, but I have found the opposite to be true. Certainly, a course predicated on flexibility demands substantial flexibility of the instructor, as classroom discussion shifts from René Descartes to Louis Pasteur to silk making to bouillabaisse to Limoges porcelain. Once the course is set up and running, however, it seems to teach itself—with much help from the students. Although I have seen colleagues spend months compiling course Web sites with links that are outdated by the time their course is offered, in Tours de France, students benefit from an ongoing process of surfing the Web in French, zeroing in or stumbling on information of interest and collectively finding far more than I ever would alone. Ultimately, I find Tours de France appealing to teach because it can accomplish so much, so efficiently.

IMPLICATIONS

What are the broader implications of this pedagogical experiment? To be sure, what makes sense in one place may not elsewhere. Small liberal arts colleges and large research universities, public and private institutions, undergraduate and graduate programs offer different combinations of advantages, disadvantages, constraints, and possibilities. Still, Tours de France addresses widespread, central concerns about humanistic pedagogy, course design, and curricular design—concerns all the more urgent in French studies as it walks a tightrope over the abyss of decreasing enrollments.

Despite my enthusiasm for *Le tour,* not everyone will want to organize a course around this one text. Moreover, *Le tour* could go out of print again just as suddenly as it came back in.[4] The question to ask then becomes, in keeping with the author's optimistically pedagogical spirit, What lessons can we learn from such a course? Such lessons might include looking for materials in unlikely places and trying novel combinations of materials; integrating language-skills acquisition strategies like small-group work, journal writing, or language-lab practice into higher-level courses; making judicious use of both primary source materials and contemporary instructional technologies; articulating more thoroughly among the study of language, literature, and culture; and framing course designs that are both rigorous and responsive—that can retain their conceptual and intellectual integrity while adapting constructively to change.

My experience teaching Tours de France in fall 2002 and 2003 bears out this last point in particular. Teaching the course again after the terrorist attacks of September 11, 2001 and hostilities in Afghanistan and Iraq, I found that perspectives had changed somewhat. Reflections in *Le tour* about patriotism, national identity, and the ravages of war, which before had struck many students as abstract and uninteresting, now seemed relevant, even urgent. Amid airplanes crashing into skyscrapers, anthrax scares, corporate debacles, economic stagnation, talk of global warming, and mounting American casualties, some were more inclined to think critically about the book's optimistic pronouncements on commerce, industry, technology, and scientific progress. Yet others, like classmates in years past, were not. How, I wondered, could I use the course's existing framework to help students understand the turmoil in the world around us? I adopted a strategy of playing devil's advocate, or asking students to do so, when we considered the book's high-minded but intellectually dubious reflections on perseverance, patriotism, progress, and so forth. This strategy did indeed enliven class discussions and lab-conversation exercises and, in a more general sense, helped further cultivate students' critical thinking skills and historical perspective. Similarly, although war with Iraq is disheartening on so many levels, it offers interesting comparisons with *Le tour*, which poignantly relates the predicament of a nation caught between repeated military showdowns with the same enemy.

Beyond such specific lessons, Tours de France might also offer ways to rethink our broader philosophy of teaching. Chapter 35 in *Le tour* provides an oddly appropriate metaphor for this larger pedagogical vision. Traveling in the Jura, André and Julien marvel at the local system whereby large numbers of cows, under the supervision of just one cowherd, are made to return each day to their respective barns. Beneath an illustration of this system at work, the caption reads:

> PATRE COMMUNAL FAISANT RENTRER LES VACHES DANS LE JURA. Toutes les vaches d'une commune, dans le Jura, sont souvent conduites par un seul pâtre, et tous les cultivateurs s'entendent pour le payer: de cette façon cela coûte moins cher, et les enfants de la commune ont le temps d'aller à l'école et de s'instruire. (Bruno 78)

> VILLAGE COWHERD IN THE JURA BRINGING THE COWS HOME. In the Jura, all the cows in a locality are often tended by a single cowherd, with all the farmers chipping in to pay him: this costs less, and the local children have the time to go to school and learn.

This unusual practice offers an inspiring image of mutual trust and cooperation, of a harmonious balance between individual needs and collective goals, of diverse elements fruitfully integrated while maintaining their integrity, of fundamental order amid much divergent activity, and, above all, of a creative approach to an entrenched problem. Such an approach, it seems, need not be complicated to be effective. Straightforward, even elegant in its simplicity, this approach yields the richest of all possible rewards: education.

NOTES

I would like to thank my colleague Scott Despain, executive director of the Foreign Languages Technology Center, for his help with my descriptions of instructional technology.

1. Examples of these lessons are:

    Il n'est guère d'obstacle qu'on ne puisse surmonter avec de la persévérance (Bruno 15; "There is no obstacle that cannot be overcome with perseverance").

    Quand on a été séparé de sa patrie, on comprend mieux encore combien elle vous est chère (Bruno 24; "When you're away from home, you realize just how much home means to you").

    Un homme en danger, quel qu'il soit, a droit à notre aide (Bruno 69; "We must help any man in danger, no matter who he is").

    Le meilleur moyen de réussir dans le commerce, c'est d'être consciencieux (Bruno 101; "Conscientiousness is the best way to succeed in business").

    L'industrie . . . est une puissance bienfaisante qui travaille pour l'humanité (Bruno 108; "Industry is a benevolent power that works on humanity's behalf").

    Le vrai bonheur est dans la maison de la famille (125; "True happiness starts at home").

    Que de mouvement et d'activité, mais aussi que de peines et de fatigues dans l'existence des grandes villes! (272; "City life—what hustle and bustle, but also what toil and trouble!").

2. There are two seventy-five-minute sessions a week, for fifteen weeks. On Tuesdays, in the conventional classroom, the class discusses the current chapters in *Le tour*, recounting, rethinking, even reinventing the story, while also considering the array of places, sites, trades, industries, inventions, or notable persons (including Joan of Arc) woven into the story. Although some time is devoted to small-group work (e.g., as a warm-up activity), discussion mostly involves the whole class and is guided more or less closely by the instructor. On Thursdays, however, the class meets in the computer classroom of North Carolina State University's Foreign Languages Technology Center, which has thirty-four Internet-enabled, interlinked multimedia workstations. Students work in pairs, and discussion is much more free ranging. The multimedia language system made by Tandberg has a random-pairing function that allows them to work, successively, with many different partners without leaving their workstations. This technology does not obstruct but stimulates and focuses students' oral production: freed from the impediments of a conventional classroom—the burden of choosing partners and breaking into groups, furniture to trip over and sodas to spill, ambient noise and constant movement, social inhibitions and peer pressure—students converse with extraordinary volubility and intensity.
3. The oral parts of the midterm and final are administered at the Foreign Languages Technology Center, using the *Divace* software program. The instructor reads questions or prompts to the entire class from the console. Students answer individually, speaking into the microphone of their headset; the instructor moves on to the next item only when most students have finished. At the end of the exam, response files are recorded onto the students' workstation hard drives, then transferred to the instructor's workstation, where they are burned onto a CD-ROM. The instructor then listens to the exams on his or her computer, pausing, rewinding, or fast-fowarding as needed. Although grading for global performance (i.e., not on a points-per-question basis), the instructor focuses on very specific aspects of the students' oral proficiency and mastery of the material, notably pronunciation, intonation, and accent; grammar and structures; vocabulary and complexity of expression; content and knowledge of subject; and quality of presentation and performance. Students receive a full-page version of the scoring grid for this examination, with scores for individual categories and the whole oral exam, comments on particular strengths and weaknesses (e.g., "excellente connaissance du sujet" or "*Attention: beaucoup*" is "bo-koo," not "bo-kew"), and general recommendations for improvement.

4. In early 2002, when placing fall book orders, I was surprised to learn that the far more recent *Découvrir la France* was no longer available—its curious hybridity perhaps explaining its swift disappearance from a publishing market increasingly based on predictable categories. A large-format, amply illustrated paperback, *Découvrir la France* is a cross between a pragmatic tourist guide and a nostalgic keepsake album of national treasures (such as, say, Gilles Pudlowski's *Trésors gourmands de la France*), offering, "sous forme d'un répertoire pratique, région par région, l'essentiel des richesses touristiques de notre pays" ("in the form of a practical, region-by-region listing, our country's principal sightseeing treasures"), according to the back cover copy. *Découvrir la France*'s region-by-region organization and thorough coverage of localities aligns nicely with the itinerary of *Le tour*, and abundant "encadrés thématiques" ("thematic sidebars," e.g., on Breton *coiffes*; the battle of Alésia; laser cleaning of the Amiens cathedral; cheeses such as Livarot, Époisses, and Roquefort; shopping in Paris; and both storks and religious pluralism in Alsace) provide an interesting mix of concordance and counterpoint.

   In its place, I have tried the 2000 edition of the Michelin *Guide vert* for France and the 2003–04 *Guide du routard: Junior en France*. While up-to-date and culturally authentic, neither guidebook proved satisfactory. In some ways, the Michelin guide did not mesh well with *Le tour*. Its alphabetical ordering of destinations within the entire nation obscures regional distinctions, and it does not mention certain places of interest (e.g., Le Creusot) to readers of *Le tour*. The *Guide du routard*, written largely for parents traveling in France with children, meshed better with *Le tour*, yet had limited appeal to college students without children. However, students spent less money on these books than on their predecessor and ended up with a more practical, pocket-sized volume that some might actually use when traveling in France. Still, when I teach the course again, particularly in the light of the increasing material available online, I may drop the contemporary guidebook in favor of requiring more extensive work with Web sites. I have also been watching French satellite television and am intrigued by the possibilities. Although I would love to integrate some of this material into the course, I am not yet sure how to do so meaningfully (from the students' perspective) and manageably (from mine). But perhaps, as Mme Fouillée would have it, "Il n'est guère d'obstacle qu'on ne puisse surmonter avec de la persévérance" (Bruno 15; "There is no obstacle that cannot be overcome with perseverance").

PART THREE

Expanding Horizons: Interdisciplinary Challenges

Charles J. Stivale

From Jourdain to Trissotin: Speaking the Tongues of Theory

J'ai cru jusques ici que c'était l'ignorance,
Qui faisait les grands sots, et non pas la science.
—Trissotin, in *Les femmes savantes*

Until now, I believed that it was ignorance
That created fools, and not science.

In a volume on teaching strategies for literary studies in French, one may question what the place for literary theory is in the light of theory's apparent waning and with the rise of cultural studies.[1] At a conference in 1998, I cast myself as M. Jourdain (from Molière's *Le bourgeois gentilhomme*) as a way to suggest that in studying contemporary French literature from a sociocultural perspective, I was already doing cultural studies without knowing it (see Stivale, "Monsieur Jordain"). One participant at that conference likened this supposedly unwitting practice of cultural studies to a different Molière character, Trissotin, to imply that such a practice, less unconscious than I pretended, may lead to an unnecessarily pedantic and even presumptuous approach in relation to literary studies (see Desormeaux).[2] By citing one of Trissotin's replies to Clitandre as the epigraph, I adopt Trissotin as a figure of the double-edged risk we run in introducing theory—whether cultural studies–oriented or some other version—within the literature classroom.[3] That is, as modern-day Trissotin's wielding a certain science to combat presumed ignorance, we teachers risk assuming too much as well as too little, both about the science contained in theoretical texts and about the presumed ignorance of reading them in literature courses. Moreover, reflections by David Gershom Myers on teaching theory in English courses, to which I return below, provide considerable food for thought on the nature of the particular science of teaching literary theory.

Sufficient flexibility should be maintained in the teaching context to mitigate risks in introducing theoretical and literary texts judged difficult. The essential emphasis in this essay and in my teaching is the unstartling principle that less is more in introducing theory in the literature classroom. I have found this principle to be valid for courses taught in French (to undergraduates and graduates alike) and for advanced interdisciplinary courses taught in English. Adherence to this principle is neither a wholesale rejection of theory in favor of some nostalgic return to the text nor an oblique mode of dumbing down my courses. Rather, adhering to the less-is-more principle inspires students toward sustained reflection about literary and cultural texts without intimidating or alienating them with verbiage that might obstruct the possibility of enriching that reflection. This principle is also valid whatever might be the definition one gives to the term *text* and whatever the theoretical approaches are that one adopts, explicitly or implicitly, in working with texts. Finally, although the choice of texts is crucial in our courses, the students' engagement with these texts will advance meaningfully only with a well-designed discussion and assignment structure that adequately helps students develop a fuller understanding of the chosen texts (see Paesani's essay in this volume).

I consider here how texts that I have strategically chosen to use in particular pedagogical contexts have functioned with various degrees of success in undergraduate and graduate literature courses. Although I have also taught several courses and independent studies on literary theory, my focus is on courses in which literary and cultural texts have played a role in relation to the theoretical texts introduced. However, considering the essay by Myers leads me to confront unexamined presuppositions maintained in the development of these courses. Myers distinguishes between theory courses in which the instructor conducts a taxonomic survey of theoretical approaches and ones in which a heuristic model based on the students' developing critical strategies for interpreting texts is adopted. Myers notes the strengths and disadvantages in each approach, and even argues that adopting an oppositional role as a means to present and confront different theories has drawbacks.[4] These cautions are important considerations for constructing and teaching a course on literature, and I support Myers's view that we need to lead "our students to struggle against the authorities that we ourselves have placed in their hands" (334). Still, Myers's cautions about introducing theoretical perspectives overlook several important issues about course development and about students, specifically, the local context, the students' varying levels of preparation, and curricular and institutional needs. I return to these crucial elements in reviewing the less-is-more principle in relation to the courses outlined below.[5]

DEGRÉ ZÉRO DE LA CRITIQUE / CRITICAL ZERO DEGREE

In a senior seminar on the theme of narrative desire, course participants demonstrated a rare zero degree of receptivity; in an advanced undergraduate–graduate course on the nineteenth-century French novel, I regularly maintained a near zero degree of literary critical content. The outcome of the first course was quite painful, for me as well as the participants, yet ultimately yielded lessons from which I have learned ever since. The organizational approach of the second course has been increasingly satisfactory for reasons that relate to my university's local curricular needs and to our students' levels of preparation. However, the choice of including minimal literary critical content other than close reading certainly remains a topic open for discussion, one that I continue to review.

In the senior seminar on narrative desire at Tulane University in 1987, I developed a capstone course for undergraduate French majors through an overview of French narrative. Situated in a limited critical framework, the overview consisted of a wide range of primary texts and periods considered through the thematic perspective of *le désir narratif*.[6] Besides requiring oral and written assignments, I provided the students with suggestions for preparing oral presentations and with study questions for general discussion to help orient their readings. Finally, I provided a list of critical texts as suggested readings only, from which I would draw material for my own presentations in class. Different factors combined to make a promising course very difficult. In retrospect, I believe that at least two fundamental errors contributed to the gradual disappearance of goodwill from a number of the students.

First, I had not thought through sufficiently the implications of the narrative-desire theme either as a multifaceted stylistic device or as an element of the plot structure in the selected texts. Specifically, I had not carefully prepared questions for the students that would have helped them discern the various aspects of this theme. Thus, their confusion was quite understandable, since I was in some ways developing my own understanding of the theme's different facets as we went along, using the class as a kind of laboratory to do so. This pedagogical situation created frustrations on both sides; the tension that developed manifested itself in some students' responses to my comments during oral presentations or on their written assignments.

Second, by simply providing the list of suggested additional readings with no further guidance, I did not offer students the means to judge which, if any, of the texts on the list would be the most helpful. I now think that selecting fewer critical texts might have alleviated some of the frustration. For example, a careful reading and discussion of even one chapter from Peter Brooks's *Reading for the Plot* might have contributed to the students' comprehension of narrative desire. Thus, the primary readings could have been balanced with one or two critical texts to inform the students more directly about the implications of the course's focus.

In another course that I teach with some regularity, the main survey course on the nineteenth-century French novel (French 6810 at Wayne State University), I faithfully adhere to the less-is-more principle in assigning readings in literary theory (see the syllabus at *Web Support*). As we know, the length of many important narrative texts in the nineteenth century makes some primary reading assignments quite demanding. To add even brief theoretical texts reduces time for discussion of the primary texts and burdens the discussion with technical critical considerations. Another factor at Wayne State University is that an instructor never knows before the course begins what the ratio will be of advanced undergraduates to graduate students, a consideration for assigning primary as well as critical readings (see Harter's essay in the volume).

Presented with a syllabus that includes close to a dozen narrative texts,[7] the students read each text with reference to study questions that I prepare in advance for the assignments. The questions address issues related to plot and character development, stylistic traits, and thematic elements (see *Web Support*). In the light of the discussions generated by these questions, I develop in class various issues implicitly related to theory and, when appropriate, try to draw out some of these theoretical issues more fully.

One goal of the course is to situate the literary works in their sociocultural context, for which I provide supplementary information. Yet I insist also that this context is not sufficient to derive an understanding of the literary text. I have found this caveat to be especially necessary for students tempted to provide literary interpretations based primarily on biographical information about the author. Discouraging biographical interpretation is usually easier in class discussion than in students' papers, since the study questions already lead students away from such an interpretation based on biography alone. In their written assignments, the tendency toward biographical interpretation requires vigilance on my part to help students find interpretive alternatives, that is, to remain fundamentally close to the text as they develop their readings. I have adjusted the course organization to require selected critical texts for graduate students but have made these readings optional for undergraduates. One rationale for this adjustment is that graduate students have critical texts assigned on the MA and PhD reading lists. Selecting critical texts for inclusion on the syllabus is an important component of the course, but undergraduates should not take on this extra critical reading unless they are interested.

DEGRÉ N *DE LA CRITIQUE* / CRITICAL *N* DEGREE

In the two undergraduate seminars discussed here, I focus on the intersection between literary texts and theoretical topics. The critical approach of these courses was situated in interdisciplinarity rather than nineteenth-century French studies and was designed for students from different departments and from backgrounds in diverse literary traditions. The first course, an honors seminar entitled Semiotics and Society, organized for the Tulane honors program, allowed me to orient students toward an array of theoretical materials and to discuss different kinds of texts. Besides providing the basic premise of the course and the required texts, the syllabus contained a general statement of the course's purpose. This colloquium was "intended to provide the participants with an understanding of the links between social sign systems and their study as developed by the challenging field of inquiry, semiotic theory."[8] The second course was a women's studies senior seminar, Women's Textualities, offered in the Tulane Center for Research on Women. This course focused on the thematics of women's textualities and juxtaposed different critical readings with a number of literary texts. I stated the course's premise as follows:

> The aim of this seminar will be to examine various practical examples of feminist theory applied to works of fiction and cinema and to

> familiarize the participants with the theoretical negotiations which have occurred, and are still taking place, between French and Anglo-American approaches to feminist studies.[9]

Both seminars gave the students considerable opportunity to develop their knowledge of the theoretical readings through class discussions and through preparation of synopses and presentations of assigned and optional readings. In Semiotics and Society, one exercise was to read Paul Theroux's *Mosquito Coast* à la Barthes's *S/Z*; that is, students examined how the novel engendered its codes, and they discerned what significations these codes could help us construct. This exercise opened up possibilities for understanding Theroux's novel but also helped students better understand Barthes's seminal text, particularly as one constituting a crossroads between structuralism and poststructuralism. Then, by juxtaposing the novel to the film adapted from Theroux's book, we considered the problems of film adaptation, a productive exercise in the light of the textual work we had already studied. In the women's studies seminar, class discussion based on the reading assignments was especially important, since there was novelty, even risk, in having a male professor lead such a discussion. In the syllabus, I explicitly addressed this problem and asked the students, through weekly preparation in advance of the class, "to take responsibility for responding actively to the weekly material as well as to assist and even to lead the site of vested institutional authority, the (male) professor, in elucidating and questioning the various topics considered."[10]

As for the courses' assigned readings, the two syllabi suggest that I had not yet arrived at the relative serenity of the less-is-more principle. I felt that in the context both of an honors seminar, namely, with the most talented students in the humanities on the campus, and of a women's studies senior seminar, with students especially motivated to explore a range of texts in feminist theory, the opportunity to provide them with access to textual, theoretical, and critical resources justified being bold instead of frugal in assigning readings in theory. The students were eager to engage with whatever I presented to them and welcomed the opportunity to meet and learn from speakers invited to campus for the course.[11]

UN JUSTE MILIEU?

To achieve a *juste milieu* between primary and critical readings in the literature courses I have taught, I was fortunate to develop different graduate seminars in nineteenth-century French literature with varying thematic foci (see *Web Support* for the different choices of primary and critical texts). In this context, I wish to discuss two particular seminars developed at Wayne State University, La Question Femme au Dix-Neuvième Siècle and Autour de Rimbaud. Although these courses achieved a balance, I admit to experiencing ambivalence in arriving at it. In an earlier seminar at Tulane, called L'Irréel du Réalisme, certain sessions were divided between a brief discussion of key critical points and discussion of the primary work. In other sessions, students made presentations and then reports on larger literary issues related to the realist, naturalist, and decadent movements. The less-is-more principle would have served me very well in this course. For example, I realized only in retrospect that I had assigned three separate activities for four of the thirteen sessions (discussion of both a literary and a critical text as well as an exposé or a presentation) and also had students prepare two written assignments beyond the weekly readings. The retrospective critique of this course helped me understand better why the weaker students (two in particular) tended to struggle while the stronger students rose to the challenge of the tasks assigned.

Hence, in the seminar La Question Femme, I was able to link one course goal—developing the students' understanding of the literary texts as models for undertaking their own critical work—to another goal, which I approached by structuring the course according to an academic-professional model. The participants developed their research paper following the three steps to which academics often adhere in developing an article: writing the abstract, preparing the project as a short conference talk, then fleshing out that talk into a written text with considerably more research. As examples, I provided the participants a sample of one of my abstracts, the conference talk from the abstract, and the journal article that I developed (see my "*(Se) Rendre Compte*"). I thus situated the specifically literary critical focus of the course in terms of a professional development model, and, because the results of the course were successful (one student's final paper became the basis of a subsequent master's essay), I have repeated the model.

In Autour de Rimbaud, I not only used this same development model but also oriented the seminar in two directions simultaneously: in a more traditional and textual direction, I asked the participants to focus on close readings of poems by Charles Baudelaire and Arthur Rimbaud; I then asked students to juxtapose those readings to critical interpretations (see Fowlie; Paliyenko; and Laurence Porter, *Crisis*). By judiciously choosing critical texts for the syllabus, of course, I limited the range of possible reference texts and helped the students develop their own analyses. This choice also helped me, especially with Wallace Fowlie, caution the students about critical readings of poetry that dwelled too insistently on biographical anecdotes as the lever for critical interpretation. The other direction of the course was an attempt to situate Baudelaire's and Rimbaud's poetry both in relation to the intertextual, symbolist entourage (i.e., Verlaine and Mallarmé) and in relation to different examples of twentieth-century artistic creations inspired particularly by Rimbaud's literary production.[12] The introduction of these intertextual influences in the final weeks of the course fulfilled a specific pedagogical goal: the students had already worked on selecting subjects and preparing abstracts for their final term papers earlier in the semester, but during the final weeks, when they were undertaking the research and preparation of their texts, the intertextual presentations gave them considerable respite from the intense textual and critical preparations of the earlier part of the course.

TEXTS AND CONTEXTS, LEVEL AND NEEDS

Returning to the figure of Trissotin, I recall the response Clitandre made to Trissotin's affirmation of belief in the benefits of science vis-à-vis ignorance: "Vous avez cru fort mal, et je vous suis garant / Qu'un sot savant est sot plus qu'un sot ignorant" (Molière 574; "You believed quite incorrectly, and I can assure you / That a learned fool is more foolish than an ignorant one"; my trans.). The fundamental issue regarding the choices and uses I have made of different texts in different contexts is whether these choices maximize the possibilities of student learning. In reviewing the courses I organized and the syllabi I produced earlier in my career, I do indeed relate to Clitandre's candid reference to Trissotin as "a learned fool." Most important, I wonder to what extent I either facilitated or hampered my students' access to a better understanding of literary texts through the occasionally lumbering and occasionally gargantuan task of reading literary theory. My experiences teaching different courses and reading reflections on teaching by Myers (as well as in Sadoff and Cain) have provided additional food for thought. That is, they have helped me better recognize the fine line that I walk as a "learned fool." On the one hand, I increase the students' skills as readers of the literature that they are, finally, meant to enjoy. On the other hand, I provide them with the critical tools useful in advancing in this ever more skillful reading.

My tempered approach allows me to account for other elements that have an effect on every course, and here my perspective differs somewhat from that of Myers, which focuses more on distinct critical approaches than on students' needs. The less-is-more principle, at once flexible and effective, allows me to respond to the specific characteristics of students in an urban public institution, especially their varying goals in preparing for an undergraduate or graduate degree. For those students who desire to undertake advanced literary studies, the critical tools increasingly become a necessity. Moreover, should some students seek employment in academe, strong preparation both with these tools and with the primary literary and cultural texts is altogether essential. The less-is-more principle also makes me attentive to how each course fits into Wayne State's curriculum, that is, how the content and approach in my courses complement the work that students, undergraduate and graduate alike, have completed in other courses in their program of studies, particularly those courses that may include strong emphasis on critical theories. Finally, we teachers should not neglect another important aspect of the teaching process, our own learning as readers, teachers, researchers, and critics. This process continues as we intensely engage with our classes; that we continue to enjoy and learn from the texts we teach affects our students in immeasurable ways.

With the less-is-more principle in mind if not always in hand—that is, with the freedom to employ it flexibly when I need to—I try to make the objects of the students' studies accessible. In some courses, accessibility has meant adhering to the relative zero degree that I outline above, but in other classroom situations it may mean something entirely different. In other words, the variety of institutional settings and demands makes any doctrinaire statement on teaching theory in the classroom entirely inappropriate. I believe that the most we can accomplish—and this is significant enough—is to open students to the possibilities of the theoretical tongues that we have come to use with some level of comfort without blocking out by dint of theoretical zeal the tongues of the primary texts that students read. Even if, in North America, the tongues of French theory are ultimately of our own creation, as Sylvère Lotringer and Sande Cohen have cogently affirmed, our task can still be that of language teachers. That is, our purpose remains to open students to all levels of linguistic, stylistic, and theoretical possibilities along carefully defined and well-developed paths that lead to science—in other words, knowledge and learning. Our purpose is thus to banish willful ignorance, but with the humility of knowing there will always be much more to learn and new tongues to speak.

NOTES

Epigraph from Molière 574; my trans.

1. By the "apparent waning" of literary theory, I refer to the situation described in books by Cusset; Rapaport; and Readings and in the essays collected in Butler; Guillory; and Thomas. See especially Culler. Other scholars have reflected on teaching theory, notably in Myers; Showalter; and the essays collected in Sadoff and Cain.
2. Desormeaux's paper was a response to my paper "Monsieur Jourdain Meets Cultural Studies."
3. This statement presumes knowing what theory is, that is, agreeing on a definition of an extremely mutable and even contested domain (see Butler, Guillory, and Thomas, Preface). In some ways, my essay recounts how I have implicitly coped with the mutability of theory over two decades in the classroom.
4. Myers outlines the following disadvantages: the taxonomic approach is untheoretical in its inherent normativity (326–27), and, although the heuristic approach "produces results, in the form of readings," it constitutes "the abandonment of theory. . . . To study literary theory for the purpose of extracting from it a useful interpretive strategy, then, is to turn aside from the adventure of questioning and trace one's steps back to an earlier stage of unquestioned norms" (328). Furthermore, both these approaches, Myers argues, "subtly encourage a pedagogical regime of authoritarianism" (329). As for the oppositional approach, which "reattaches the knowledge of how to *do* theory to knowledge that theory is *about* something in particular" (329), the approach not only is fundamentally monist in "dedicat[ing] itself tirelessly to the goal of radical change" but also problematizes some notions, such as "the special category of literature, individual authorship, the claim to social autonomy" and not others, "class, real relations, social constructedness" (330–31).
5. The syllabi and resources for selected courses discussed here are located on this volume's Web site (see *Web Support*). I must add one caveat: I offer these syllabi and course materials only as tools that have functioned variously in my courses and as works in progress.
6. The texts included in the course were *Le roman de Tristan et Iseut*; Mme de Lafayette, *La Princesse de Clèves*; l'Abbé Prévost, *Histoire du chevalier des Grieux et de Manon Lescaut*; Chateaubriand, *René*; Honoré de Balzac, *La peau de chagrin*; Guy de Maupassant, *Nouvelles choisies*; André Gide, *L'immoraliste*; Boris Vian, *L'écume des jours*; Alain Robbe-Grillet, *La jalousie*; Marguerite Duras, *Moderato Cantabile*; Michel Tournier, *Le coq de bruyère*.
7. Germaine de Staël, "Mirza"; Chateaubriand, *René*; Claire de Duras, *Ourika*; Balzac, *Eugénie Grandet*; George Sand, *La petite Fadette*; Gustave Flaubert, *Madame Bovary* and *Trois contes*; Maupassant's selected tales; Émile Zola, *Au bonheur des dames*.
8. Required books for this course were: Barthes, *Mythologies* and *S/Z*; Dick Hebdige, *Subculture: The Meaning of Style*; Kaja Silverman, *The Subject of Semiotics*; Paul Theroux, *The Mosquito Coast*; and extensive readings available in a coursepack.

9. Required texts were the following: Margaret Atwood, *The Handmaid's Tale*; Shari Benstock, *Women of the Left Bank: Paris, 1900–1940*; Ursula K. LeGuin, *The Left Hand of Darkness*; Toni Morrison, *Sula;* Adrienne Rich, *On Lies, Secrets, and Silence*; Virginia Woolf, *A Room of One's Own*; and additional readings available in a coursepack.
10. In both courses, the students benefited from campus lecturers and from visits to the courses by different guest lecturers: in the honors seminar, Ana Lopez (Tulane Univ., Dept. of Communication) and Lawrence Grossberg (Univ. of North Carolina); in the women's studies seminar, Alice Jardine (Harvard Univ.) and Carole Spitzack (Tulane Univ., Dept. of Communication).
11. In the conference version of this essay, I included in this section two graduate courses I developed at Wayne State University—Socio-cultural Semiotics (1996) and French Cultural Studies (2000)—that corresponded to the department's modern languages PhD interdepartmental minor in literary criticism and cultural studies. However, since neither of these courses dealt primarily with literary texts (which is the focus in this essay), I have not retained them for detailed discussion but have provided Web links to them (see *Web Support*). I note one key aspect of the first course on the sociocultural semiotics of the 1990s culture wars, with essays from Bérubé's *Public Access*; Grossberg, Nelson, and Treichler, *Cultural Studies*; and other readings. As critical supplement to class discussions, I organized a series of meetings entitled Professional Issues for Languages, Literatures and Cultural Studies, with three invited guest speakers who provided texts for discussion and five additional meetings on professional issues (see www.langlab.wayne.edu/CStivale/Courses/FRE777SuppMeet.html; see also Stivale, "*(Se) Rendre Compte*"). In the second seminar, which grew from my research on French cultural studies (see my "Cultural Lessons," "Acker/Rimbaud," "Cajun"), I was able to respect the less-is-more principle more readily than in the first seminar, thanks to readings selected primarily from two collections, by using a set of complementary texts focusing on difficulties involved in defining cultural studies (Lentricchia and McLaughlin; Le Hir and Strand). To this material I would now add selected readings from Cusset.
12. These creations included essays and poetry by Antonin Artaud and André Breton; musical works by the Doors and poetry by Jim Morrison, linked to video material from Oliver Stone's *The Doors*, the documentary by Gordon Forbes entitled *The Doors: A Tribute to Jim Morrison*, and Francis Ford Coppola's *Apocalypse Now*; and a comparison of poetry and prose by Kathy Acker (particularly, *In Memoriam to Identity*) with poetry and music by Patti Smith. I would now supplement this material with readings from Noland.

Loosening the Knot: Professing Sexuality in Nineteenth-Century French Studies

Garett R. Heysel

KNOTS AND BELTS

Many readers may have seen a card by the cartoonist Gary Larson that pokes fun at perceived interest in seventeenth-century French drama. Barely noticeable in the northernmost part of an outline map of the United States (just south of western Ontario) and distinctly apart from other special-interest regions of the United States such as the Bible Belt, the People Magazine Belt, and the Garfield Belt, lies an irregularly shaped region bearing the label "Seventeenth-Century French Drama Belt." The humor I find in Larson's geography comes not from the specialty represented (indeed, I debated at great length between a dissertation topic treating seventeenth- versus early-twentieth-century texts), but from the very queerness of specialization and subspecialization altogether. In the same spirit, a belt depicting interest in teaching gay, lesbian, bisexual, and queer nineteenth-century French studies courses at the graduate and undergraduate level would appear remarkably smaller by comparison. The interest zone shrinks and becomes barely perceptible once we begin to pose such questions as, How far have we professors come in our willingness to explore issues of homosexuality in our teaching of French literature and culture and to design entire courses around these issues?

In contrast, even a cursory review of Nineteenth-Century French Studies Colloquium programs would indicate our willingness to talk about issues of same-sex desire and sexuality among our peers. Queer panels, papers and panels about lesbian and gay male writers, and panels focusing on texts treating lesbian, gay, bisexual, transgendered, and queer (LGBTQ) subjects or themes appear regularly[1] and enjoy a healthy attendance by a variety of colleagues interested in exploring the relation between sexuality and textuality. In fact, one conference, Rhetoric of the Other, grew out of a desire among many of these panels' participants and attendees to organize entire colloquia devoted to LGBTQ issues in French and francophone literature.[2] But to what extent and in what ways our research and interest in LGBTQ studies translate into the courses we might offer remains a question. What, if anything, is at stake when we attempt to square the pedagogical challenges of LGBTQ studies with institutional and curricular issues? For, as broad as these questions may seem, they are vital today when university administrators and promotion and tenure committee members extol the importance of bringing research into the classroom.

The topic of creating bridges between research and teaching is certainly an important one, and it has particular resonance for those of us who work in LGBTQ studies and negotiate the space between the classroom and our research interests. On the one hand, life in many academic settings progresses more easily when we leave the queer interests out of the classroom. On the other hand, personal identification with the material we teach, in addition to a desire to share with students what we find interesting in a text, makes closeting our research seem false. Each scholar will navigate differently the pull between personal research interests and professional teaching expectations, as well as the ethical implications of transforming the personal into active pedagogy. One solution, according to Eve Kosofsky Sedgwick, might be to allude to gay and lesbian themes in passing, perhaps even in veiled terms so as to resonate directly with our in-the-know learners. Such a "professing-to-the-cognoscenti" approach, however, is a form of dismissal, similar to those that dominated scholarship and teaching in the early days of gay theory, because it reflects same-sex-centered interest without daring to engage the inquiry into LGBTQ issues directly (52–53). Another approach might be to ignore specific readings to expound on the universal qualities and themes of a given text. Put another way, given only a limited amount of time to teach, for example, a selection of Proust to an undergraduate class, how justifiable would it be to concentrate on the dynamic between Charlus and Jupien in *Sodome et Gomorrhe*? What if our students debated this aspect of Proust but ignored the more crucial scene of the madeleine? At first glace, both the approaches mentioned above seem innocuous enough; however, they also involve censorship—not necessarily of the text but of the teacher of the text. Textual choices have very real consequences to those of us who dwell in the belt today.

In fact, as early as 1951, a founding pioneer of the queer nineteenth-century French literature belt, André Gide, forewarned of grave risks of closeted professing. In a translated letter appearing in the preface of *Homosexualities and French Literature,* Gide identifies one possible downside to being evasive about our passions:

> Whether it comes from the right or from the left, whether it be political or religious, falsehood tends to suppress human personality by depriving it of the right to free inquiry. It is the stifling of the individual with the hope of an illusory advantage to the herd. Each of us is asked to abdicate his critical spirit in order to make it easier to strangle himself. (qtd. in Stambolian and Marks 13)

All grim and guilty connotations aside, the inclusion of Gide's letter in the preface to the earliest and most influential collection of essays on gay and lesbian approaches to French literature offers two lessons. First, Gide's cautionary statement demonstrates the longevity of the dialogue on professing one's true (research) interests—a debate that is far from over. Second, when the warning is extended to the classroom, it demonstrates that by being untrue to ourselves we compromise our students' engagement with and critical thinking about the text.

In the spirit of rallying against falsehood, I should begin with some acknowledgments and disclaimers. Many people have contributed to my exploration of this topic, and they are all represented in some way in what follows.[3] Also, I do not wish to propose any one best way to teach and design courses focusing on representations of homosexuality in French studies. The variables of individual teaching styles, comfort levels, student response, campus culture, tenure, and personal research interests render absurd dictating a single approach. Rather, I offer here an individual response and the insights, strategies, advice, and materials of colleagues currently engaged in professing sexuality issues in a variety of academic settings.

THE STATE OF THE LGBTQ/NINETEENTH-CENTURY FRENCH STUDIES BELT

Although my efforts to search the Web and request course syllabi from colleagues in the belt are unscientific, they have led me to conclude that few if any instructors are teaching what could be considered a queer nineteenth-century French studies course or a course that treats exclusively texts about or by homosexuals. This conclusion is especially true if we narrowly define such a course to include only gay, lesbian, or bisexual authors writing in French or only those texts that speak directly to nonheterosexual desire. A handful of instructors offer courses that problematize same-sex desire in nineteenth-century French texts and culture or that investigate head-on issues of gender and sexual difference through the lense of nationalism, languages of desire, or melancholy. Most people teaching queer studies French courses offer nineteenth- and twentieth-century literature surveys (or twentieth-century surveys alone) with an emphasis on culture. Some include texts dealing with homosexuality and underscore the role of sexuality in nineteenth-century France or include queer studies readings in their syllabi and lectures. Many professors assist students who choose to explore same-sex desire in a text even if the courses' teaching and syllabi do not include or emphasize that particular avenue of inquiry.

With all these permutations of teaching the queer nineteenth century, one commonality consistently rises to the surface. Those of us professing sexuality in the nineteenth-century French studies classrooms all seem to be committed to contextualizing sex and text. The thread of culture runs predominantly throughout all the curricular approaches I present below. To varying degrees, the convergence of culture and sexuality informs and forms our teaching in undeniable ways. In all cases I was able to document, the syllabi seem to speak for themselves. Consequently, I have linked what might be considered a course catalog from the belt to this volume's Web site (see *Web Support*). Readers will find syllabi that directly address aspects of sexuality in nineteenth-century French studies. These examples suggest that colleagues teach sexuality broadly, and not only gay or lesbian sexuality.

Syllabi, like the texts we so carefully and deliberately select to include in them, are open to infinite forms of interpretation. Whereas a syllabus viewed in the context of a department's or a program's curriculum might complement or contrast with other course offerings, an individual instructor's syllabus viewed in isolation seems more authoritative and perhaps defiant. And yet this is precisely how many of our students read and follow our syllabi, assuming, for example, that since certain books are on the syllabus, the instructor must believe they are indispensable to an understanding of the subject and that what a student learns in a course is not related to what that student might be examining in other courses—or even worse, anywhere else in life. Both these reactions seem troubling, and I return to them after sharing other comments from the belt.

VOICES FROM THE BELT

Beyond what syllabi and course descriptions reveal about the approaches and rationale of each class and its instructor, instructors' commentaries on their teaching underscore the importance of culture. Michael Lucey, considering LGBTQ content in nineteenth-century French studies, makes a distinction between courses he would or would not be drawn to teach and his penchant for thinking about "queer texts or the 'queer' content of mainstream texts." For Lucey, offering a course with a title such as Queer Writing in French holds little appeal: "I'm more interested myself in understanding and teaching about the place and function of sexuality in a complex cultural landscape than I am in teaching texts that might be associated with any particular kind of sexuality." The complexity and variety in sexual culture and "the imbrications between sexual, cultural, and all other parts of life in [nineteenth-century] France" structure how Lucey thinks about teaching sexuality in nineteenth-century French studies. The result, he feels, is a body of syllabi that are "centrally about developing and employing a critical matrix that allows one to perceive sexuality, and its complicated place within a larger culture" instead of what might typically be considered LGBTQ courses. Because Lucey widens the cultural scope of his courses to include sexual culture, Lucey's students stand to gain a broader perspective on the relations between sexuality and other cultural phenomena, such as nationalism and music. Better still, by professing sexualities, Lucey's approach seems to draw from what students know (i.e., sex, sexual difference and tension, desire, etc.) to illuminate what they most likely know much less about (i.e., melancholy or nationalism).

In a phone interview, Gretchen Schultz spoke of an overwhelmingly positive experience teaching her course titled Altérités Sexuelles, Perversions Littéraires ("Sexual Alterities, Literary Perversions"). Her reading list is focused on specific gay male and lesbian texts and sexuality, although she greatly emphasizes nineteenth-century French culture through her choices of critical works. What interests Schultz in contrasting Charles Baudelaire's lesbian poetry and Renée Vivien's poems is how sexuality is constructed and then reclaimed in nineteenth-century France. Schultz focuses on subjectivity in this course. She asks her students to talk about their own subject position and how their perspective as readers with a specific subjectivity influences their interpretation. In designing the course, Schultz said, she felt it critical to give equal time to lesbian and gay male problematics; doing so offers her the opportunity to reconsider and teach texts and authors she normally might not teach. She also found that the course made more sense for her and her students if it covered more recent sociopolitical issues such as the Pacte Civil de Solidarité ("Civil Solidarity Pact," a French civil-partnership agreement) instead of offering a course on gay, lesbian, and queer French writing from 1850 to 1950. In this way, students shorten the distance between the present and the past or bridge the gap between their own situation and understanding of what it means to be gay, lesbian, queer, bisexual, or transexual and an author's or critic's perspective.

Another factor in designing such a course underlined by Schultz was the culture of the campus and the students in her class. Culturally sophisticated; somewhat elite; generally liberal; and almost without exception lesbian, gay, or in some way queer, her students readily identified with the authors and texts. One student offered that he was "glad to able to read about himself." In the Rhetoric of the Other 2 conference held at Miami University, Ohio, in 1999, Schultz led a panel specifically dealing with queer pedagogy. She stated that many participants echoed the belief that campus culture played a major if not the most important role in professing queer. At a conservative, religiously affiliated institution, for example, many of the courses presented here could simply not be offered. That is not to say that where we teach necessarily determines either what or how we can and cannot teach. I have had the pleasure to teach in devout Utah, conservative Pennsylvania, and liberal Connecticut. Whether in a research institution or a small liberal arts college, I did little to hide or obscure my research interests. In fact, I found that my students appreciated knowing what being a French professor involves beyond teaching language.[4]

Another approach I employ in my courses in nineteenth-century French studies is to select a body of work and then explore the texts in it thematically from a variety of critical discourses, including queer studies. At the beginning of the course I state my intention to go beyond plot summary and to engage contemporary criticism. I also involve the instructional librarians in the design and execution of the curriculum. For the first few texts, I make a point to present to my students a few starkly opposing readings of a particular text. I might assign them to debate either side as if they had written the article themselves and their entire career depended on having the most convincing understanding of the novel, play, or poem. Later, since I generally have small classes at this level, students benefit from spending a good deal of time developing a critical dialogue with the texts and, then, doing research. Daily reading journals reveal how my students interact with the text and respond to class discussion. My responses to their journals are designed to tease out and narrow their research topics and to encourage them to engage relevant critical resources. Sometimes, it takes considerable time and effort to lead students toward their angle or critical approach, but they benefit from being encouraged to care about an interpretation.

Once students have chosen the text they are drawn to, the goal is to help them render meaning to that text. Along with the instructional librarians, I generally spend at least two class meetings working in the library combing through the stacks to show students sources that resonate with their own research. Once they have begun pursuing a thesis in the context of a helpful critical discourse, I generally offer a queer reading of a text as just one more example of how different communities of readers make texts matter. When possible, students will present their final paper at an informal colloquium held at the end of the semester with a French literature class from another area institution. By bringing students together in the role of experts on material, they better appreciate both the relevance of and various critical approaches to literature. No longer are they performing for the professor; they are presenting what they understand and, more important, why it matters to them.

OUT-ER BELTS AND OTHER BELTS

In comparison with professing sexuality in other humanities departments, doing so in French studies seems tame if not closeted. A special issue of *College Literature, Queer Utilities: Textual Studies, Theory, Pedagogy, Praxis*, offers one striking example of the debate about teaching queer studies. But there are many others. Jonathan Silin states that he wastes little time outing himself in his classroom since he feels "obligated to reveal the way that sexual identity informs [his] understanding of how social institutions function in our society" (96). Of course, there are many takes on just how out one needs to be in the classroom, and the debate is livelier in English departments than it is in French. *The Lesbian and Gay Studies Newsletter* solicits and publishes queer course syllabi; Deborah Meem's course Lesbian Literature and Psychology, at the University of Cincinnati, promises to "focus on one 'landmark piece' of lesbian literature, plus related commentary" each week (Meem 7). Queer studies, however, never found a substantial following in France or among French academics. For David Caron, French academe's reluctance

> reminds him of an old-fashioned but ever present discourse that is based upon a misunderstanding of the identity question. It makes me think of those French intellectuals who assume that gay and lesbian studies and queer theory seek to reduce Proust to his sexual orientation. It is absurd and often in bad faith.
>
> (Caron; my trans.).[5]

Yet there exists a clear difference between politicizing a classroom and contextualizing a reading list. Saying that the texts on a syllabus will be analyzed through the thematic contexts of difference, desire, or sexuality is quite distinct from teaching queer landmarks solely as a bold political statement. Identity politics, just like falsehood, has its dangers. Professing queer should not be understood as a call to contribute to the commodification of queer theory in academe. There is indeed great merit to theoretical debates informed, for example, by Urvashi Vaid's analyis of the dangers of virtual equality or the appearance of acceptance and parity in society. Lisa Downing, Helene Meyers, and Eric Savoy, among others, have pulled significantly on the hotly contested theoretical knots that describe discussions involving the proliferation of queer theory in academe and elsewhere. Loosening the knot, however, involves the nuts and bolts of teaching at particular institutions. I readily admit and strive to avoid the dangers of imposing particular ways of reading on my students. Neutrality, however, seems equally naive.

The challenge, therefore, becomes that of contextualizing to engage students—to teach the processes, means, and codes of identification with a view toward energizing inquiry of a text or a course of study. Contextualizing has both risks and rewards. Many students, especially undergraduates, hope to understand texts the way they perceive their professors want them to. When we encourage our students to develop their own critical tools by introducing them to powerful critical approaches, students aim not to please the professor but to develop the skills of literary analysis. To be sure, my own thinking about teaching literature owes much to a course I took as a graduate student with Gerald Graff. Entitled Introduction to Graduate Studies, it was designed around what he articulates as the "teach the debate" model in *Beyond the Culture Wars*. Graff calls for judiciousness in debates over "politicized teaching" (146) and sees his own role in the classroom as "concerned more with clarifying debates over politics than pushing a particular commitment" (147–48). Although his is a laudable goal, I tend to reveal my literary bent to foster the development of my students' approaches to texts. The balance might be more delicate, yet once my undergraduates have grappled with bringing critical meaning to their reading by exploring their reactions through journal writing and dialogue, they are generally enthusiastic to participate actively in critical debate. I am inspired by Graff's model to invite one of those bad-faith French intellectuals into my seminar room next time I teach.

What then do we risk when we choose to profess sexuality in the French studies classroom? One potential loss is the breadth of the mainstream canon. Most of the French majors at Lycoming College will take only one course in nineteenth-century French literature. But that fact is perhaps as much a reflection of the institution as it is of the instructor. Given our resources, our heavy general education requirements, and our modest but healthy enrollments in French, I find offering a broad-ranging, canonical, nineteenth-century French literature survey course inappropriate. When it comes to choosing texts, less is indeed more. I am comfortable limiting the view of the nineteenth century as the price paid to engage my students more ardently, a goal that is justifiable in any teaching context but especially in the small liberal arts college. I strive to design my reading lists in such a way that literature will begin to matter to my students. It seems more respectful to ask them to understand fully a limited corpus from their own self-evolving perspective than to fill them with the masterpieces of literature in some imagined ideological vacuum. Better still, the canonical authors on my syllabus—Honoré de Balzac, Charles Baudelaire, Jean Lorrain, Alfred de Musset, and George Sand—appeal widely to students and easily adapt to multiple critical approaches.

"To attempt to be funny," Larson writes, "is a very scary, risk-laden proposition. . . . But if there was ever an axiom to follow in this business, it would be this: Be honest to yourself and—most important—respect your audience"

(Larson, "On-line"). Gide and Larson appreciate the risks, respectively, of being out and out there. Both writers weighed individual loss against collective pleasure. Do my students lose by understanding not only my passion about French studies but also how it figures in my personal life? The answer is no. Students have much more to gain from engaging with my real motives, since these define why I teach: to help students realize their own passions through reading, profess them in writing, and turn them into knowledge.

NOTES

1. LGBTQ is a commonly accepted inclusive acronym. I use the term *belt* not only to make reference to the Larson cartoon but also to invoke the image of a distinct, self-identified community with specific, common interests, such as professing sexuality in the classroom. Teaching in the belt, however, may not always be comfortable. As Lawrence Schehr writes, "To teach *Old Goriot* using gay and lesbian theory is to introduce students to radical rethinking of the ideas of gender and sexuality as these ideas relate to narrative. Since the field is somewhat controversial, such an approach also means that an instructor needs to engage the students and the text while realizing that there may exist prejudicial barriers to understanding" ("Queer Theory" 118).
2. The Rhetoric of the Other conference was first organized in 1997 by Martine Antle and Dominique Fisher and sponsored by the Center for European Studies at the University of North Carolina, Chapel Hill. The organizers have produced an edition of selected proceedings from this conference that include excellent essays on queering pedagogy by Schehr and Delvaux.
3. Both through discussion and sometimes debate, Frédéric Canovas, David Caron, Lisa Downing, Philippe Dubois, Michael Lucey, Judith Mayne, José Santos, Larry Schehr, and Gretchen Schultz have all demonstrated graciousness and support. With their permission, I have included some of our discussions in this essay. It is especially important to underscore the generosity of David Caron, Philippe Dubois, Michael Lucey, and Gretchen Schultz.
4. When I have to postpone classes to attend a conference, I often post my paper on my Web page so that students can see what I am working on outside the classroom. Certainly not every student chooses to look at the site or read my presentations, but at least the mystery of what a professional conference means to the average undergraduate becomes solvable. Those whose curiosity spurred them to look at my research had favorable reactions. One student naively remarked, "I hope you don't expect my research paper to look like that!"
5. "Ça me rappelle un certain discours français, assez démodé mais toujours présent qui repose sur une incompréhension de la question identitaire. Ça me fait penser à ces intellectuels français qui prétendent que les gays and lesbian studies et la queer theory cherchent à réduire Proust à son orientation sexuelle. C'est absurde et souvent de mauvaise foi." Caron is also quick to point out that things are changing rapidly in France. Didier Eribon and Marie-Jo Bonnet, for example, are two notable participants in the French queer studies debate. Even the word *queer* has become popular in France.

Cultural Diversity and Nineteenth-Century French Studies

Doris Y. Kadish

The new concept of the francophone world, which has been extended to encompass a plurality of racial, ethnic, and gender identities, has led to revised curricula and hiring practices of French departments throughout the United States and other countries and thus to a whole new way of studying and representing French literature and culture. Concomitantly, developments in postcolonial studies have laid the theoretical groundwork for expanded notions of national identity, and feminist studies have come to focus increasingly on issues of gender and sexuality for women of Third World as well as First World countries. Regrettably, however, francophone studies have been largely confined to the period since 1950. French scholars and teachers in general, and in nineteenth-century studies in particular, have been slow to apply the new, broader definition of the francophone world to earlier centuries. These centuries tend to be treated in many academic settings in a traditional manner that predominantly if not exclusively relies on canonical texts from hexagonal France. This essay suggests how to identify, locate, and use culturally diverse materials to enrich the curriculum of courses in nineteenth-century French literature and culture.

There are two compelling reasons for making the effort to expand the current conception of nineteenth-century French studies. One is the centrality of the subject of colonialism in French history, a subject that too often is eclipsed in courses that dwell exclusively on formalistic, psychological, theoretical, and other literary concerns. Although it is now widely acknowledged among historians that the revolutions in the French West Indies, and the events leading to the independence of Haiti in 1804, transformed the Atlantic world, French students often know nothing of these events. Similarly, nineteenth-century French literature courses often pay little attention to the existence of slavery in the French islands, its abolition first in 1794 and then in 1848, and the postcolonial dramas that mark the rest of the nineteenth century. These colonial and postcolonial dramas are essential not only for an understanding of nineteenth-century French history but also for francophone literature of the twentieth century, in which stories from the past under slavery play a central and recurrent role. As specialists in French studies, we have a responsibility to lay the groundwork for historically enlightened readings of that literature. Failure to meet that responsibility might be explained in part by our training, which in most cases focused on the aesthetic properties of literary texts. Also, we have tended to take our lead from the canonical authors we study, most of whom belonged to the system that produced colonialism, failed to acknowledge race as an integral part of the economic basis of their society, and made ambiguous if any references in their works to the racial issues of their times. By not following up on the references found in those works and by not seeking to deconstruct the texts or critique the worldview of the authors we study, we repeat their silences and omissions. We thus become complicitous with what postcolonialists would call the will to forget or the voluntary amnesia that has prevailed both in the former colonizing countries and their former colonial territories until recent decades.

The second reason for broadening the concept of what it means to teach nineteenth-century French literature concerns the students we are teaching, as well as those who will be taught by the future teachers we are training. Students today live in an increasingly complex and diverse society that requires a heightened consciousness of and sensitivity to issues of race and gender. Part of our mission as teachers should be to provide skills in analyzing complex social phenomena, including ways to deal intelligently with the elements of Eurocentrism, racism, or gender bias that may arise in literature from the past and present. Moreover, some of our students are persons of color: indeed, we may be teaching in or training teachers to teach in schools that have significant proportions of students of color. For those students, it is important to acknowledge the central role that persons of color have played in literature and history as literary characters, symbols of oppression, writers, audiences, political leaders such as Toussaint Louverture and in many other ways. Speaking about gender as it applies to race, Naomi Schor admonishes teachers to make issues of diversity part of foreign language teaching. As Schor observes, "today's students need no longer check their subjectivities at the door" ("Studies" 281). It is essential that we take the time to provide appropriately diverse materials for foreign language students so that they do not reach the inaccurate and potentially insulting conclusion that only whites or males have produced or figured prominently in the literature that is studied in our classes.

One of the chief difficulties in promoting cultural diversity in French courses arises from its marginalization in the curriculum. In exit interviews I conducted for my department's outcomes-assessment evaluation, in which I asked students who majored in our department if they had been exposed to issues of race in their courses, they typically said yes. However, then they identified the composition and conversation courses in our department as the ones in which they recalled those issues being raised. Undoubtedly the reason cultural diversity enters the curriculum mainly in such courses is that authors of textbooks and anthologies for them make a concerted effort to include diverse materials. Although that effort is to be applauded, an unfortunate result is the marginalizing of cultural diversity in a limited part of the curriculum. In addition to courses in composition, conversation, or civilization, issues of race typically arise in nonrequired courses in francophone or Caribbean literature that treat writers who write about race. Again, the existence of those courses is laudable. But the unfortunate result of their existence is that those classes that deal with "real literature"—canonical European works—are left intact and untainted. Relegating issues of race to special classes sends out the message that race plays no significant role in French literature.

Another difficulty results from the lack of readily available materials for more advanced literature or culture courses. This difficulty can be best addressed by gaining familiarity with the wide range of steadily growing materials accessible electronically. Let me illustrate some of the resources that are currently available for my own particular research area, slavery and abolition in France and the French Caribbean, although I understand that these resources change all the time and that new resources will be available in the future. An extensive set of materials has been developed by Dominique Chathuant, a historian of Guadeloupian origin teaching in France, to enable high school teachers in France to incorporate materials about slavery into their curricula. Chathuant's site offers primary and secondary texts, biographies, chronologies, student essays, graphic representations, and other interesting materials, such as examples from *manuels scolaires* (textbooks) from 1956 to the present time that analyze their significant omissions and biases in discussing colonialism. The existence of such materials can be a significant resource for our classes as well as a lesson to future teachers about how technology can serve to diversify the curriculum and meet the needs of different kinds of students.

My own Web site provides access to various nineteenth-century texts in French that deal with issues of race. It includes links to texts by eighteenth- and nineteenth-century writers such as Jean-Antoine Caritat, marquis de Condorcet, and Alphonse de Lamartine, who are known for their positions on racial issues. Their texts can be compared to illustrate the abstract eighteenth-century discourse of a writer like Condorcet ("Quoique que je ne sois pas de la même couleur que vous, je vous ai toujours regardé comme mes frères. La nature vous a formés pour avoir le même esprit, la même raison, les mêmes vertus que les blancs" ["Although I may not be of the same color as you, I have always seen you as my brothers. Nature created you with the same capacity for reason, the same virtues as whites"]) and the more pragmatic political ideas of Lamartine, who was writing in the years preceding emancipation in the French colonies in 1848 ("Nous voulons introduire graduellement, lentement, prudemment le Noir dans la jouissance des bienfaits de l'humanité auxquels nous le convions, sous la tutelle de la mère Patrie, comme un enfant, pour la compléter et non pas comme un sauvage pour la ravager!" ["We want to introduce the black man gradually, slowly, judiciously to the benefits and triumph of humanity that we invite him like a child under the tutelage of the mother country to acquire, not like a savage to destroy!"]). An especially useful resource is the Code Noir, which was issued in 1685 as the legislative basis for treatment of slaves in the French colonies. The sixty articles of the Code Noir ostensibly protected slaves from abuse and injustice by detailing their rights to proper food, clothing, housing, baptism, medical care, and other things. In reality, however, it was never used to better their condition and stands as a shocking statement of the denial of their basic rights. Reissued in 1724 for Louisiana, the Code Noir of Louisiana was retained under Spanish rule (1768–1803) and continued to influence legislation in Louisiana in the nineteenth century. Both documents are extremely useful primary source materials that could be meaningfully integrated into a variety of courses in French literature, history, or culture. For additional understanding of the Code

Noir, one can consult Louis Sala-Molins for detailed analyses of and comparisons between each of the articles in the original French and Louisiana codes.

It is also possible to gain access electronically to texts such as Claire de Duras's *Ourika*, Germaine de Staël's *Mirza*, George Sand's *Indiana*, and Olympe de Gouges's "Réflexions sur les hommes nègres" and *L'esclavage des noirs* through the Bibliothèque Nationale's *Gallica* (gallica.bnf.fr.) or through my Web site, which also includes some of my published articles on *Ourika* and *Indiana* that discuss issues relating to race. But gaining access to texts is just the beginning. We also need to make a conscious attempt to go beyond the surface resistance that these texts put up in their efforts to conceal and render ambiguous their racial underpinnings. We need to work at bringing out the social, political, and economic issues that constitute the historical context of these works. In studying *Ourika*, for example, we should note that during the French revolutionary period in which the story is situated, there were as many as 5,000 blacks living in France (Peabody 4). Those blacks who sought legal redress in the courts for their freedom, invoking the principle "que le sol de la France affranchit l'esclave qui le touche" ("the slave who touches French soil is free"), were typically successful. Whereas we tend to accept Ourika as a sort of pet who has no legal status, who is neither free nor a slave but who is the dutiful and grateful recipient of Mme de B's enlightened and aristocratic tolerance of blacks, she was one of many persons of her race living in France at the time, some of whom successfully exercised agency and resistance against white owners and oppressors. As Pierre Pluchon has shown, during the first half of the nineteenth century, laws regarding how long blacks could stay in the country or whom they could marry changed frequently. Failing to call students' attention to the historical complexities of the situation of blacks in France in the late eighteenth and early nineteenth centuries is a missed opportunity to meaningfully integrate history and literature into our courses. Similarly, in studying *Indiana*, we need to consider that Sand uses the word *Creole* to describe both Indiana and Noun, despite the traditional use of *Creole* as a noun in French that meant a "person of pure white race born in the colonies" (*Grand Larousse* 635). To call both Indiana and Noun *Creole* is curious since there is no direct evidence in the novel that Noun is white and since there are hints in the text that she is black or of mixed race. Surprisingly, however, critics have often maintained a virtual conspiracy of silence regarding racial issues in *Indiana*. Such silence is strange when you consider that the novel takes place in part in the French colonies in the years preceding emancipation, when Noun was more likely to have been a slave than a mere servant or confidant, as she appears to be in the novel, and when you consider that the novel's white heroine has a name connoting the nonwhite race of Indians.

Having mentioned a number of works by white writers, I turn now to the difficult matter of identifying texts from the nineteenth century written by persons of color. Much of what exists consists of speeches, petitions, pamphlets, and other political material published by literate persons of color who assumed a public role around the time of the French and Haitian revolutions—for example, the impassioned plea for freedom delivered by the military leader Louis Delgrès in 1802, shortly before his death and the reimposition of slavery in Guadeloupe. Other examples, available through my Web site, are two letters by women dating from around the time when slavery in the French colonies was abolished, on 27 April 1848, two months and two days after the institution of the provisional government of the Second Republic, headed by Alphonse de Lamartine (see Kadish). Both these texts can be attributed to or connected with the white abolitionist Victor Schoelcher, who rose to prominence in the Second Republic and who was revered by persons of color in the Caribbean as the author of the emancipation decree. A wealth of information is contained in Schoelcher's *Histoire de l'esclavage pendant les deux dernières années*, a compilation of newspaper articles calling for immediate emancipation and documenting the failure of the reforms instituted by the Mackau Law of 1845, which included such supposedly ameliorative but ultimately ineffectual measures as improved religious instruction and greater opportunities for self-purchase by slaves. Many of the articles in *Histoire de l'esclavage* focused on stories or testimonies of women's suffering, which Schoelcher foregrounded to gain sympathy for his abolitionist cause by focusing on the personal side of slavery. Other materials, such as the *Revue des colonies*, published in France by free persons of color from 1834 to 1842, can be found only in specialized collections and thus are inaccessible for use in classes. However, some Web sites do provide useful primary source information. For example, the Center for the Public Domain maintains the database of Louisiana slaves created by Gwendolyn Midlo Hall (www.ibiblio.org/laslave/), and another site provides genealogical information about persons of color in nineteenth-century New Orleans (www.gensdecouleur.com). Secondary sources are another way to fill the gap and at least acknowledge the existence of writing by persons of color in the nineteenth century. For example, in *Islands and Exiles: The Creole Identities of Post/Colonial Literature,* Chris Bongie provides an analysis of the political issues surrounding the publication of the *Revue des colonies,* including the granting of full rights to mulattoes in the French colonies in the years preceding the abolition of slavery in 1848. Bongie pays special attention to the bitter polemic between Cyrille Bissette, the mulatto editor of the *Revue des colonies,* and Schoelcher.

Some literary texts are available in modern editions, for example, Raphaël Berrou and Pradel Pompilus's *Histoire de la littérature haïtienne,* which contains a considerable number of texts by Haitian writers from the nineteenth century. Another example is a 1979 bilingual French-English edition of the poetry published by a group of poets of color from Louisiana in 1845 under the title *Les cenelles,* which means the fruit of the hawthorn bush or holly tree. As the translators and editors of this edition explain, quoting one of the poets, R. L. Desdunes,

> The small size of the volume shows the modesty of our writers; and the hawthorn, 'a thorny shrub bearing white or colored flowers' expresses, we believe, the difficulty of the undertaking for those who were forced to work in the midst of an environment so discouraging to their poetic inclinations. (Latortue and Adams xxi)

In studying the works of these writers, one generally encounters the same tendency to sidestep issues of race and slavery that is evident in *Ourika* and other texts by white writers of the time. Some exceptions include Victor Séjour's short story "Le mulâtre," originally published in the *Revue des colonies,* reprinted in the *Revue de Louisiane* (1972), and translated in the *Norton Anthology of African American Literature.* For the most part, however, these writers considered themselves French by speech and culture and thus turned to France for literary inspiration. Moreover, as members of an economic and cultural elite, some were slaveholders and were not inclined to address issues of social injustice directly. It is possible and indeed enlightening to analyze the racial *nondit* of their poetry, the veiled allusions to their situation as persons of color writing in America before the abolition of slavery, and of their treatment of voyage, exile, separation, suffering, poetic inspiration, social class, nature, beauty, and sexuality. Especially useful for considering the social context of their writing is Christopher Benfey's *Degas in New Orleans,* which contextualizes the *Cenelles* poets and brings a wealth of cultural and historical information to bear on these texts.

Available materials in French do not of course compare with the rich supply of nineteenth-century American slave narratives, for which there are no French-language equivalents. In "The Slave Narrative and the Black Literary Tradition," Martha K. Cobb cites two French slave narratives. One is by Julien Raimond, a free person of color who distanced himself strongly from slaves and did not favor the abolition of slavery. The other is composed of recollections by a white woman, Hannah Farnham Lee, about Pierre Toussaint, a slave born in Haiti and brought as a young boy to New York, where he lived for over sixty years. But neither really qualifies as a slave narrative. There are numerous reasons for the lack of slave narratives in French. First, literacy in the francophone colonies was confined to members of an elite, mulatto class who were not eager to dwell on their connections with slavery—even though they wrote pamphlets and other works demanding their rights. Second, French abolitionists, unlike their American counterparts, focused their attention on obtaining rights for free persons of color, not on recording or making known the lives of slaves to help the cause of abolishing slavery. Most important, in France there were few individuals, with the exception of Schoelcher and Bissette, or institutions that promoted the publication of writings by former slaves, as did the Quakers and other religious groups in the United States.

Another alternative in literature courses is to include available works by twentieth-century writers who dwell on the history of nineteenth-century persons of color. André Schwarz-Bart's *La Mulâtresse Solitude* is one especially appropriate example: it is short, deals with a key moment in the history of blacks in the Caribbean, and focuses on a woman of color as heroine and thus raises issues of both race and gender. In teaching this novel, one might want to contrast Ourika, whose African roots are erased and replaced by European values, and Solitude, who never forgets that she is the product of her African mother's rape and who consciously rejects any complicity with the cultural standards of her masters. Another example is Maryse Condé's play *An tan revolisyon* (*In the Time of the Revolution*), which was performed at the Fort Fleur d'Epée in Gosier, Guadeloupe, on 11 November 1989. (It is available in French [see Kadish] and in English translation [see Condé]). Reflections on slavery in the francophone world appear throughout Condé's work, including her widely acclaimed two-volume novel *Ségou* (1984–85), a saga of African history from the seventeenth through the twentieth century; her celebrated novel *Moi, Tituba, sorcière . . . noire de Salem* (1986; I, Tituba, Black Witch of

Salem), the story of the female slave from Barbados who was at the center of the infamous Salem witch trials; and her two volumes of historical and literary essays from the late 1970s—*La civilisation du bossale* ("The Civilization of the African Slave") and *La parole des femmes* ("Women's Writing")—as well as numerous other published essays and interviews. Unlike *Ségou* and *Tituba, Revolisyon* deals specifically with slavery in the French colonies, deconstructing masculinist depictions of the heroism of Haitian leaders and highlighting instead the roles of women and slaves. It thus constitutes an especially valuable resource for studying the history of slavery and abolition in a French context. It also sheds light on current issues in France. In an interview, Condé states that her goal in writing the play was to make the people of Guadeloupe understand that they, who had been denied privileges and reenslaved following the events of 1789, had nothing to celebrate for the bicentennial of the French Revolution (Nesbitt).

Considering postcolonialism is another way works by twentieth-century writers of color can enrich the teaching of nineteenth-century literature. The work of Edouard Glissant provides a valuable resource in French for teaching some of the postcolonial concepts developed by Homi Bhabha and others writing in English. By focusing on such forms of cultural mixing as hybridization and creolization, Glissant provides a theoretical basis, indebted in part to Gilles Deleuze and Félix Guattari, for rejecting stable identities and roots-oriented identity politics. Since Glissant applies the theoretical concepts he develops to nineteenth-century subjects in works such as *Le quatrième siècle,* his theory and literature can be useful in reaching the goal of introducing postcolonialism into the teaching of nineteenth-century literature and in raising questions about the existence and the function of the past in relation to the present. Secondary sources can also be valuable resources. A recent attempt to provide an overview of the topic of postcolonialism in France is Jean-Marc Moura's *Littératures francophones et théorie postcoloniale,* which, although general and largely nontheoretical, is a useful tool for undergraduate or survey-type French courses. Other useful tools are available electronically: www.lehman.cuny.edu/ile.en.ile/antilles/index.html, for example, provides a broad range of literary, cultural, historical, and other materials.

I argue here for an expanded concept of the French nineteenth century that includes materials more culturally diverse than are usually found in our literature and culture courses. I believe that the time is right to move in the direction of that expanded concept, since the Internet has made a wide range of materials easily available to us. With the plethora of materials at our disposal, teaching the nineteenth century in the twenty-first need not and should not be the same as it was in the twentieth.

Marie Lathers

Sculpted Texts

Interdisciplinarity in teaching strategies seems often to suffer from what has become known in feminist theory as the add-and-stir method. This method constructs the category *women* as a group of white, middle-class, Western, and heterosexual beings, to which diverse subgroups such as African Americans, working-class women, non-Western women, and lesbians are added.[1] Teachers of literature who aim to interdisciplinize their courses may easily fall into the similar trap of merely adding paintings, photographs, films, and book illustrations to their course materials. In such cases, the literary text remains the primary text—the default text—of the course, just as the white woman has remained in many instances the default woman of feminist studies. We add in visual examples and stir, but that literature taste continues to dominate.

I propose a reassessment of interdisciplinarity that reads literary and visual texts together, as interconnected in a matrix constructed by students and teacher.[2] My example involves the sculptural reading of three nineteenth-century literary texts that foreground the art of sculpture: Honoré de Balzac's *Sarrasine*, Prosper Mérimée's "La Vénus d'Ille", and Auguste Villiers de l'Isle-Adam's *L'Eve future*. I propose that the history of sculpture and its reception in the nineteenth century be studied concurrently with the reading of these texts. I also explore how the metaphor of the writer sculpting the work of literature and its characters forms a central image around which a course or course unit may be developed. The undergraduate French studies course thus moves from cross-disciplinarity to true interdisciplinarity, as the visual work is transformed from a marginal or illustrative example into a central, ever present, object of inquiry.[3]

Despite the dominance of painting during the nineteenth century, sculpture maintained its position as an important art form, partly because a keen interest in classical sculpture had been inherited from the second half of the eighteenth century. Perceived and real connections between sculpture and history also explain the continuing interest in statuary art. Early-nineteenth-century archaeologists and museum administrators busily amassed examples of Greek, Roman, and Gothic sculpture and set about constructing a history or heritage of France based on these. We should also remember that the nineteenth century was the era of sculptural reproduction; in particular, miniature reproductions or statuettes, made using the Collas method (invented in the late 1830s), were ubiquitous. Finally, modern sculpture developed slowly over the course of the century and culminated in the work of Auguste Rodin.[4]

The painting-literature relation has been debated often by art historians and literary critics; it is my contention that an opposition between sculpture and painting has always lurked behind it. The association of sculpture with the material, the three-dimensional, and movement—that is, the association of sculpture with the body—has been cited as a cause of painting's preferred status in the West (see Read 46). Sculpture is a dirty, hands-on, manual art form; to use Alex Potts's term, it is "awkward" (ix).[5] Sculpture has also been labeled a conservative art because of its dependence on political regimes for patronage and its public mission in the nineteenth century, whereas painting enjoyed for many reasons a more liberal status. Finally, sculpture has also been disparaged as a decorative or industrial (applied) art, in part because of techniques of reproduction that developed during the nineteenth century (Boime 4–5).

Balzac's *Sarrasine* (1830) is a fine starting point for a course unit or entire course on the sculpted texts of nineteenth-century France, because its protagonist, Ernest-Jean Sarrasine, is a sculptor. The young Sarrasine's brief career is typical of an artist educated in the eighteenth century: Sarrasine travels from the provinces to Paris, studies in the atelier of the sculptor Bouchardon, and sets out to study in Italy in 1758. Although there is no real analysis in Balzac's tale of Sarrasine's method or of the working conditions of Bouchardon's studio and those of French students in Rome, providing background about the situation for art students in Balzac's own day helps explain to students the naïveté of the singularly talented Sarrasine.

Sarrasine creates his masterpiece, a nude statue of a female, La Zambinella, from memory: having watched the opera star perform, clothed, he returns to his studio and creates first drawings, then a statue. The artist thus participates in the time-honored tradition of creating an ideal from memory, an ideal that always already clashes with the real. The resulting clay statue is acquired after Sarrasine's death by Cardinal Cicognara, protector of the castrato La Zambinella, and a marble cast of it is placed in the Albani Museum. Sarrasine is killed on his discovery of La Zambinella's secret, that she is really a he or rather a sterile monster that belongs to no one gender. Yet Sarrasine's art lives after Sarrasine and yields offspring: the marble cast; then a painting of Adonis done after this piece by Vien (in Balzac's revised version); and a subsequent painting, Girodet's *Endymion*, which is based on the Vien version. A change of gender accompanies the change in genre: whereas the two statues are of the female body, the two paintings display male bodies, or rather ephebes—those feminized images of men favored by the neoclassicists.

Sarrasine's story provides the opportunity to weave painting into a course's matrix of the verbal and visual. The literary text is born of painting (the *Endymion* is the impetus for the tale); the painted image is born of the sculpted one. Thus Roland Barthes's remark in reference to *Sarrasine*, textual realism, and painting—"Every literary description is a *view*. . . . Thus, realism . . . consists not in copying the real but in copying a (depicted) copy of the real"—must be modified if one is to read for the sculptural (54–55).[6] The painted text does not replace and contain the sculpted one, as Barthes contends, but masks the statue in a continuing battle between painting and sculpture, a battle that is itself masked by the more obvious painting-literature opposition. Indeed, the statue has already "contained" and "pacified" (Barthes 207) La Zambinella—difference—by turning a clothed man into a nude woman, a transformation that completes the castration of the singer.

Sarrasine also allows teachers to introduce the sculptural metaphor of the literary text. The first scene of the novella, in which the narrator describes the ball given by the Lanty family, sets up a series of antitheses: inside/outside, light/dark, life/death. This scene prepares the reader for the eventual revelation of La Zambinella as a being who oscillates between the poles of male and female, truly belonging neither to one category nor the other. The images of the living and dead that meld in the mind of the narrator in this scene are reminiscent of the danse macabre theme in art, in which both life and death are depicted as one woman. The ability of sculpture to fool the viewer by presenting several sides of a scene or both sides of an opposition—something denied painting—is reinforced in *Sarrasine* because La Zambinella is a castrato. The castrated body serves easily as a double of the carved statue: La Zambinella is carved up, his body polished and smoothed, and then served up as the ideal female. He is sculpted as a castrato and opera star and then recast in stone and painted versions.

Literary critics, like Barthes (and like Balzac himself, some would argue), have displaced sculpture in favor of painting. Sculpture thus continues to be victim of a critical blind spot, a blind spot that causes us to ignore the material, three-dimensional, even archaeological nature of Sarrasine's obsession. Balzac's text is itself constructed as a three-dimensional sculpture, a piece we must observe from all vantage points before settling on an answer to the enigma of sexuality. Human experience is not two-dimensional, Balzac implies, but three-dimensional—one may extrapolate that gender is not a matter of easy oppositions. Two-dimensional painting, which emphasizes width and height at the expense of depth, reminds us of the narrator's position, for he only sees two sides of the artwork or story. But Balzac tells us that a third term, a conspicuously awkward one, has inserted itself into the equation, lending it depth. Therefore, the artist who first depicts La Zambinella must be a sculptor, although later painted versions of the opera singer as an ephebe may be produced.

In Mérimée's *La Vénus d'Ille*, an antiquarian, the narrator, arrives at the town of Ille prepared to assess the archaeological finds of the area with his host, M. de Peyrehorade. He is excited to learn that a bronze statue of Venus has recently been unearthed in Peyrehorade's garden, but the imminent marriage of his host's son Alphonse de Peyrehorade to a young beauty from a nearby town interrupts his plans. On the day of his marriage, Alphonse places the wedding ring intended for his betrothed on the finger of the statue. On returning home, he endeavors to remove the ring from the statue but is unsuccessful; he must therefore give another, lesser, ring to his bride. As he heads to his bridal chamber, he extracts from the narrator a promise that the ring will be removed. The narrator reneges on his promise, however, convinced that Alphonse's fears are mere superstition. In the morning, the bride emerges from a fainting spell and discovers her husband's lifeless body on the floor. The young woman recounts that the Venus paid a visit to them in the night, strangled Alphonse around the waist, and left the ring on the floor next to him. She is considered mad, but the cause of the groom's death is never established and the narrator leaves the village empty-handed. He discovers afterward that the statue has been melted into a church bell.

Mérimée introduces an important aspect of the sculpture question in nineteenth-century France, an aspect that I call the archaeological impulse. This impulse arises from the desire of postrevolutionary regimes and individual collectors to unearth and assess stone remnants both in and to the south of France (Spain, Italy, Greece, and Turkey). Maurice Agulhon has referred to this impulse as *statuomania*, a term that recalls a pathology or psychological state.[7] Mérimée is a good example of the amateur archaeologist who was swept up by this French impulse to recover fragments of sculpture. From 1834 to 1860 he was inspecteur général des monuments historiques and in this capacity regularly visited the departments of France to assess both ancient and medieval monuments, often then housed in provincial depots or lapidary museums. He was also named to the Commission des Monuments Historiques in 1837, the year of the publication of *La Vénus d'Ille* in the *Revue des deux mondes*.

Mérimée is doubled in the tale's narrator, who wishes at the end of the text to install the statue in a museum, following the opposition established in the tale between the museum (state) and church, the modern and the medieval. The narrator is an antiquarian, an expert from Paris who is astounded at the provincials' crude manners and his host's naive interpretations of the Venus statue's inscriptions. That he is also, like Mérimée, a bachelor puts him in an odd position with respect to the triangle of statue, bridegroom, and bride: at times, the marriage seems to him an impediment to his archaeological quest; at other times, he seems to pity the bride and to fancy himself a better match for her. By offering a reading of the text with the narrator's complex motives in mind, instructors can enlighten students about the multiple political and aesthetic motives of archaeologists and museologists in the nineteenth century.

Students can learn that the archaeological impulse comes from the desire of revolutionary and postrevolutionary France simultaneously to destroy (through vandalism) the past and its stone monuments and to preserve (through restoration) these ruins in new museums such as the Louvre, Alexandre Lenoir's Musée des Monuments Français, and the provincial depots:

> While in the other countries of Europe the metamorphosis from the Old to the New World came about through a slow and progressive replacement of the structures of the past, according to a rhythm that

> did not exceed that of previous historical mutations, France approached the nineteenth century in an immense field of ruins. . . . Nowhere more than in France was the impulse to save—out of which the museum grew—so closely connected with the act of destruction.
> (G. Bazin 218; see also Nochlin; McClellan)

There also arose a new appreciation for the art of the Middle Ages—the quattrocento or primitives of Italian art, as well as Gothic architecture (one has only to think of Victor Hugo's novel *Notre-Dame de Paris*, itself an impetus for the restoration of the cathedral). As fragments and pieces of antique and medieval monuments and statues were gathered in depots, these historical periods were, if not collapsed, at least merged in the new search for a national history or past that occupied French artists, politicians, and writers.

It comes as no surprise, then, that the basis of Mérimée's tale of a Greco-Roman statue is a Roman legend set down first as a full narrative by William of Malmesbury in the early twelfth century and subsequently by Gautier de Coincy, Vincent de Beauvais, and others (see Baum; Ziolkowski). The apparently willful confusion in *La Vénus d'Ille* between the medieval and the ancient and the further confusion of Rome and Greece reveal that these histories were linked in the first half of the nineteenth century. Students benefit from understanding the multiple archaeological threads woven into the story, as Mérimée creates a Venus that responds to France's desire for both national (medieval) treasures and classical works, the latter cited by many as evidence of France's historical connection with ancient Rome and ultimately Greece. Mérimée's *Venus* is French (found in the Midi) and medieval—and thus a fine objet d'art for a provincial depot—and at the same time ancient and classical, because she is called "la Romaine" but is also presented as a work possibly sculpted by a descendant of Myron, the famous fifth-century BCE Greek sculptor. The statue, both virgin and Venus, melds two images of woman and thus reinforces the status of Venus as a medieval and classical icon.

Another nineteenth-century variation on the Venus myth that can be studied alongside Mérimée's is found in Émile Zola's *L'œuvre*. In Zola's novel, the sculptor Maheudeau's *Vendangeuse*, broken into pieces on the atelier floor, seems to be restored and brought to life in the marriage bed of Claude and Christine: Claude feels Christine to be a dead stone weight beside him in the moments before his suicide. A reading of excerpts from *L'œuvre* alongside *La Vénus d'Ille* provides an opportunity to introduce students to the role that recurring myths play in literature and how certain myths become national.[8]

In Villiers's *L'Eve future* the protagonist, Lord Ewald, has just returned from an expedition to Abyssinia (Ethiopia); he is identified, then, as being afflicted with the archaeological impulse. The novel's other male character, Thomas Edison, delivers a lengthy soliloquy on history that revolves around the notion of retrospectivity, which had occupied French thinkers and writers for a century. The significance of this notion relied on the power of sculpture to evoke the past. That sculptures, unlike paintings, may be readily broken into pieces, forming fragments (often body parts), is just one aspect of their powerful ability to translate the passage of time for modern writers: they make and break time and history at the same time as they are made and broken by archaeologists, collectors, sculptors, and writers.

L'Eve future may be read as a culmination of the nineteenth century's archaeological impulse toward sculpture and thus of its statuomania. Lord Ewald's journey to Abyssinia has apparently left him empty-handed, but, on his crossing of the Atlantic to meet with his friend Edison, Ewald is presented with an archaeological find—a masterpiece uncovered in Edison's laboratory. This treasure, named Hadaly, closes up history by representing both the past and the future: she looks like the *Venus de Milo* and she is made by a sculptor, yet she is an android. In this tale, the android becomes the modern sculpture, the scientist the modern sculptor. Ewald's confusion of Hadaly and her flesh-and-blood model, Alicia, recalls Sarrasine's hesitation before the work of art that is La Zambinella. Sarrasine must decide if La Zambinella and his ideal are one or if La Zambinella is in effect too multidimensional to be contained in a work of art. Ewald must decide if Hadaly the android is really a distinct and independent being or a mere copy, a sculptural reproduction of Alicia. Sculpture is, because of its three-dimensional simulation of life, the perfect medium for the representation of hesitation between life and death, masculine and feminine, work of art and machine. Sculpture, because of its hesitation effect, is a propitious art for texts that display elements of the fantastic, as do each of the texts discussed here.

Students find the competition between real woman and android in *L'Eve future* compelling and relevant, since this is a competition they see played out regularly on the big screen (*Blade Runner* is a good film to show along with this novel) and in the media (cloning is, of course, a sculptural technique). What students might miss by considering contemporary examples is the importance accorded sculpture as an art form in the history of the phenomenon of the inanimate brought to life, of the double woman. Cast as androids and cyborgs since the twentieth century, ideal women have long been fictionalized as statues awakened on command. Villiers's reflection on the role technology might play in the construction of the ideal woman brings the Pygmalion myth into modern times. Yet Villiers's work of art, Hadaly, would not be complete or as enigmatic were she not also the perfect copy of an ancient work, the *Venus de Milo* (called the *Venus Victrix* by Villiers).

The *Venus de Milo,* discovered on a Greek island in 1820, acquired for Louis XVIII, and installed in the Louvre in 1821, was heralded as a statue from the fourth or fifth century BCE, considered the height of Greek statuary. France, which already possessed a good collection of Hellenistic and Roman pieces garnered from Napoleon Bonaparte's campaigns (although many were returned to Italy after the fall of the empire), was anxious to own Greek classical works, particularly after the Parthenon marbles went to the British Museum in 1816. Although doubts concerning the attribution and dating of the *Venus de Milo* arose early on, it was not until late in the century that the *Venus* was definitively identified as a Hellenistic work of the first or second century BCE (see Lathers, "Goddess"). From its discovery, the *Venus de Milo* attracted the praise of a nation: beautiful women were referred to as bearing the *Venus*'s lost arms, poets and artists wrote odes to the statue, photographers of the nude adroitly placed reductions of the work in their photos, and the Louvre became more and more a temple to this *Venus*. Students, most familiar to some degree at least with this statue, benefit from learning its history and the connections among diplomacy, museum politics and the restoration of artworks, and the legitimacy of the Restoration government that may be read onto this work of art.

L'Eve future is the nineteenth century's most extensive literary musing on this statue. And the most significant sculpted scene of the novel occurs, not surprisingly, at the Louvre, home to the *Venus de Milo*. Lord Ewald takes his beautiful but inadequate lover Alicia Clary to the museum, hoping that she will recognize herself in the *Venus de Milo* and develop a depth of character to accompany her faultless body. She fails miserably, however, by noting that she possesses arms and "[is] more distinguished looking" (46). On leaving the museum, Alicia displays to Ewald her bourgeois and utilitarian understanding of the significance of the statue: "Well, if they spend all that money on this statue—then—I may do well too?" (46).[9] For Alicia, the aspiring virtuosa, statuary serves the practical purpose of increasing one's renown. She is therefore easily duped into posing for Edison, who claims to make a statue of her for display in London. Thus *L'Eve future* presents the fin de siècle's contradictory view of the value of sculpture: for Ewald, the *Venus* continues the beauty of the past into the present—this is the historical function of sculpture, its function as connection to the past. For Alicia, sculpture represents the practical, decorative art of the present—its function is to allow for the reproduction of images of the famous and would-be famous. In Ewald's view, the absent arms become symbols of the ideal (versus material) quality of the statue; in Alicia's view, the lack of arms limits the statue and allows Alicia to imagine herself superior to it.

As critics have pointed out, Edison's construction of Hadaly is more verbal than visual: the reader and Ewald begin to envision Hadaly as Edison explains her interior and exterior workings to Ewald (see Schefer). The amount of space in the text devoted to Hadaly's interaction with Ewald is minimal compared with the amount devoted to her verbal construction. Nonetheless, running parallel to this verbal construction is the actual sculpting of Hadaly. In several scenes, Edison and his helper Sowana (an "unknown sculptress" [*Tomorrow's Eve* 151]) are presented as sculpting the statue of Alicia that will serve as the body of Hadaly. Edison and Sowana sculpt and thereby construct the ideal of the future, for this text is about the process of sculpting as much as it is about the recitation of Hadaly's creation. When the sculpting is finished, the text ends—it must end, because the chiseling of the future Eve, as android and as text, is complete.

Although it is difficult in a literature course not to allow the written text to dominate other texts, including visual and tactile texts, it is possible to attenuate the additive quality of much interdisciplinary teaching. By attending to the multiplicity of meanings generated by sculpted texts such as those of Balzac, Mérimée, and Villiers, we may open students' eyes to the close relation between the written word and sculpted image that the nineteenth century in particular worked to consolidate.

If an entire semester is devoted to sculpted texts of the nineteenth century, I would also suggest the use of the following texts and film: Balzac's *La cousine Bette* (or excerpts from it), for its depiction of the July Monarchy sculptor Wenceslas Steinbock; Alexandre Dumas fils's *L'affaire Clémenceau*, the story of a sculptor driven to murder his wife and model; Alphonse Daudet's short tales concerning sculptors in his *Femmes d'artistes*; the film *Camille Claudel*, for a study of the female sculptor (although the film often foregrounds Rodin at the expense of Claudel); and Octave Mirbeau's "L'octogénaire," a short story based on an anecdote from Rodin's atelier. For secondary materials, I suggest essays such as Baudelaire's "Pourquoi la sculpture est ennuyeuse"; theoretical texts such as Michel Serres's *Statues;* studies of the relation of sculpture and politics such as Albert Boime's; technical accounts such as Arthur Beales's; and museum exhibition catalogs such as *Le corps en morceaux*, edited by Anne Pingeot. Many of the Salon publications on the annual exhibitions of sculpture are also valuable and accessible. In addition, scandals concerning sculpted works, such as Auguste Clésinger's *La femme piquée par un serpent* (exhibited at the 1848 Salon), may be introduced to underscore the cultural weight that sculpture carried in the nineteenth century. Finally, short texts of literary and art historical criticism useful to students include articles on Balzac and Rodin by Naomi Schor, Judith Robinson-Valery, and Pingeot ("Sculpture"). Although this list of primary and secondary sources is not exhaustive, it is evident that a wide variety of materials exist that may be used to open the minds of our students to the engaging and beneficial merits of interdisciplinary learning.

NOTES

1. Spelman refers to "the ampersand problem in feminist theory." See "Gender and Race."
2. I borrow the term *matrix* and the idea of interconnectedness from Collins, who uses them to discuss the relation among different forms of oppressions (18).
3. Interdisciplinarity is a topic that has received much attention lately, especially in research collaboration. See Hutcheon and Hutcheon.
4. On many of the necessarily general statements here, see Haskell and Penny; Potts. Pingeot demonstrates that there was also a connection between the rise in literacy in the nineteenth century and the rise of sculpture in literature ("Sculpture").
5. "Sculpture is a category so obvious that it is usually taken for granted, and at the same time a little awkward, partly because it disrupts the pervasive logic of the two-dimensional image in modern culture" (ix). See also James Hall's study on the general status of sculpture in Western art.
6. "Toute description littéraire est une vue. . . . Ainsi le réalisme . . . consiste non à copier le reel, mais à copier une copie (peinte) du réel" (61).
7. The term is used by Agulhon, as by others before him, to refer exclusively to the penchant for producing and erecting monumental statues of famous men. Here I mean to extend its meaning.
8. To expand this unit on sculpture and the archaeological, the texts of Théophile Gautier, especially *Le roman de la momie*, *Le pied de momie*, and *Arria Marcella*, are appropriate. These reflect another sculptural myth that is related to the Venus one, that of Pygmalion.
9. "Mais, si l'on fait tant de frais pour cette statue, alors,—j'aurai du SUCCÈS?" (816).

Cynthia Running-Johnson and Judith F. Stone

French Identities in Film: An Interdisciplinary Approach to French Culture

Our collaborative, interdisciplinary course, Movies in Europe: French Focus, grew from several different sources. Most immediately, it began through conversations between us, two good friends, both teachers at Western Michigan University, Cynthia in French literature and language and Judy in French history. Our shared passion for film led us frequently to talk about movies, discussions that often concluded with our saying, "Wouldn't it be great to teach a film class together?" Putting this idea into action arose from another source. Like many universities these days, Western Michigan University is eager to promote interdisciplinary studies. Although its broad integration into the curriculum has not been fully accomplished, steps have been taken to encourage the interdisciplinary approach. In the mid-1990s, for example, the university instituted a program of hiring faculty members with origins or significant experience in a foreign country. This program was meant in part to promote cooperation in research and teaching among different disciplines through the common language in use or the culture under study. Through this and other efforts, led most often by the College of Arts and Sciences, there has been some increase in interdisciplinary coteaching and more generally in the degree of contact between faculty members in different departments. In practice, of course, the reality of economic demands and the strength of existing curricular structures have made this and other interdisciplinary initiatives difficult to pursue to their full extent. The large number of students to teach has made it complicated for departments to release faculty members from their normal assignment of courses to explore interdepartmental coteaching opportunities. Because of the financial bottom line, departments and colleges are often reluctant to assign two professors where one might do. In addition, the system of courses and of requirements for majors, minors, and the university degree as a whole is slow to adopt a more collaborative point of view. But the university and the college have stated their commitment to pursuing interdisciplinary work in pedagogy and research. Moreover, when it has seemed financially feasible, ideas for collaborative courses and for collaborative programs have been welcome. Recent years have seen the creation of a program in American studies, the development of the women's studies program, the reorganization of Africana studies, reinvigoration of the minor in world literature, and initial discussions about minors in film and in Canadian studies.

In the context of this institutional interest in interdisciplinary work, our department chairs were open to our proposal for a discussion-based, three-credit-hour class with a maximum enrollment of thirty students. They approved the course, to be listed under separate titles in each of our departments: Studies in French and Francophone Culture (French 510) and Topics in History (History 400). To appeal to a broad audience, we agreed that class discussion and written work would be in English and that there would be a discussion group and some readings in French for French students. In both departments, this was an elective course for the undergraduate major and minor. Two years passed from the time of our first conversations to our actually teaching the class.

The benefits of bringing our two disciplines together were evident for all concerned. Cynthia felt that, in a historically oriented course such as this, the French students would be able to study French culture in a more focused and in-depth way, gaining a better sense of historical developments than they do in civilization survey classes. In particular, the course offered a chance for them—and for Cynthia—to examine more closely those twentieth-century events that have powerfully shaped contemporary France: the Popular Front, World War II, Vichy, collaboration, Resistance, postwar modernization, the Algerian War, and May 1968. Judy thought that, in a context that included consideration of French language, mentalities, and representations, history students would have more tangible contact with varieties of French culture. They would be better able to discover ways to connect political, economic, and social developments with individual lived experiences. Film seemed to offer an ideal space for exploration by both the literary and the historical imagination. We felt that such a dual investigation would enable us to fully examine the various, often competing elements that constitute French society.

Both of us had had experience using film in our classes. Cynthia included movies as a component of advanced undergraduate readings courses in which the students investigated parallels between literature and film. In advanced undergraduate history classes, Judy introduced movies as illustrative sources. Each of us viewed film study as important for our students and for us. Film has both represented and shaped French culture and may be considered the preeminent medium of the twentieth century. We also assumed that our students all had exposure to movies as a source of entertainment. We hoped that this experience would facilitate their exploration of this medium as an artistic and cultural object. In addition, this new course offered us the possibility of moving away from conventional uses of film in our two disciplines. Cynthia wanted to be able to concentrate more on the historical development of movies and to examine the content of films in a larger historical and cultural context. Judy saw the chance to escape the typical (and always inadequate) use of movies in history courses simply as illustrations of the past and thus to explore film as film.

For the students who would be taking the class for French credit, there was the added linguistic element to consider in the organization of the course. Since the class was open to students who were not necessarily proficient in French or who might have no knowledge of it, working in French as a group would not be an option. We tried to come up with a way in which the students studying the language would still have as much exposure to it as possible. We planned an extra, forty-five-minute discussion section to be held in French each week for the seven students who were taking the class for credit in French (see *Web Support*). Since it was a 500-level (advanced undergraduate / graduate) course, students would have the necessary competency to carry on fairly nuanced discussion in the language. In preparation for this forty-five-minute session, held just after one of the two regular seventy-five-minute periods per week, Cynthia sometimes asked the students to do reading in French—for example, an article written by a French survivor of a concentration camp when the class was seeing the documentaries on the World War II years. Most often, the French group would pursue the themes that had appeared in the full-class conversation preceding it or comment on a particular scene that Cynthia had chosen from the film currently under study. In addition to participating in the discussion group, each student was expected to present (in English) a French text to the class as a whole. The selections included interviews with François Truffaut from the *Cahiers du cinema,* excerpts from Agnès Varda's autobiographical writings, and sections from the memoirs and conversations with Resistance fighter Lucie Aubrac. These activities—participating in the discussion group and summarizing and commenting on the French texts—took the place of different types of presentations done by the other members of the class.

We developed the French-language elements of the course gradually and in several stages. Since we wanted the appreciation and interpretation of films to be the central activity, we began our work by compiling a list of our favorite movies. At the same time, we communicated with colleagues at Western Michigan and at other schools with whose work with film—especially French film—we were familiar. Their suggestions and our further bibliographic research led us to a number of articles and books that provided us with additional ideas for the framework as well as some of the practical details of the class. An article that we consider useful is "Teaching French National Cinema," by Christopher Faulkner. The author believes that in studying a national cinema, one should pay attention to Homi Bhabha's view that the nation is "an 'impossible unity' " (89). Film both reflects and is part of the conflict and division, the constant change, that constitutes national and personal identity.

After reviewing this information and thinking about our students' experiences and interests as well as our own, we decided to organize the class as a loose chronological survey. We were interested in examining in depth several important moments in the development of French cinema through most of the twentieth century. We aimed to include the artistic, commercial, and even some technical advances for which France is known. This approach meant showing the work of the internationally recognized filmmakers Jean Renoir, François Truffaut, and Jean-Luc Godard. At the same time, we wanted to include movies by directors who, for various societal reasons that we hoped to discuss, have been less celebrated, filmmakers such as Henri Clouzot and Agnès Varda. To arrive at our list of movies, we were able to preview films through our university's collection and those of local video stores. We used funding that Judy had received as part of a teaching award to purchase other movies to preview, mainly through Facets Video. This fund was also the source for buying the main copies of the films that we eventually chose. We selected movies from the 1920s through the 1980s: films from the interwar period, the new-wave movies of the 1950s and 1960s, and more recent films in which the directors reflect on France's immediate past.[1]

The emphasis of the class was the study of films as representations of French identity, including a consideration of how certain formal aspects of film contribute to these representations. We hoped to develop our students' and our own abilities to analyze formal elements of film: setting, character development, camera angles, lighting, the score. Thematically, we agreed that the mid-century experiences of war, defeat, occupation, and civil war had profoundly shaped French identities and their representations in movies. We chose a number of films because they reflected on these historical experiences: the documentaries *Nuit et brouillard* by Alain Resnais and *Le chagrin et la pitié* by Marcel Ophuls, as well as Truffaut's *Le dernier métro*. In the light of this focus, we selected Henry Rousso's book *The Vichy Syndrome* as a core text to accompany the movies. This work is significant not only because it discusses the World War II period but also, and more important, because it deals with the construction of memory of the past. Rousso demonstrates that film has a privileged place in this construction.

We also assembled a packet of articles that we used throughout the course, consisting of the following essays:

Victoria de Grazia's study of the effect of Hollywood on the development of the European movie industry introduced the theme of the relation between Hollywood and French movies to which we would return throughout the course. Providing an initial historical perspective, de Grazia's article was especially useful, since she examined the issues of cinema as a component of national identities and of the movies as an industry, underscoring the economic dimension of filmmaking.

Chapters from Jill Forbes's book *The Cinema in France after the New Wave* gave the students a brief overview of the emergence and decline of new-wave cinema and an analysis of what followed.

Chapters from *Jean Renoir* and *French Cinema* by André Bazin introduced this pivotal figure in the post–World War II renaissance of French cinema.

Sections of Annette Insdorf's biography of Truffaut allowed us to underscore the dominant position of this director.

Selected material related specifically to the two documentaries, *Le chagrin et la pitié* and *Nuit et brouillard*, created a necessary context for each film.

In our study of *Le chagrin et la pitié,* we asked students to consult selections from the film script, an exercise that rendered more accessible this long film, which has many conflicting interviews. We chose the opening chapter of Kristin Ross's book on post–World War II modernization, *Fast Cars, Clean Bodies,* in part because she affords an important place to film in her study of this period of social transformation.

Finally, pertinent sections of Jeremy Popkin's textbook on modern France helped us cover the period from 1930 to 1980.

When we taught the course a second time, we made some changes to this reading list. We chose as a main textbook Charles Sowerwine's *France since 1870: Culture, Politics, and Society,* which provided a more solid guide to the historical developments of the period we were discussing. Approximately a third of the students' reading came from this text. For the course packet of articles we then deleted the sections of Popkin's textbook, incorporated pertinent parts of Rousso's *The Vichy Syndrome,* and added articles on the more contemporary films that we included in this subsequent teaching of the class. (See Everett; Marie; Rollet; Triggs; and Vincendeau for works added to our list of readings.)

In planning the course, we knew that we wanted it to be based on considerable student participation. In this respect, the instructors' experiences—Cynthia's with communicative techniques in teaching language and Judy's with electronic conferencing—complemented each other well. Instead of assigning individual journals as a way of engaging the students in the material and of monitoring their progress, we asked them to go online to participate in a computer forum. They submitted weekly journal-type entries to the class electronic conference, commenting on the film that we were viewing. We strongly encouraged them to read all the contributions and to respond to them online. We organized the syllabus and calendar around a variety of student presentations—scene analyses and the leading of discussions of assigned readings. In addition, as explained above, the students who were taking the class for French credit gave presentations on articles that they had read in French and met once a week to discuss in French the films and readings. The students wrote a final paper that they began a third of the way through the semester, revised several times, and presented to the class in the last week.

Given the schedule of student presentations, our brief commentaries on the historical context, and general discussion, there was no time to view films during class. We came to value this approach, since it treated film in the same way as we approach literature or a historical text. There was a public screening of each film approximately one evening per week, and copies of the movies were available for students to check out. Students therefore had greater choice about when and where they would view the films.

The ease and success of the practical aspects of the course—showing the movies and having them available for student checkout—depended greatly on the organization and goodwill of the staff in the language and computing laboratory, who were extremely helpful. Other material details were facilitated by careful planning. We arranged to hold the class in the main building used for foreign language teaching, where we could show films on a large-screen video projector (half-feature-sized); have the students check out videos from the main office; and conduct discussion in a small, comfortable library equipped with a VCR and monitor as well as a slide projector. We did the weekly screenings ourselves, but the support staff was available to help us with the occasional malfunctioning of equipment.

We count this class as a success. The final enrollment was a group of fourteen, seven who had registered under the French listing, seven under history. They were generally advanced, articulate speakers and writers. Most were French and history majors, but we also drew students from English and even occupational therapy. All unquestionably gained a greater and more sophisticated appreciation of French culture, and many were able to develop their ability to see the relations between large social and political events and people's lives. Significantly, the students arrived at this new understanding through their own work and especially through interactions and discussions with one another. As instructors, we were often gratified and sometimes moved by our students' work.

There was, to be sure, a range of reactions to the course. Some students were intensely engaged and completed outstanding work. Others, while contributing to discussions and apparently learning, were unable to keep up with the written assignments. A few were overwhelmed by the requirements of the course and resisted active participation and engagement with the films and their classmates. The greater degree of difficulty experienced by students seemed to be unconnected with their disciplinary background (French or history); perhaps the difficulty had more to do with idiosyncratic personal problems and with the expectations that a film class would involve watching and not much analyzing. The strong students had in common a certain open-mindedness, an interest in areas outside their major, and a commitment to the work of the course.

For the most part, the French students were pleased with the discussion group, where they had a chance to speak the language. Conducting this discussion session immediately after the main class facilitated participation in one way: the group could continue talking about the same subject, but in French. An inevitable fatigue factor did arise, but it was mostly countered by the *bonne volonté* of this group of students. Some of the readings gave them a sense of the value of knowing the language, particularly untranslated work such as a book of slogans from May and June 1968 and the articles and interviews that they read individually and reported on to the class as a whole. Indeed, this kind of awareness of the power of their knowledge may not occur so often in classes in which everyone understands French. Students also felt empowered during our discussion in English with the entire class, since their knowledge about French culture could add information on language and attitudes gained from studies and experiences abroad.

The success of the course was due to the quality of the class presentations and discussion; the students' involvement with the electronic conference; and, fundamentally, the power of the films themselves. There were three types of presentations and discussions: the French students' reports, pairs of students leading a discussion of a text that the entire class had read, and individual students showing and analyzing a scene from the film of that week. Not surprisingly, the presentations that most engaged the students were the scene analyses. The students had the visual representation before them, and almost all were willing to comment on what they had just seen. For the most part, the presenters had minutely studied their scene and pointed out subtle, easily overlooked elements. This approach permitted us to explore the formal aspects of film and to appreciate the art of moviemaking, as we discussed elements such as Godard's jump cuts in *A bout de souffle* or Varda's use of mirrors in *Cléo de 5 à 7*. The students were also able to prepare close readings of major themes, such as the camaraderie and conviviality of the POWs' table in *La grande illusion*. During these exercises, we were convinced that our students' familiarity with movies permitted them to be adventurous and to have confidence in their insights. However, we also recognized the importance of having asked them to look at movies in a new, analytic way.

The journal entries on the electronic conference provided most students with an opportunity to communicate a wide range of responses. Students were able to express themselves in ways not always possible during class time and still share their ideas with the others. One student's reaction to *A bout de souffle*, for example, showed his emotional connection to the movie and indicated his understanding of the film's mood and methods: "My face feels flush. I'm nervous; I'm not sure what to write. I feel all mixed up, excited, and I don't even have the words to truly say how I feel. I'm stupid and crazy and I know too, too well how Jean Seberg (Patricia) must have felt." Classroom discussions were extended into the conference exchanges; immediate strong reactions to a movie were noted and then considered and reconsidered in the written commentaries. We believe that the very high level of this discussion had several causes. First, the students demonstrated a variety of genuine talents. Second, we stayed out of the online conference as instructors. That is, although we did enter comments intermittently, we did so largely to encourage the students to engage in further discussion and to assure them of the quality of their work. Finally, the students supported one another and were able to disagree. The printed version of the semester-long electronic exchange constitutes a 96-page, single-spaced document. On the volume's Web site, we provide additional brief examples of these entries, each citation originating from a different student (*Web Support*).

The students' response to the films—both in the electronic conference and during general class discussions—was not always what we had expected and enlightened us both about their point of view on the world and about the content of the movies. For example, we had expected students to have difficulty with the notions of class difference in *La grande illusion* and to find *La règle du jeu* somewhat obscure. We also feared that both of these films from the 1930s would seem old-fashioned and distant from them. Although we were correct as far as our assumptions on the question of class difference were concerned, we were surprised at the students' depth of engagement with both movies. They connected with the films on an emotional level. In addition, they were sensitive to the political and social contexts and to the artistic aspects of the movies. We were also pleasantly surprised that *A bout de souffle* had a contemporary feel and therefore appealed to our students. As far as *Week-end* was concerned, we had expected them to be shocked by the pornographic language in its opening scenes. Instead, they ignored that and reacted strongly to the violence in the movie. Viewing the films with them also revealed interesting juxtapositions and parallels that had not been evident to us before: the presentation of the French educational system in such otherwise dissimilar films as *Les diaboliques, Les 400 coups,* and *Le chagrin et la pitié;* the revealing scenes of the killing and eating of rabbits in *La règle du jeu, Week-end,* and *Le chagrin;* and the use of the Beckettian pairs of *clochards* in both *La grande illusion* (an influence on the playwright?) and *Week-end.*

The electronic conference not only encouraged students to think carefully and seriously about the movies but also provided a space in which they could express deeply felt, immediate emotions. For the scene presentations, we had asked students to focus analytically on the films, and we have no doubt that the variety of feelings evoked by the films energized the class and enabled several of the students to engage in fairly sophisticated interpretation. As far as the readings for the class were concerned, the contribution was more problematic. At most, the selected texts provided useful background information for the films. Although providing background had been our intention in assigning some texts, we had hoped that they would spark greater debate than they did. The most effective texts were those specifically addressing the biographies of filmmakers or outlining particular eras and genres in filmmaking, those by Forbes, Bazin, and Insdorf. The historical readings were more difficult to integrate. Judy felt that the excellent de Grazia article needed a better presentation to the class and should not have been the first reading assignment. The subject of Europe-Hollywood relations that it introduced could have been developed more sharply as a theme throughout the course. Similarly, the provocative and insightful views of Ross on postwar France required more preparation. In teaching the course a second time, we addressed these difficulties by reordering the articles under discussion and including more reading on the cultural and historical context of the films, with the addition of the textbook by Sowerwine.

Although the readings assigned to the class as a whole had varying success, the final paper for those who completed the assignment worked very well. However, some students had the inevitable difficulty of meeting deadlines, and almost all the papers could have benefited from more thorough research. The topics ranged from a focus on an individual filmmaker, Godard, to a formalist comparison between Clouzot's *Les diaboliques* and the recent Hollywood remake and to a study of French films portraying the Holocaust. The last paper was first-rate and explored history and memory in film. We encouraged the student to submit the paper to a journal, and it is currently under consideration.

The class benefited all of us, even though it inevitably suffered from some of the awkwardness and mistakes in organization that are part of every course in its initial offering. We did succeed in exploring the intersections of French culture and history as represented in twentieth-century film with a genuinely student-centered course structure. For Cynthia (in French) and especially for Judy, who sometimes teaches large lecture-based courses in history, the class depended more on student initiative and contribution than our other courses. Most students met or did significantly more than meet this challenge. As Cynthia had hoped, the class helped both her students and her learn much more about modern French history, and especially about the concept of difference in the construction of modern French identities. For Judy, the entire experience underscored the tensions between historical analyses and the formal elements of film. That is, movies are inescapably in the present; no matter how many times one views them, the images remain unchanged, even when they represent the past. Instead of being an obstacle, this past-present tension offers the possibility of developing multiple perspectives about the notion of history.

For both instructors, the course provided an added reward: it was a pleasure to teach with a colleague and a friend, to see something of the disciplinary and pedagogical approach of the colleague, and to be in a situation in which each learned from the students and from the other. Not only does this collaborative work allow us to continue to reap personal and professional benefits; it also contributes substantially to interdisciplinary pedagogy, which is often difficult to realize in the rush of university life and the press of conflicting demands.

NOTE

1. We arrived at the following list: Renoir's *La grande illusion* (1937) and *La règle du jeu* (1939); Marcel Ophul's 1969 documentary on the Vichy years, *Le chagrin et la pitié*; *Nuit et brouillard* (1956), Alain Resnais's documentary on remembering the world of the concentration camps; Clouzot's 1954 mystery, *Les diaboliques;* the two new-wave classics Godard's *A bout de souffle* (1960) and Truffaut's *Les 400 coups* (1959); Varda's film of the same period, *Cléo de 5 à 7* (1961); Godard's *Week-end*, (1967), a film mirroring the debates of its time; and Truffaut's *Le dernier métro* (1980). In our second teaching of the class, we added several films to emphasize the subject of French colonization, the period of the Algerian War, and more recent French society. In place of parts 2 and 3 of *Le chagrin et la pitié*, *Les diaboliques*, and *Le dernier métro*, we chose the following movies: Diane Kurys's *Diabolo menthe* (1977; "Peppermint Soda") and André Téchiné's *Roseaux sauvages* (1994), both set in the early 1960s; Régis Warnier's *Indochine* (1992) and Mathieu Kassovitz's film on life in the Parisian *banlieue*, *La haine* (1995). (See our syllabus and calendar for the course at *Web Support*.)

PART FOUR

Stitching the Quilt: Institutional Demands, Curricular Strategies

Shifting Contexts: Choosing Texts to Fit Institutional, Programmatic, and Individual Needs

E. Nicole Meyer

Gone are the innocent days when our research or teaching interests and whims ("Wouldn't this be fun?") could solely determine course content and design. Threatened enrollments, declining language requirements, and, especially, related funding cuts in many states; restructuring or downsizing; elimination of tenure lines in the face of massive retirements and a certain administrative fervor for the student-as-client metaphor—all these developments require us to rethink our choices and carefully reconsider our needs. It is perhaps no surprise, then, that since the 1998 Nineteenth-Century French Studies Colloquium's pedagogical roundtable, Nineteenth-Century French Studies within a Cultural Studies Frame, a distinctly defeatist tone has resonated not only in the context of French studies but more generally in print responses to successive phases of academic crisis. Colleagues express frustration in being unable to have appropriate expectations from students—"My students won't read long texts," "My students can't read, write, or speak in English, let alone French," among others. Despite these dire complaints, I would argue that we can require our students to read longer texts and can expect that they meet more than minimal standards. If I can still think this at my public institution dominated by first-generation, decidedly anti-intellectual students, then I believe any of us can.

Even so, we must consider very carefully institutional, programmatic, and pedagogical needs when choosing course texts. We must define our needs and how they intersect with course goals. Those of us who teach courses that serve different programs must repeatedly address these issues and will encounter varied results. One particular question to consider is how we bring our disciplinary expertise into the contemporary teaching environment of cultural studies in an interesting and interdisciplinary way.[1] Since I teach general education courses as well as the whole gamut of French discipline courses at a smaller interdisciplinary institution, I hope to bring a fresh perspective to this and other questions. At the same time, given the changing nature of the courses I teach and the programs I serve, the syllabi I make available on the volume's Web site are examples and should not in any way be taken as prescriptive (see *Web Support*).

DEFINING NEEDS

The reasons we as teachers want to teach a specific course or text usually diverge sharply from the reasons a student takes our course or an administrator wants the course included in the curriculum. Although I detest the growing incorporation of the student-as-client metaphor in the university setting, we do need to choose texts that attract the interest of our audience so that its members will actually read and discuss them. Course goals, class assignments, and assessment methods should clearly correspond to the raison d'être of a course and should be stated succinctly on its syllabus.[2]

Our needs tend to shift when considered vis-à-vis five major factors: institutional, programmatic, pedagogical, individual (the professor), and student (which I address in that order). The syllabi available on the volume's Web site illustrate my decisions in response to these sometimes conflicting factors.

INSTITUTIONAL FACTORS

Institutional factors are often imposed from above and are politically defined. Enrollment concerns typically dominate an administration's pronouncements on course offerings, faculty hirings, and budgetary funding of our programs. At the University of Wisconsin, Green Bay, we are currently in the process of refining "the compelling idea" of what a student needs and should get. Portfolio building and concrete and non-humanities-related skills dominate the rhetoric of recent directives. Many discussions with colleagues from other universities lead me to believe that all of us face similar threats (whether implied or stated) at our own institutions. My ability to offer certain courses has been hampered further by the requirement of having the catalog reflect a certain cycle (and hence repetition) of courses; two of my courses were eliminated on this basis.

An additional factor that often restricts what we can can offer is the need to honor commitments to different programs. I have attempted to address these institutional concerns by developing non-nineteenth-century related courses, including the design of a business French course, arrangement of student internships, inclusion of more twentieth-century literary works and film, and grant seeking to support the production of innovative materials for my courses. These efforts illustrate how so many of us have become jacks-of-all-trades as we diversify our expertise to survive in an environment that is sometimes hostile to our discipline.

PROGRAMMATIC FACTORS

All programmatic decisions we make are directly affected by the maintenance or improvement of student enrollments and student quality. We must address these concerns while respecting the desires and skills of faculty members and the financial resources of our institutions. I try to improve critical thinking skills and linguistic ability (written and oral) as well as provide a stimulating and fun atmosphere in my overcrowded upper-level language courses. These goals are essential, since such courses appear to entice the greatest number of majors and minors into our French program. I need to improve their skills in the upper-level language courses so that I can have the quality of interchange I desire in my literature courses. (See also Paesani in this volume.)

My introductory French surveys introduce the students to works from the Middle Ages to the present and to numerous genres. The course titles are generically bland to satisfy both my colleague who occasionally teaches his own version and the course catalog requirement mentioned above. At Elmhurst College I was faced with exceptional freedom in a moribund program. The course title What's in a Name? appealed to the curious student and definitely attracted more students than the title for the course at the University of Wisconsin, Green Bay, ever would: Representative Authors: How to Read and Understand Them. In addition to subtlely including some theoretical concepts (originality, reader-response criticism, etc.), I was able to motivate students to begin their close textual analysis with the title.[3] Even without the more engaging course title, however, the UWGB course serves similar purposes, that of providing a broad literary and cultural overview. The course stresses reading analysis, ongoing exchanges through class discussion and electronic means, concisely written responses to essay topics, and exams that force students to prepare thoroughly. Despite the course's difficulty, the variety of texts (from Perrault to Sallenave) and approaches (Louis Marin influences my reading of Perrault, Jules Brody that of Racine) provide a solid base on which to build the upper-level courses.[4]

In my upper-level French courses, I seek to increase critical thinking, linguistic skills, and other skills through small-group work based on questions I provide and through class discussions that challenge assumptions on the role of the reader. For example, in a text by Gustave Flaubert, such as *Madame Bovary*, I urge students to question Flaubert's manipulation of readers' sympathies with either protagonist and to consider how the text functions if a reader has no sympathy with either character. I also ask them to reflect on what Flaubert could have meant in stating that he desired to write a book about nothing and what this statement might mean for our own reading of the novel.

Programmatic considerations do not usually motivate text selection in my general education courses, the upper-level English major courses on world literature in translation, or the courses on interdisciplinary works. In these, I focus primarily on pedagogical goals.

PEDAGOGICAL FACTORS

Programmatic and pedagogical concerns overlap. What course goals do we set? How do we structure our courses? Which course texts do we choose? How does this selection explicitly and implicitly redefine a course's goals? What is knowledge, and how do we test it? Why would students wish to read a text? How can we get the most work possible out of them without crossing that fine line where they resist us and our assignments?

Course goals While content clearly counts, I like to think that all my courses help students develop critical thinking and the ability to comprehend and communicate in an active and spontaneous manner with their peers. "The abilities to conceptualize, organize, and verbalize thoughts, resolve conflicts, and work in teams are increasingly cited [by employers] as critical" to their future (Carnevale, Gainer, and Meltzer 7–8), since students must eventually learn how to perform their job, not simply how to furnish a list of vocabulary, memorized phrases, or dates. It is important to encourage active communication with students and make clear the goal of developing integrated skills.

From the first day, I introduce students not only to course goals, structure, and content but also to the importance of community and communication through social, community-building activities. I use various get-to-know-one-another activities and have students fill out interest cards.[5] Each course is discussion-based and relies on the students' willingness to participate fully, an approach that also calls for a rather strict attendance policy and insistence on completing reading assignments.

Course design and structure Although course content may be thematically structured (*la question femme,* alchemy as represented in nineteenth-century literature, representation of the body, power and spectacle) or designed to cover broad content (a specific century, ethnic group, gender, or genre) or even aimed at addressing theoretical concerns (see Stivale's and Kadish's essays in this volume), each of my courses shares some characteristics. They start slowly (fewer pages are assigned, there is more concentration on literary analysis, the group learns of my expectations) and build in difficulty but end with a more approachable, easier text. I find that the last week of class should be markedly easier for my students, because they tend to crash and burn at the end of each semester. If I want success on the final paper or exam, reducing their stress level even slightly produces spectacular results.

I consistently use full texts rather than anthologies. My reason is simple: I agree with Charles Stivale and Deborah Harter in this volume on the importance of close textual analysis, which for me is possible only with a fully formed text. Perhaps I am more Flaubertian than I realize and cannot conceive of form and content as separable. Close attention to narrative detail (e.g., *Madame Bovary* read and discussed over three or four weeks) helps students learn to read for themselves, that is, to ask interesting questions of the text, form original or at least sophisticated responses, and refine their reading strategies.

My course syllabi promote close narrative analysis in more subtle ways as well. Each course syllabus includes a variety of carefully placed quotes designed to be read in conjunction with the text assigned. For instance, in the French and francophone autobiography course that I teach, students reading *L'amant* by Marguerite Duras also consider Nancy K. Miller's words: "To justify an unorthodox life by writing about it is to *reinscribe* the original violation, to reviolate masculine turf" (qtd. in Heilbrun 11). Carefully chosen images (ranging from a drawing of the Venus Hottentot for a nineteenth-century course to illustrations by Kathe Kollwitz or Réne Magritte for later periods) quietly inform and enrich their readings as well.

Course text choice Choice of texts clearly depends on the course one teaches.[6] The introductory French literature survey courses I teach cover both a broad period (the Middle Ages to the present) and a sampling of genres (novel, fairy tale, epistolary novel, play, etc.) and literary movements. In alternate years I teach *Madame Bovary*, which satisfies all my requirements (including the improvement of critical thinking skills, literary analytic ability, and general knowledge) and fits well into the course because of its length. When I recently taught *René*, however, to my surprise students found the main character annoying and the text somewhat difficult (not unrelated factors, to be sure). All attempts to involve them were not as successful as I would have liked, and I will find another example of Romanticism or perhaps choose a work from another movement altogether. I have encountered this kind of resistance only on one other occasion, in teaching Emily Dickinson's poetry. In both cases, the students objected on an emotional level: "Why should we read her?—she's crazy!" My discussion of alienation, youthful yearnings, and other topics fell flat. Student discomfort reveals certain attitudes that worry me as a teacher and that I hope to address in the future in a more effective manner.

The readings in my upper-level courses were chosen to elicit interesting discussion on specific topics. For instance, the syllabus for the course Representations of the Body in Nineteenth-Century French Literature states as its goal the connection of bodily representations with scientific, cultural, and ideological developments of the period through the themes of health, illness, sexuality, textuality, and money in texts by Honoré de Balzac, Flaubert, Jules Michelet, and Émile Zola. The course syllabus further divides the readings and discussions into thematic areas.[7] Such an approach focuses students' readings and seems to provide a rich context in which they can reflect on their ideas. In this course and in the Flaubert seminar I have taught, the texts must stimulate the students to read with more sophistication, discuss their ideas at a rigorous level, and acquire basic skills and knowledge that will help them in the future.

The text selection for my world-literature-in-translation course Twentieth-Century French and Francophone Autobiography, which serves upper-level

English majors, operates similarly.[8] Two additional activities supplement this course: the oral summary and presentation of a critical article and a panel on tattooing. The panel challenges the students' notions of narrative and the autobiographical I. Each student presents a short oral summary of a critical article or chapter from a thorough bibliography provided during the first week of class. Since they receive the bibliography early, students understand—from the very beginning—the level of work expected from them in the course. The presentations occur (usually two at a time) after almost four weeks of class and continue throughout the rest of the semester. The instructions are simple: each student orally summarizes a relevant critical article or book chapter chosen from this list. The summary is followed by two questions that tie the article's topic to our readings. A presentation lasts up to ten minutes and is evaluated not only on the accuracy of the oral summary but also on the summary's and the two questions' ability both to stimulate discussion and to further expand class discussion.

Narratological, psychoanalytic, sociological, and other theoretical approaches are included in the bibliography. More important, I encourage students to pursue creative ways of approaching the presentations, for example, to consider themes discussed in relation to a woman artist (e.g., Kollwitz) or to broaden their understanding of narrative. I supplement such efforts in less traditional ways as well. The annual panel about tattooing that I organize expands students' comprehension of narrative. I invite women to discuss the inscription of memory onto their body by explaining their choice and placement of images and the process of tattooing.

My pedagogical approach and goals differ most significantly in the large general education courses for which I am responsible; I have taught each only once. The courses are remarkably similar. They were designed by the humanistic studies concentration to introduce a large, mostly first-year group of students to a vast amount of material. While maintaining the broad time span demanded by the course, my approach was to focus more on literary works than do some of my colleagues trained in history or philosophy. Only a few of us use whole works and film in our courses. The pedagogical shift away from literature is caused, as can be expected, by the beginning level and large quantity of students, the fact that each class is one of several sections, and the teaching of every text in English.

In the first half of the great books course, called Blindness and Truth, we dealt both with "the individual and fate" (*Oedipus Rex*, *Tartuffe*) and with "confronting conformity or the autonomy of the individual" (*Candide, Huckleberry Finn*), and finally with "woman's place."[9] The themes, myriad texts, and the decidedly French focus (four works were originally written in French) were effective ways of considering the literature at different historical moments and of evaluating what makes a book great in our society.[10] The next two courses offered a chance to teach in a more interdisciplinary fashion. The syllabus for the first course, Introduction to the Humanities 2, states, "Through the prism of this [notable] literature, art, and culture, we will consider the events, people, and ideas of the times" (1598 to the present). The second course states its focus slightly differently: "Foundations of Western Culture 2 is designed as an introductory study focusing on notable events, people, and ideas as witnessed through literature, art, and culture." Text choice and course structure further delineate the differences.

The first course's themes, power and desire and woman's place, clearly echo those of its more literary predecessor. Yet the course syllabus also states, "It is my hope that you use this course as an opportunity to exercise your imagination and your creativity." To foster the goal of creativity and to increase the interdisciplinary focus of the course through active learning, all the students presented a five-minute oral presentation on interdisciplinary topics (e.g., science, art, music) and wrote an essay explaining an artistic work, how it determined their cultural outlook, and why they consider it a chef d'oeuvre. Georges Braque's writings and illustrations served to further motivate them to reflect in less conventional ways. I felt that the course successfully challenged their notions of what knowledge is and fruitfully combined my disciplinary background with a more interdisciplinary outlook. Conventional means of assessment (course evaluations, number of newly declared humanistic studies majors) confirm this belief.

The Western culture course proved more challenging, for several reasons. First, the catalog emphasizes a historical approach. Second, Roy T. Matthews and F. DeWitt Platt's *The Western Humanities*, volume 2, and its accompanying reader were already ordered in the bookstore. Thanks to the very open-minded person in charge of textbook orders, I was able to replace the reader with single texts, which the students read along with selections from *The Western Humanities*. This historically organized survey book structured the course. Although I maintained a thematic organization, the themes were historical in nature (e.g., Baroque 2: Scientific Revolutions) and chronologically ordered. Discussions reflected this contextual approach. Despite what may have been an optimal opportunity to produce an exemplary interdisciplinary course, the dry nature of Matthews and Platt's work, combined with the vast amounts of material covered both in the readings and in the class, made Foundations of Western Culture a more conventional course than Introduction to the Humanities.

INDIVIDUAL FACTORS

I teach from seven to eight different courses that serve four different programs each year, so there are constraints on my time. Faculty members who are untenured or undergoing posttenure review cannot ignore the importance of preserving their employment by cooperating with supervisors and, to some extent, with students' expectations. All faculty members must also maintain enrollments and reach a certain level of success on student evaluations, while still respecting pedagogical standards. Since reducing course preparation may allow us to do more research, our familiarity with certain texts or movements, individual tastes, and ease with teaching certain approaches may also justifiably influence our overall choices in preparing a course.

STUDENT FACTORS

Student quality and level of preparation may vary from university to university, but student motivation remains an important factor in text selection. As Stanford C. Ericksen writes, "Students learn what they care about and remember what they understand" (51). However, since each institution, from the small liberal arts college to the public megauniversities, has a particular mission, faculty members must find the sweet spot between students' preparation and interest level, on the one hand, and the factors mentioned above, on the other. We must be judicious as well as tenacious in maintaining course quality while remaining attentive and compassionate to our students' needs and possible limitations.

We cannot teach without inspiring and motivating our students to participate actively in the learning process. The emphasis is not on students' knowing what they want and demanding to be served as they wish but on our providing an environment through our courses for students to become other than they were on entering our classroom. Texts must be chosen that stimulate students to ask interesting questions and then to attempt original and well-formed responses while enjoying their readings. The innocent days of yore when our interests and whims determined course content may appear less appealing, indeed entirely mythical, as we rediscover the excitement that inspired us to embrace our profession in the first place.

NOTES

1. For a more general discussion of French cultural studies and other perspectives on the present and future of cultural studies in general, see the special issue of *Contemporary French Civilization* on French cultural studies; Stivale, *Disenchanting* and "On Cultural Lessons"; Le Hir and Strand; Grossberg, Nelson, and Treichler; and Grossberg.
2. See Meyer, "Ten Tips," for similar suggestions in a business French context. For more on the active learning of integrated skills in a business French context, see Meyer, "Active Learning."
3. Course texts include *Aucassin et Nicolette*; Jean Racine, *Phèdre*; Voltaire, *Candide*; Chateaubriand, *René*; Albert Camus, *L'etranger*; and a selection of poetry.
4. Although the course lists do vary somewhat over the years, Representative French Authors: How to Read and Understand Them includes both Béroul's and Thomas's *Tristan et Iseut*, Racine's *Phèdre* or Molière's *Le Tartuffe; ou, l'imposteur*; Françoise de Graffigny's *Lettres d'une Péruvienne*, Flaubert's *Madame Bovary*, Annie Ernaux's *La place*, Charles Perrault's "Le petit chaperon rouge," and Nathalie Sarraute's "Le mot amour." Representative French Authors: How to Place Them in Context features *Aucassin et Nicolette*, Molière's *Les femmes savantes*, Voltaire's *Candide*, Chateaubriand's *René*, Flaubert's *Un coeur simple*, Mariama Bâ's *Une si longue lettre*, Danièle Sallenave's *Viol*, Perrault's "Le chat botté," and selected poems by Guillaume Apollinaire.
5. See Holden-Avard, Nusbaum, and Verdier for suggestions of such activities (343–45). The interest cards that I use for all courses help me get to know the students better. Given the large number of students I teach, the cards provide an opportunity to flip through their names and prepare to greet each one personally. For classes with over sixty students, I also use photographs of the students to help jog my memory.
6. The courses I teach fall into eight major categories: language, business, introduction to French literature in French, upper-level French literature, world literature in translation, women's studies, general education, and great-works or interdisciplinary-themes courses that focus on one to three works. The Flaubert seminar focuses on this major nineteenth-century French novelist's works and their significance. We consider Flaubert's "contributions to the development of the novel and to the political and social thought of France." The last course, Great Works: Flaubert's *Madame Bovary*, centers on one work, but the amount of time devoted to it permits me to bring in other materials, including film, and to introduce an array of literary approaches. This course also serves to introduce the French discipline to an entirely new audience.
7. I organized the two-day course (75 minutes each) along the following themes. Weeks 1–2: L'argent et le corps de l'avare (money and the body of the miser); weeks 3–10: L'argent et le corps de la femme (money and women's body); weeks 11–15: Corps et savoir (body and knowledge). The course (last taught in fall 1992) is a

simplified version of the Duke University course of the same name. The major change is reducing Flaubert's *Bouvard et Pécuchet* to shorter extracts and eliminating Joris-Karl Huysmans's *A rebours*. Both choices were made for my particular audience, whose level of analytic rigor is less developed than that of my former Duke students. The course is still challenging, includes heavy reading of lengthy texts and a complete bibliography of critical works. Course texts included Balzac, *Gobseck;* Michelet, extracts from *L'insecte, La mer, La sorcière;* Barthes, *Michelet par lui-même;* Maupassant, "Le signe," "Les soeurs Rondoli," and "Histoire d'une fille de ferme"; Zola, *Nana;* and Flaubert, *Bouvard et Pécuchet* (including his *Dictionnaire de idées reçues*). The course entitled Representation of the Body in Nineteenth-Century French Literature is a modified version of a Duke course I designed as well.

8. Required texts were the following: Simone de Beauvoir, *Une mort très douce;* Ken Bugul, *Le baobab fou;* Colette, *La naissance du jour;* Marguerite Duras, *L'amant;* Ernaux, *Une femme;* Nathalie Sarraute, *Enfance;* Heilbrun, *Writing a Woman's Life*. Also viewed in class were Diane Kurys's films *Diabolo menthe* and *Entre nous* and Jean-Jacques Annaud's *L'amant*.
9. Other works included *Aucassin and Nicolette;* Dickinson, *Collected Poems;* Flaubert, *Madame Bovary;* and Zora Neale Hurston, *Their Eyes Were Watching God*.
10. The great-books course was replaced. From what I understand, some colleagues were uncomfortable with the broadness of the time span covered (from ancient times to the present) and the literary emphasis. I found those two constraints quite stimulating and organized the readings around two central topics with several subthemes. Furthermore, as the only woman to have taught the course, I felt my effect and choice of works to be quite significant, despite the removal of the course from the program.

Balancing Acts: French Studies and the Graduate and Undergraduate Classroom

Deborah A. Harter

In the waning weeks of summer, college professors often find themselves tinkering with the syllabi they have constructed for courses they will teach in the fall—thinking once again about which texts to read, the right quantity of work, the appropriate balance between primary and secondary readings, and the optimum order in which to take these up. Nowhere, however, is the task of getting it right more delicate than in those seminar courses open to both graduate and advanced undergraduate students. Here, professors must find creative ways to blend the different strategies that guide the rhythm and tone of their teaching when they work with graduates and undergraduates separately, design courses of study that are challenging and pedagogically viable for constituencies with differing backgrounds and expectations, and find effective ways for meeting both the graduate student's need for theoretical depth and the undergraduate's abiding interest in the primary text.

Such pedagogical challenges are common here at Rice University and at institutions like it, where undergraduates are particularly strong and where the faculty is relatively small so that course selection is limited. It is not unusual to find in a single classroom graduate students hungry to tackle theoretical, political, and cultural perspectives that are the foundation of most graduate programs and bright, highly motivated undergraduates anxious to push their intellectual experience of French studies beyond the limits available to them at the undergraduate level. Successfully negotiating this mix of students is crucial for the effectiveness of such courses and for the health of a department's larger curricular program.

THE ADVANTAGES OF INTERDISCIPLINARITY

The challenge of bringing together students of differing levels can be addressed, in part, by introducing greater interdisciplinarity into one's program at all levels. When undergraduates perceive that the idea in their courses is not only to become familiar with a certain literary canon but also to reflect on the texts they read from multiple disciplinary perspectives, they begin to value the kinds of knowledge that have traditionally been the province of the graduate student. With this strategy in mind we launched, at Rice University, an interdisciplinary program in French studies in 1990 to situate French literature and culture, for all our students, in the broadest possible context of European and world thought and to emphasize the dynamic interplay among literature, history, art, philosophy, and social science. For our undergraduates we wished to maintain a firm grounding in French literary and cultural works—the sort of grounding one acquires in courses such as The Lyric Genre from Baudelaire to Bonnefoy or Masterpieces of French Theater from Corneille to Sartre. But we also hoped to enable their going beyond the literary text to tackle materials in such areas as gender, film, philosophy, and art. To this end, we put together courses such as Modern French Painters and Their Writers, Society and the Sexes in Modern France, and French Utopianists.

Interdisciplinarity was given even greater emphasis in our graduate program as we designed courses that were more ambitious, theoretical, and compact. In Contemporary French Thought: Towards a Symbolic Economy, students explore notions of production, exchange, and consumption in anthropology, semiotics, psychoanalysis, and literature. In Western Traditions / Postcolonial Challenges, they consider discourses of cultural affiliation in modern literature, painting, and film from Africa, the Caribbean, and France. In The Meaning of the Sacred in French Thought from Surrealism to the Present, students examine the significance of the rise of a posttheological notion of the sacred in modernity. We hoped that in the courses we offered, our graduates would gain the tools needed to work with not only the most canonical of literary texts but also the most modern intellectual and cultural debates.

However bright one's undergraduates, patient one's graduates, and interdisciplinary one's offerings, blending the needs of graduates and undergraduates remains an enormous pedagogical undertaking. Interdisciplinarity itself presents curricular challenges. Among undergraduates (whose vision we wished to widen) we found, on occasion, a resistance to texts and issues beyond the literary, especially when we leaned toward the theoretical. With our graduates the difficulty was precisely the reverse. We found ourselves having to remind our students that the heady theoretical and interdisciplinary reflections that dominated many of their seminars were not intended to be replacements for the literary text.

We began to reconsider our syllabi as we worked to build courses that would allow us to hold on to outstanding undergraduates in graduate seminars without lowering the stakes or the discourse of the graduate classroom, ensure a sophisticated body of knowledge, and accommodate multiple approaches without creating schizophrenia of purpose. And we began to look afresh at our pedagogy.

PRINCIPLES FOR THE UNDERGRADUATE CLASSROOM

For undergraduate students, it is critical that readings and lecture be accompanied by active verbal and written engagement. Only in this way are undergraduates able to synthesize and make their own the linguistic nuances, interpretive richness, and political and historical contexts of the texts before them. For these students—even those with the strongest linguistic backgrounds—it is critical that one maintain a balance between introducing new material and allowing students the necessary time to explore and digest this material in depth. In my own courses I have found that I am able to take my undergraduates furthest when I focus sharply in class on a small number of texts or portions of texts (a single poem, a chapter in a novel, a few scenes from a play), so that students may gradually develop the critical tools they need for understanding and rigorously analyzing each text's linguistic and literary structures. It is not always an easy task, refraining from exposing one's students to a broad range of wonderful texts in favor of allowing them to master more deeply a select few. But an in-depth discussion of a single poem—Victor Hugo's "Demain, dès l'aube," for example, or Charles Baudelaire's "La cloche fêlée"—often provides, even in a ninety-minute session, far more than a superficial study of three or four poems by one of these writers. In the frame of close reading, one has time to unpack and explore the nuances of language, integrate matters of language into the larger project of interpretation, and point to broader contexts in which the text resonates.

At home, too, students' preparation should be thoughtful and intense rather than passive and superficial, and it should be geared toward preparing for a classroom discussion focused on questions and exchange. Such discussion requires a classroom environment where students are able to support each other as well as to disagree and where they are unafraid to make mistakes. Nowhere is it more true than in the undergraduate classroom that learning is at its best when it is a dynamic process of discovery rather than an occasion for reviewing the analyses, readings, and wisdom of others.

Undergraduate courses are most successful, finally, when one assigns texts that are not only accessible and important but also engaging. When I teach Baudelaire, I introduce poems such as "Une charogne" and "Hymne à la beauté" before assigning the more abstract "Correspondances." Students enjoy immensely Guy de Maupassant's brief, fantastic tales ("Lui," "La nuit"); Jacques Prévert's moving "Rue de Seine" and hilarious "Chanson des escargots qui vont à l'enterrement"; and Gustave Flaubert's "Légende de Saint-Julien l'hospitalier." I am mindful, as I teach, both to build meaningful connections between the texts we read and to discuss the larger contexts in which they might be understood—the way a text expresses a certain Romantic sensibility, its place in the development of the novel, its relation to the fin de siècle or to surrealism. But these connections are only vivid to the degree one brings the text to life. I like to imagine that my students carry with them, when they leave the classroom, scenes such as the one in Georg Buchner's *Danton's Death* where Danton and Camille and their companions joke and dream about their impending deaths or the one in *Madame Bovary* in which Emma pricks herself on her wedding bouquet, throws it into the fire, then watches as its paper petals flutter up the chimney like black butterflies.

PRINCIPLES FOR THE GRADUATE CLASSROOM

Graduate students, just as much as undergraduates, crave texts that will engage them. Assigning readings that are provocative and rich is as fundamental at the graduate level as it is at every level of the undergraduate curriculum. But an even more critical challenge in the graduate seminar is the one of achieving the right balance between primary and secondary readings

—between readings that view the texts as literary and cultural artifacts and readings that offer perspectives (theoretical, historical, political) with which to engage such artifacts. I make a point never to teach theoretical texts or literature alone but to teach both simultaneously and in dialogue with each other, so that in a course on literature and psychoanalysis, I might teach Marcel Proust's "Combray" and Franz Kafka's "A Country Doctor" alongside Sigmund Freud's *Interpretation of Dreams*, Baudelaire's "Une martyr" and "L'héautontimorouménos" ("The One Who Strikes Himself") with Jean Laplanche's "L'aggressivité et le sadomasochisme" ("Aggression and Sadomasochism"), Émile Zola's *Nana* with Jacques Lacan's "Le stade du miroir" ("The Mirror Stage"). These are literary and theoretical texts that work together to illuminate common ideas and that bring to life the rich ways in which literature and theory inform each other.

Not surprisingly, I often find that my most successful seminar sessions are those in which we identify the threads connecting the texts before us. Discovering these threads makes preparing for class a less daunting task for students, ensures that they sharpen and deepen their skills in a variety of domains, and modulates the pace and tone in the classroom. It prevents the student's losing sight of the literary text in his or her quest to master the theoretical paradigms, a quest that can centrally occupy the graduate seminar. Most important, combining literary and visual texts with theoretical readings provides students with ongoing opportunities to use, as tools in their discussion and writing, the critical paradigms to which they are exposed. In other words, it helps them understand how theoretical texts illuminate certain dimensions of the literary and visual and how, in turn, literary and visual texts illuminate—sometimes even engender—the theoretical.

Graduate seminars, unlike undergraduate courses for majors, are often forums for significant lecture. Yet here, too, students benefit greatly when they participate more actively, know there will be time and space to express their ideas, have opportunities to work through material with their peers as a class in a joint effort of discovery and exchange, and are required to give oral presentations in a pedagogically productive environment that discourages readings calculated to impress the professor.

BALANCING ACTS

I have suggested that teaching courses that enroll both graduate and undergraduate students poses especially difficult problems. Not only are there issues of choice of texts but also questions of level and focus, of pace, even of comfort. Undergraduates are often intimidated by their more advanced counterparts and inclined to become quiet, whereas graduate students are sometimes irritated with the lesser language skills of undergraduate students and worry that their presence in the graduate classroom jeopardizes the level of discourse.

Some of these issues are best resolved through professorial fiat. There should be no ambiguity, for example, about the level that will be targeted in any given course. I teach my graduate seminars as graduate seminars, explaining to my undergraduate students that I will require less written work from them but that in every other way they can expect the course to take place at the highest level. Conversely, in the advanced undergraduate classroom, I explain to the graduate students who attend that I will be happy to provide them additional reading and writing opportunities but that the level of the course will be geared, at all times, to the undergraduate.

When it comes to oral presentations, I find that seminars with a mix of graduate and undergraduate students enjoy real advantages. In the context of my insistence that presentations demonstrate a student's best efforts at good pedagogy, graduate students often appreciate the presence of undergraduates as an appropriate (although certainly unnecessary) excuse for aiming at simplicity and directness. Undergraduates, in their turn, can be remarkably good at rising to meet the heady challenge of addressing their more advanced classmates.

The question whether to conduct class in French or English is the most difficult issue in seminars that enroll students of different levels. French language proficiency tends to divide graduate and undergraduate students in stark ways, whereas intellectual ability (especially at universities where undergraduates are particularly strong) is a place where the two groups come together more. When one adds nonfrancophone students from other departments to this mix, language barriers become almost insurmountable. Teaching a graduate seminar in English is often the only effective means for attending to the needs of students who in fact share a great deal in terms of interest and intellectual talent but whose language abilities are varied. With English as the lingua franca, there is greater common ground among undergraduate, graduate, francophone, and nonfrancophone groups and one less obstacle in setting the highest possible intellectual tone for the seminar. Undergraduate French majors, one hopes, continue to be immersed in the French language in their undergraduate courses, while graduate students of French sharpen their ability (an especially important exercise for graduate students from abroad) to articulate viewpoints with confidence in an English-speaking environment. One succeeds, finally, in accommodating students from other departments, many of whom have already been introduced to French theory and criticism in their own programs. Graduate students from outside French studies, moreover, add both richness and breadth of background to the intellectual tone of a seminar. They bring with them a different set of assumptions; a view from another discipline; and a validation, in the end, of the very project of French studies.

It is certainly true that language shapes not just the objects we teach but the ways in which we think about them. In the undergraduate course for majors, the study of French literature and culture in French cannot be replaced. Still, as Judith Ryan suggests, we need to encourage occasional changes of vantage point. Such changes, she writes, need not destroy that "special aura, that sense of being initiated into a secret science that makes learning about foreign literature so appealing" (18).

Finally, in the classroom that brings together a heterogeneous group of students, a weekly response paper (a single, journal-like page of reflections addressing one or more of the readings that week) becomes an important tool, allowing the professor to remain tuned to the pulse of student interests and difficulties. Such papers make possible a dialogue between the professor and every class member—whether graduate or undergraduate, student of French studies, art history, or English—that can take place at the appropriate level and address the issues each student finds most interesting.

ADJUDICATING THE CONFLICT: A FEW SYLLABI

Although a list of principles may be useful, at some point it is more efficient to look at sample syllabi of the courses we teach and to consider the successes and the difficulties that have attended them. In this spirit, I would like to discuss three courses I have taught in the past two years in which there was a mix of graduate and undergraduate students (the syllabi are available at *Web Support*). The first course, Women and Women's Voices in French Literature, was an undergraduate seminar taught in French (as are all undergraduate courses at Rice) in which fourteen French majors enrolled along with two graduate students from French studies and one graduate student from art history. We read a selection of fiction (Lafayette's *Princesse de Clèves*, Duras's

Ourika, Sand's *Indiana,* Mérimée's *La Vénus d'Ille,* Colette's "La main"), a selection of poetry (from Desbordes-Valmore and Baudelaire), several historical texts (excerpts from Michelet's *Révolution française,* revolutionary writings by de Gouges), and very short selections from several theoretical texts by Simone de Beauvoir, Luce Irigaray, and Elisabeth Badinter (collected in Tondeur). There was no question but that the course belonged to the undergraduates, who seemed to enjoy the presence of the graduate students rather than to be intimidated by them. But the graduate students also fit right in, adding depth to our discussions and relishing, I think, the opportunity this undergraduate seminar provided them to dwell at greater length on a body of primary fiction. I made it clear to them in outside conferences that I would direct them to issues beyond the scope of the course on an individual basis but that the level of the course, in the classroom, would be strictly geared to the needs of the undergraduate students. I also encouraged them to write a single research paper for the end of the term rather than the required set of short papers. In this I found added opportunity to encourage exploration of materials beyond the immediate scope of the course.

Not every problem arising from the mix of students in this class was solved so easily. On the first day, several students from Rice's program in Studies in Women and Gender appeared who had hoped the course might be conducted in English. But with fourteen undergraduate French majors and our department's commitment to the importance of teaching undergraduate courses entirely in French, our nonfrancophone students could not in the end be accommodated (with the exception of the graduate student in art history, who remained in class and whose comments in English added immensely to the scope of our discussions).

In a second course, a graduate seminar that examined nineteenth-century fiction through its discourses of displacement—its depictions of nostalgia and of homelessness in the first half of the century and of the crowd, the flaneur, and hysteria in the second (From Nostalgia to Hysteria: Balzac, Stendhal, Flaubert, Maupassant)—it was clear from the outset that it would be best to conduct class in English. There were eleven students enrolled: seven French graduates, two French undergraduates, and two graduate students from the English department. The undergraduates were extraordinarily bright but had limited background in reading dense theoretical texts. The French graduates, representing several nationalities (French, American, Romanian, and Russian), were quite advanced in the French language but less so in English. The English graduates were remarkably at home on issues pertaining to literary theory but were of course unfamiliar with much of the French literary tradition.

Negotiating the different needs of this challenging mix was not without hazard, and here again the most difficult issue was language. Although there was no question that conducting class in English was critical for the success of the course, the two undergraduates occasionally yearned to practice their French, while one of the graduate students in French was less adept in English than I had realized and thus participated less energetically than she might otherwise have done. Finally, the bureaucratic headaches of securing texts in two languages were a regular burden. And yet the use of English also allowed this seminar to take full advantage of its rich mix of students and to develop into a course that was, in many important respects, exhilarating. On the one hand, the French graduates enjoyed enlightening their fellows from the English department about the contexts and richness of the French texts we read. On the other hand, the English graduate students challenged their peers to broaden the stakes of their ideas and to include a wider range of literary and critical frames of reference. The four bright undergraduates, meanwhile, were at no disadvantage when it came to engaging in and contributing to the discussion. One of these, a double major in French and history, offered unusual insights into several historical issues that became pertinent along the way, outlining these in one of the best oral presentations of the course.

In a third course, finally, a graduate seminar on literature and psychoanalysis, there were twelve students enrolled: eight French graduates; two French undergraduates; and, again, two graduate students from English. Like the graduate seminar described above, the mix of students was more an enrichment than a distraction. The English graduate students brought to our discussions outstanding insights from a course on this subject taken previously in their department. The undergraduates worked mightily to keep up with the reading. My efforts to select engaging primary texts that would speak interestingly to our theoretical readings and provide the balance I find so indispensable produced a course that allowed for diverse comparisons and in which we read works not just from Baudelaire, Zola, and Proust but also from Kafka, Edgar Allan Poe, and Thomas Mann.

But in this course, unlike the other two, my strategies for success ran into conflict. One of the graduate students from French studies was deeply dissatisfied with the comparative selection of texts ("Why in the world should I read Kafka?"). He was unhappy that I had admitted undergraduates ("Surely they will lower the general level of our inquiry"). He was displeased with the presence of graduate students from the English department ("What does French studies, after all, have to do with them?"). In his view undergraduates were nothing less than infiltrators whom I was encouraging and accommodating by conducting class in English ("If this goes on any longer, I'll have forgotten my French by next year!"). Many hours of discussion with this student failed to allay either his disapproval or my anxieties at the possibility of our having betrayed French studies. I spent a long weekend making significant changes to the syllabus and ordering additional books, only to find on Monday that the student had dropped the course.

In the forcefulness of this student's reaction (even if extreme and atypical), I was reminded that the decisions we make cannot be taken lightly and that there is a price to be paid when we adjust a course to fit not only intellectual issues but also enrollment trends. I realized as well that this particular student (an American whose French is impeccable and who took his BA at a French Canadian university) reflected a kind of parochialism that is no longer an option for foreign literature departments. We can neither compete for survival in a market of diminishing foreign literature majors nor enjoy the benefits of working with other departments when we have opportunities to reach out to their students, if we do not see ourselves and some of our courses as participants in a dialogue in which differences—in language, level, and specialization—are opportunities for productive collaboration.

This search for productive collaboration is why I will find myself next August fretting once again over the syllabi, strategies, and choices of texts I planned for courses in the fall and spring. In the end, our syllabi are the skeleton on which we build our courses, focus our readings, and guide our discussions. They determine the body of works with which we tackle the challenges that face us each semester as we work to create engaging environments of learning; as we seek to expose our students both to the specificities in our field and to the wider contexts of which they are a part; and as we negotiate the problems, possibilities, and promise of interdisciplinary dialogue, whatever the lingua franca and the risks we take in doing so.

Overseas Engagements: The Presence and Futures of Study Abroad

Gayle Zachmann

This essay reflects on the potential of designing study-abroad programs to stimulate interest in and enhance the quality of undergraduate French sections. The topic almost inevitably invokes what colleagues nationwide regard as the major issues affecting French studies today. That is, besides the logistical affairs of deciding on a place (francophonie or metropolitan France), space (staying in a home or dormitory or touring), time (summer, semester, or academic year), and institutional context (at state and private institutions alike) for study abroad, approaches intersect with a range of philosophical and pragmatic paradigm shifts that affect French sections and departments across the country.

I first focus on the efforts at my home institution, the University of Florida, to mount a study-abroad program; I then analyze the creation and structure of our program as responses to cultural, curricular, and administrative realities. The ambit of my remarks shows how the overseas program offers a speculative microcosm in which many of the issues facing the future of French studies compete for discursive and curricular space; an occasion for productively addressing many of the transformations that preoccupy undergraduate educators of French language, literature, and culture at our *début de siècle*; and a propitious opportunity for enhancing faculty development of site-specific and interdisciplinary courses.

For French departments with long-standing study-abroad programs or French sections that wish to create them, the value and need for study abroad seem almost too obvious to merit discussion. And yet coming from a major state institution that has had a study-abroad program in place for only five years, I must admit that the banal details of setting the program in motion and the results of this process have proved much less self-evident than previously imagined. Indeed, our modest endeavor moved rapidly beyond logistical considerations.

In the fall of 1994, when I arrived at the University of Florida, there reigned a national atmosphere of anxiety in and about French studies. As legislative and administrative practices in many state institutions moved to a corporate model for the analysis and management of our schools, it seemed that in the humanities in particular our productivity was in question, that in French our enrollment and major numbers were not considered competitive. Our section also lived with the atmospheric pressure of a doomsday, somewhat fin de siècle discourse that ran rampant in the mid-1990s. The slogan "the end of French studies" was buttressed by false questions from critics of French programs in and outside academe, inquiring why we continued to reproduce a decidedly imperialistic and hegemonic tradition rising out of seventeenth-century France. It is in this context that I address our initial corporate math problem of enrollments and number of majors and the challenges we faced in designing our study-abroad program.

In 1994 French at the University of Florida was stable. Although coming into that academic year the program had consistently hovered between thirty-five and forty-five majors, there existed a growing feeling of anxiety about future enrollments, the need to justify replacement lines, and administrative support for French—campus- and nationwide. Among different strategies taken to ensure the future of our French program, the section began to consider initiating a study-abroad program. This endeavor, however, met with reluctance, which was caused by other administrative realities. In the mid-1990s, the trickle-down, downsizing corporate model of the 1980s seemed to mean a trickling down and up of administrative tasks to faculty members. We were thus a section faced with many administrative duties while trying to assert the validity of our sections at a moment when Spanish was booming in Florida and elsewhere.

Furthermore, so-called literature courses were being questioned now, and the legitimacy of French studies was under attack despite growing interest in francophone literatures, cultures, and cultural production. In this context, we supported the view that a study-abroad program was one of the measures that would both strengthen our section, its curriculum, and its students and address a number of the mounting pressures mentioned above. This initiative would also respond to what had become a student demand at the University of Florida and, not insignificantly, to a task requested of me by the department chair. Although the effort to establish the University of Florida in Provence has been daunting at times, it has become the occasion to question many issues, including the place and role of French on our campus and in the field.

In 1998, I began seriously to construct viable models for a program. By general consensus among the members of my section, support arose for summer as the proper time frame to adopt. After analyzing a number of top-rated summer programs and sounding out my colleagues, I devised a wish list of program characteristics that included but was not limited to the following:

a program with a family stay for students to encourage an authentic experience of interaction with French daily life and meals (thereby avoiding the fish-bowl effect that regularly occurs when students remain in dorms or tour France without integration into the French university system)
a program that would provide numerous excursions and cultural activities
a program that would offer a wide range of rotating interdisciplinary and site-specific courses in French that were not offered on our campus
a program that would encourage faculty development
a program that would allow our faculty members to teach in the program
a program that would not repay use of such faculty expertise with the dubious reward of traveling to Europe with three to four dozen twenty-year-olds in culture shock
finally, given that we were truly starting from scratch in our organizing efforts, a program backed by the full support of a host institution to facilitate our plan.

Although this list may appear basic, logical, and logistical, it calls up many issues. First, where was the program to take place, in the Hexagon or in a francophone region? Not surprisingly, this question emerged in my nationwide poll as one of the most important issues to French studies today, that is, the place of francophonie and francophone studies in our curriculums, departments, and institutions. We addressed this issue in pragmatic albeit summary terms. Since my chair had specifically requested that I explore possibilities for a program in France, some colleagues never considered the possibility of locating it anywhere else. Others chose to consult programs that had established or considered locations outside France. Most colleagues and students alike judged that France still held (and still holds) enormous attraction for a successful program. The attitude suggested that the exportation of France's greatest national products, French culture and allure in all their grandeur, was still a draw. Because numerous University of Florida programs and exchanges already existed in francophone regions through our African and Asian studies unit and because a solid base of our faculty still considered France as its primary research ground, we decided to locate the program in France.

We then had to decide where in France to locate it. Although Paris was my first choice, both for draw and research opportunities, our choice to initiate a program during the summer made the Paris option difficult, for lack of facilities and home-stay support during the vacation months. After consulting with colleagues in Paris programs, I began to make contact with a number of host institutions outside the capital and found one that facilitated realization of every one of our wishes. That was the easy part.

The next major decisions I faced were integrally linked to a second issue: we sought to create a program to encourage faculty members to stay in France and students to travel abroad to improve the quality of their fluency as well as the expanse of their contact with French culture and its global legacies. Yet how could we form better students and build stronger enrollment numbers and curricular offerings for French majors and minors while not destroying our program in Florida by depleting what already seemed dwindling numbers and thereby contributing to the nationwide trend of downsizing French? Finally, in the light of the growing critique of French isolationism, perhaps particular to our campus, how could we justify locating this program in France's borders as an effective means of deploying more open models of French studies?

At this point, we developed the strategy of a two-site program and, more specifically, a two-site interdisciplinary program. The two sites for the University of Florida in Provence were a function of both philosophy and reality: after careful analysis and by polling colleagues around the nation, I realized that we could accommodate faculty desires, work with the logistical circumstances of the host institution, and provide a conduit that might replenish depleted French enrollments. Most important, we could create a program that would encourage intercollegiate and interdisciplinary collaboration across campus locally and thereby address many issues affecting French studies today.

We chose both Aix-en-Provence and Avignon as sites. Avignon is our intensive interdisciplinary French site. The program there is specifically designed to afford students at the lower course levels a chance to study with University of Florida faculty members. Instead of the junior studying abroad, we were targeting the first- or second-year student who might come back to campus and declare a major with us. We thus instituted an intensive intermediate French course that would bring students back to our third-year classes. We also offered site-specific and interdisciplinary upper-level courses for our majors and minors. Finally, we decided to do our best not to duplicate courses—that is, to give equivalencies—on our home and abroad campuses but to make the courses abroad desirable for students and faculty members alike.

Still, this model alone (with the intermediate-level intensive course) would not make up for reduced enrollments in our upper-level courses. Thus, our goals for a second program site focused on the future growth of the campus program and on cross-campus and cross-disciplinary outreach. At Aix-en-Provence, we offered courses to students drawn from across the University of Florida campus. Students enrolled at Aix do not have a minimum language requirement, and content courses there are offered and conducted in English. A program site was selected that would provide a conduit back into the French major and minor at Florida and that would encourage interaction with faculty members and colleges across campus.

The results in the first year were as follows: we took 44 students to France in 1999, coming from 26 different majors and 8 different colleges. Consequently, the presence of the program on campus has brought French out of its corner and into the minds and conversations of members of our Florida campus. Indeed, after only one summer, the program's projected future actually became realized in the present. Not only can we move students more quickly through the tracks by having them study French during the summer but also many students who would have minored in French have declared a major as a result of having more faculty contact. On a campus with over 45,000 students, one simply cannot overestimate the effect of our strategy of developing the feel of a liberal arts college atmosphere in our section.

Finally, many students have decided to major in order to apply for scholarships available only for French majors. Some of these students, who are either minors or just a few credits shy of the major, were thus given the impetus to take extra steps to be eligible for one of our program-specific scholarships. Notwithstanding the program's brief history, this approach has proved to be statistically significant: in fall 1997, we had 57 majors. Then, just before we informally talked up the program during spring 1998, 61 majors were enrolled. Following the first year of the University of Florida in Provence, we returned from France in fall 1999 to 83 majors. Growing to 85 at the beginning of the spring 2000 term, the number did not include new majors recruited during the program application process that term. In other words, between the semester before we announced the program and the spring following its first year abroad, there was an approximate 33% increase in majors, from 57 to over 90. Even more significant, since many of these new majors are also either double or dual majors or students placing into our intermediate and upper-level courses earlier in their academic careers, we are attracting students of a higher caliber and a more diverse student body in our classes.

Although study abroad at many institutions is deeply embedded in the history of the departments and curricula, after five years the French program at the University of Florida is experiencing the effect that such a program can have, which is an increase in the quality and quantity of students and the stronger presence of the French section and French studies on campus. Admittedly, the dramatic growth in majors may be due to any one of several factors or all of them in combination: the immediate logistics of actually developing and maintaining a summer program; the distribution of fliers all over campus and in the newspaper bearing the name of the program, the section, and the department; and even the enthusiasm created by the rapid administrative support with which the program began. We not only received two faculty lines for the summer to start the program but also, in our second year, expanded with a line outside the department. That is, for three years the English department contributed alternating lines for courses in French and francophone film and cultural studies–comparative literature to be taught at the Aix-en-Provence site. This kind of appointment was our first step toward having other departments and colleges join the program, and we had a number of faculty members from other departments and colleges interested in collaborating in the future.

Since that initial phase, several international programs at the University of Florida have been reorganized. The University of Florida in Provence program is no longer solely a financially self-sufficient endeavor maintaining its cooperation with English and film and media studies. The program has expanded further by joining with faculty members from the Department of Political Science to create an additional political science track. This track has courses and enhancement activities expressly designed to include guest lecturers who address political issues relevant to any understanding of contemporary French politics. The newest addition affords students the opportunity to visit local and regional government sites to explore, hands-on, both regional politics and the place of France within the European Union and beyond.

Of course, established quickly, the program has posed enormous challenges. Complications include the budget (there are five different budgets), the organization of advising and equivalencies for what is now over twenty courses, student orientation, and visa matters. All these activities have brought new life into the section. They have also helped us continue our process of rethinking the courses that we offer at the University of Florida and abroad and what we view as the principal goals in the program for our students. Moreover, the summer program not only makes shaping the future of French studies on our particular campus appealing to faculty members but also highlights the links among enrollments; the quality of programs; and interdisciplinarity, which is increased because students take classes with a broad range of subjects while in France. Thus, our program, both in Provence and on the University of Florida campus, constitutes a space in which the significance of the French language and the importance of French and francophone history and cultural production for myriad disciplines are alive and evident to our campus population. This vitality, in turn, has motivated students to come back to campus and to register for upper-level content courses in the target language.

Turning more particularly to the development of some of the site-specific and interdisciplinary nineteenth- and twentieth-century courses in our program, I address yet another issue important to French studies, the role of curriculum development in meeting the challenges of increased interdisciplinary and cultural studies. Since the inception of the University of Florida in Provence program in the summer of 1999, faculty members have been creating courses that question the boundaries of the disciplines and seek to profit from the locations of the program. These courses, most of which are at the intermediate level, have widely expanded our third-year offerings. They have had great success, inspiring students to return to register for more intermediate and advanced courses in French in our section. The courses are a major attraction for our students and a motivation for faculty members campuswide to participate in the program.

In our Provençal literature course, La Prose d'Inspiration Provençale, through a selection of texts by Alphonse Daudet, Marcel Pagnol, Jean Giono, Henri Bosco, and Jean Carrière, students are given a progressive initiation to regional literature. Site visits to Fontvieille and Manosque allow them to understand better the literary inspirations of Provençal literature. Not surprising, our theater course uses the Avignon theater festival as its backdrop to bring to life the dramatic texts presented in the classroom. Students on the program have been able to meet with directors and actors of the festival in addition to pursuing their study of texts. My own course, Revolutions, Arts, and Literatures of the Nineteenth and Twentieth Centuries, presented a survey of the Romantic, realist, impressionist, and surrealist revolutions. It provides a historical and critical introduction to comparisons between literature and the visual arts and a study of selected writers, painters, and photographers. I paid particular attention to the paradoxical effect of photography on interartistic relations and the aesthetic production of verbal and visual creators and made every effort to take advantage of the site-specific collections in regional museums and exhibits as well as of the Arles Photography Exhibit.

At our Aix site, besides adding the political science enhancement track, we have been offering newly created film, cultural studies, and comparative literature courses. One example, Narrative Developments in French Film, examines the history of narrative form in French film, concentrating on three distinct periods: characteristics of the early sound period, the *nouvelle vague* (new-wave) filmmaking of the late 1950s and the 1960s, and recent French cinema in its recall of the features of these two earlier periods. Works of the most famous film directors, Jean Renoir, Marcel Carné, Jean Vigo, Robert Bresson, Jean-Luc Godard, Agnès Varda, François Truffaut, are among the films analyzed. Because the site of the course is Aix-en-Provence, some films selected are set in the region. Another recent addition to our interdisciplinary courses is Visual Narrative Culture in International Comics. This experimental course examines the theoretical and methodological possibilities that arise in analyzing visual culture from the perspective of internationally circulated comic books and comic strips. The emphasis of the course, taught in summer 2001, was on using methods of cultural, visual, and ideological analysis developed in relation to theorists such as Jacques Lacan, Jacques Derrida, Roland Barthes, Christian Metz, and Joan Copjec.

Although it is not an upper-division content course, my six-credit Intensive Intermediate Language, which actually meets five to seven hours a day, four days a week, is truly innovative. To maintain this quality, the course has been revamped each summer since its inception in 1999, almost tripling the contact time for students and increasing fourfold their outside activities. Focusing on the development of auditory, oral, written, and reading skills, this course takes students out of the traditional classroom environment to practice and test their language skills and cultural competence in real-life, everyday, academic, and professional situations. Exposed to a combination of contemporary French culture and French-language courses, these students prepare vocabulary and form lessons around themes that focused on French history, culture, and everyday life. For example, when studying a particular vocabulary and grammar lesson dealing with World War II, students went to see Jean-Claude Grumberg's *L'atelier* and met with the actors and directors. When studying the Algerian conflict, vocabulary dealing with immigration, and the past tenses in French, they met with the lead actor of *The Arab and the Jew*, who is a son of an Algerian family that immigrated to France in his youth. Students were also required to describe crimes they witnessed (and the culprits) to actual police officers. They met with regional journalists; were given private tours of art collections and historical monuments in the region; interviewed citizens on the streets and their French host families; and, in addition to oral, auditory, and cultural competence activities, devoted no less than two hours each day to intensive writing activities.

From the nationwide sampling poll I conducted regarding major issues affecting undergraduate French studies today, it became evident to me that the responses reflected paradigm shifts in the profession and mirrored many of the issues raised by our program: meeting the challenge of decreased enrollments in French courses, effectively emphasizing increased interdisciplinarity, exposing students to experience outside the classroom that is meaningful for their understanding of globalization, countering growing concerns about American isolationism and its effects, and demonstrating the importance of language in contexts other than teaching. Finally, how do we address an additional issue affecting French studies today, the place of francophone studies in a program located in France? It is true, certainly, that France still holds great attraction for students, which results in creating great demand for the program. However, since the University of Florida in Provence students are at once exposed to the history and culture of France, contemporary urban and rural life, and the demographics of the French population, they have the opportunity to gain a greater understanding of the significance that cultural production has played in ideological imperialism outside as well as inside the Hexagon. In fact, since lived experience in many ways disrupts the idealized vision of France and liberal French culture, students are exposed to what one of our French hosts referred to as both the "good and the not-so-good of French civilization." Thanks to a faculty with varied interests and approaches from both the hosts and our institution, students understand and accept that today French and francophone culture and heritage—inside and outside France's borders—embrace much more than the mythical visions of the France of Versailles.

These are lessons and insights that students can bring back to the home campus; share with their classmates in the different courses in our program and across the curriculum; and, best of all, communicate as informed and culturally aware citizens to friends, families, and employers in the broader social arena. From this perspective, then, the program goes well beyond meeting head-on the challenges facing French studies today. Our mission embraces the possibility of enhancing students' understanding of the world and of educating students through cultural experience informed by an active textual and pedagogical practice.

NOTE

In the spring of 2003, Gayle Zachmann proposed the creation of the University of Florida Paris Research Center, which she now directs. With a mission to facilitate international research and exchange, the center welcomes ideas for international research endeavors and international partnerships and exchanges and for the development of colloquia, workshops, independent research projects, and study-abroad programs from University of Florida departments and colleges campuswide.

French Today: The Relevance of Undergraduate French Studies, to Teachers and Their Students

Nathalie Rachlin

NAPOLEON'S CUFF LINKS

Several years ago, a senior member of the psychology department at Scripps College, the women's college where I teach, published an article in the student newspaper that provoked controversy. It questioned the necessity of having a language requirement and thus of maintaining costly foreign language departments at Scripps. The author's argument was based on two claims: first, that people are biologically incapable of learning a foreign language (therefore it is a waste of time and money to teach languages); second, that the languages taught at Scripps (French, German, Italian, and Spanish) have become irrelevant to the lives of our students. If we can safely dismiss the first as groundless, the second claim—however demagogic its intent may be—cannot be so easily rejected. That my colleague proceeded to propose we replace the currently taught European languages with Navajo does not diminish the importance of the challenge that his second claim poses to us, professors of French: Is French, as a discipline, still relevant today?

To this question, my ever provocative colleague had the following answer: learning French is as relevant and useful to our students today as the golden cuff links on Napoleon's coat. Mere remnants of a former model of higher education in which French represented high culture and a form of European elitism, French departments, his article suggested, have become obsolete in a globalized world where English has become the de facto lingua franca.

Maintained out of habit and the constraints of the tenure system rather than out of necessity, French in the curriculum has become, as my colleague's comparison implied, purely decorative, the residue of an outmoded finishing-school curriculum.

This attack on our discipline could be rejected as simply incendiary if it did not reflect a pervasive attitude toward the teaching of languages in this country today. In fact, it has never been more urgent to take seriously the question of the relevance of French in the United States undergraduate curriculum. If we fail to provide convincing answers, our profession may indeed soon share the fate of Napoleon's cuff links.

THE LOGIC OF LATE CAPITALIST EDUCATION

Over the last thirty years, the humanities have lost the privileged place in academe that was theirs from the 1920s well into the 1960s. Today, the humanities have been not only downgraded but also downsized.[1] In this context, the article published by my colleague reflects not an idiosyncratic view of the place of foreign language departments in the undergraduate curriculum but a view prevalent among administrators, university regents, and boards of trustees who have applied contemporary corporate models to the management of universities and colleges. This form of management is viewed as a way to modernize and render more efficient the delivery of education to an ever increasing number of students. According to the logic of this model, the goal of higher education in the United States today is to provide as cheaply as possible a growing student population with useful knowledge and marketable skills. Education as a service industry aims to produce not future citizens of a democratic nation but consumers in a global economy, and it caters to the perceived preprofessional needs of these consumers.[2] Just as consumers in a free-market economy make choices that determine the success and failure of businesses, students' choices in the market-model university legitimize and determine curriculum offerings. As a result, the criterion for shelf space in the university supermarket has become largely demand-driven and utilitarian. Although the demand comes first and foremost from the students and their parents, it is also increasingly driven by transnational corporations from different industries—telecommunication, biotech, pharmaceutical technologies, and others (see Press and Washburn). These industries, by funding research conducted at universities starved for public funds, are shaping not only these universities' research agenda but also, in the end, their curriculum.

The questions implied by my colleague's remarks—Why should we have French departments today? What use are they? What is their marketable value? What added value do they bring to an undergraduate education?—now seem to be pragmatic because they not only reflect the traditional utilitarian strain of American education but also fall in the logic of a new post-modern view of education:[3] what educational consumers want has value, what they do not want needs to be taken off the shelves and thrown into the trash can of academic history or, perhaps, like other refuse of consumer capitalism, sold at a discount to some Third World market.

Given this mutation in the goals and management of higher education in the United States, French departments in colleges and universities (as well as in high schools) have addressed the question of the relevance of French in one of two ways. Some decided to adapt to the new situation. They developed new rationales for the existence and value of French in the market-model university and have developed new programs to fit better the educational and preprofessional needs of their new clientele. Others chose simply to ignore or even denounce the situation, retrenching behind a traditional notion of liberal arts education in which the study of French language and culture, because of its universal claims, must and does feature prominently. I discuss these two recent developments to point to some pitfalls (instrumentalization and passéism) that we will need to avoid as we chart new territories for French studies in the twenty-first century.

SELLING FRENCH

Many in the profession have risen to the challenge posed by the market model of higher education and have attempted to answer explicitly the question, Why study French today? The American Association of Teachers of French (AATF), for example, launched a commendable campaign directed at both teachers and students to promote the study of French (see American Assn.). In this campaign, teachers and professors of French are essentially provided with sales tools—or rather sales pitches—that might help persuade their students to study French. They are told that they need to be more proactive about selling French if they want to halt the national downward trend in French enrollments. They can no longer be complacent about the value of studying

French, because that value, once requiring no demonstration, is no longer evident to their students. Such a campaign does not simply rehearse the old arguments for learning French: the beauty and sophistication of the language and the importance and the prestige of the cultures it represents. Rather, it proposes a new set of utilitarian reasons why French has a legitimate place in today's higher education curriculum. For example, Tennessee Bob's home page, one of the best sites for French resources on the Web, includes an article written by Bob Peckham, "On the Importance of Knowing French." The article lists seventy-five reasons to study French. These reasons are based predominantly on France's economic, financial, and technological power, as well as on France's preeminent role in the international arena.

This way of promoting French fits very well in the postmodern strain of today's higher education: the potential usefulness of French for career advancement or opportunity is emphasized to the detriment of the humanistic value of studying French.[4] By pointing to the marketability of French in a global economy, these campaigns show an astute awareness that the allure of money sells a discipline in today's educational marketplace. In their article entitled "The Market-Model University: Humanities in the Age of Money," James Engell and Anthony Dangerfield deduce that the basic rule for disciplines' success in today's market-model university is, "academic fields that offer one (or more) of Three Criteria thrive; any field lacking all three languishes." These three criteria are a promise of money (the discipline or field is perceived as a means to improve one's career opportunity and one's chances of securing a lucrative job), a knowledge of money ("The field itself studies money, whether practically or more theoretically, i.e., fiscal, business, financial, or economic matters and markets"), and a source of money (the field receives significant external funding from government, foundations, or corporate sponsors). French departments, following the AATF model of promotion, have repositioned themselves as belonging to a field that satisfies the first criterion. The introduction and the popularity in the French curriculum of French business courses are revealing. This repositioning of French may help make French the most widely taught foreign language in the United States, since Spanish no longer constitutes a foreign language and is de facto, although not yet de jure, the United States' second language.[5] This promotion of French may, however, have the perverse effect of instrumentalizing our discipline. The proliferation of language-across-the-curriculum (LAC) courses underscores this instrumentalization. These courses at the Claremont colleges are taught by two instructors. There is usually a main instructor, who is in a discipline other than French (political science, for example), and a professor of French (or any foreign language faculty member), who takes the French-speaking students enrolled in the class for an extra hour of conversation each week. During that hour, the students read and discuss, in French, documents and primary sources or texts germane to the class topic. The main instructor provides the more substantive part of the course, while the expertise of the language faculty member is seen as ancillary, that is, merely linguistic.

The risk of instrumentalization does not reside solely in French business or LAC courses. Even the cultural competency that we hope to give our students through the teaching of French literature, history, and culture in our more traditional French curriculum can be instrumentalized, especially when it is viewed by our administrators or students as a means of fostering better understanding between trading or business partners or between customers. But this repositioning of French in the curriculum validates, at least in part, my colleague's statements that French literature and culture no longer have any value in and of themselves. Conforming to the logic of the market-model university, this repositioning may also confirm that logic without contesting it. In fact, French as a discipline may lose the critical edge it has often had in the United States curriculum. Some may argue that this is the price we have to pay for the survival of our discipline, but I disagree. I think that there is a way to sell French without selling out.

CULTIVATING HUMANITY IN THE ACADEMIC-INDUSTRIAL COMPLEX

For those who reject the current commodification of education, for those who refuse to abandon the noble but perhaps outmoded ideals of a liberal education designed to produce an informed citizenry, the temptation is great simply to retrench behind these principles and dig in one's heels. However, at a time when state sovereignty is being eroded by supranational entities, such as the United Nations, the World Trade Organization (WTO), the International Monetary Fund, the World Bank, and the European Union and by a network of global corporations freed from state regulations, the goal of producing responsible citizens of a democratic state through a well-rounded liberal education that includes the knowledge of foreign language and culture seems to belong to a long-gone era. When vital decisions that affect the citizens of a country are made elsewhere and sometimes behind closed doors (as was true of the WTO meetings), an educated citizenry may no longer be as essential to the good functioning of the state or society, and it may therefore no longer need to be one of the goals of higher education.

Of course, a liberal education does more than educate citizens. It also helps students develop into well-rounded human beings capable of participating actively in their communities and of enjoying life to the fullest. This concept of the goals of education, drawing on the Socratic ideal of the examined life, purports to produce people who can decide for themselves what the good life is and who, as Seneca prescribed, have learned to cultivate their humanity (see Nussbaum). But despite their ritual evocation at commencements and convocations, these lofty goals have largely been jettisoned, since they rarely influence either curriculum reforms or allocation of resources in the university. Thus such an appeal to the values of the old liberal arts tradition to justify the teaching of a discipline like French has today little purchasing power in our postmodern university. Although I share the sentiments expressed by Eyal Press and Jennifer Washburn in defending the values of a liberal education,[6] I am afraid that a recourse to traditional justifications of the importance of French as a humanistic discipline is woefully insufficient to shore up the viability of French departments in the market-model university. I also think a fortiori that in the light of the current decline in French enrollments, it is a mistake to retreat, as some of our colleagues still seem to do, behind the antiquated notion of the civilizing mission of French culture. An appeal to an abstract and seemingly changeless notion of what a liberal education ought to be will not convince the administrators who run our schools of the relevance of French.

A reassessment of the goals of a liberal arts education is nothing new, of course, since the meaning of liberal education has always been contested and retooled to fit circumstances, the aspirations and values that obtain in a certain social formation at a certain historical moment. In United States universities during the 1920s, for example, the study of French literature (as belles lettres) and culture (especially the fine arts) provided upper social classes with what Pierre Bourdieu calls cultural capital and was seen as essential to the formation of a cultivated American elite (see Kritzman). Today, the United States enjoys an uncontested economic, political, technological, and cultural supremacy while French culture's *rayonnement* ("prestige") in the world has lost much of its luster. In between these two moments in the history of French in United States academe, French professors and scholars have had to expand the parameters of their fields. They have invented new objects of study relevant to the lives of their students, for which they have articulated new rationales. The latest expansion occurred in the last generation and allowed the humanities, including French, to reassess what a liberal arts education should do to remain vibrant and relevant to our students' lives.

Reflecting on the latest mutation, the classicist and philosopher Martha Nussbaum, in her book *Cultivating Humanity*, argues that the introduction of the study of non-Western cultures into the liberal arts curriculum, as well as a concern for gender, class, and race issues in it, does not constitute a radical politicization or a watering down of higher education, as conservative critics of academe have argued, but has had an invigorating effect and is essential for producing what she calls "citizens of the world." Nussbaum's strategy is to shift the goals of a liberal education from that of producing citizens of a state to that of producing "world citizens" (9), a move allowing Nussbaum to justify as vitally important the introduction of issues of multiculturalism, transnationalism, and cross-cultural understanding into the curriculum. Of course, in the absence of a political entity that might be called *the world*, her notion of what a world citizen might be can only remain vague and abstract; this vagueness is one of the problems of her approach. But Nussbaum rightly argues for the relevance of the principles and ideals of a liberal education reshaped to address the needs of a student population that is more culturally diverse than ever (438).

In the field of French studies, we have seen, not without trepidation, the introduction of the subfields of French cultural studies and francophone studies (see Petrey, "French Studies"). As in other fields in the humanities, areas of research that had hitherto been on the periphery of our discipline have taken center stage. In the last ten years, the relatively great number of tenure-track jobs in an otherwise depressed job market that call for scholars in francophone studies and to a lesser extent cultural studies suggests this strategy of adaptation has worked well for us, at least in terms of resource allocations—the main criterion, alas, today. More important, this expansion has allowed the discipline of French to redefine itself by charting new territories for new investigations.[7]

FRENCH STUDIES GOES GLOBAL

The cultural turn that opened the door to issues of race, gender, national and transnational identities, and previously subaltern fields in the United States curriculum (including French studies) took place in the 1980s and 1990s, when the world economy was just beginning to become globalized. What can we say of the future of the humanities, and more particularly of French studies, at the beginning of the twenty-first century? Which way should French studies go? It should go global.

Of course, global studies can exist neither as a discipline nor as a subfield in a discipline because its object of study, globalization, is far too recent and far too complex a phenomenon. I see it as a program of research that aims at a better understanding of the tremendous changes that have occurred in the last fifteen years. Global studies is interdisciplinary in nature and should draw from an array of disciplinary expertise: economics, of course, needs to play a large part, but so do politics, law, sociology, anthropology, demographics, environmental studies, cultural studies, religious studies, history, media studies, and modern languages. Today many researchers in different disciplines are engaged in understanding the phenomenon of recent intensification in global interconnectedness and interdependence. As Anthony McGrew suggests, globalization is the product of a number of factors that have recently coalesced to form a single system. According to McGrew these factors are

> the dynamics of the global financial system; the tremendous expansion of transnational corporate activity; the existence of global communications and media networks; the global production and dissemination of knowledge; the escalating significance of transnational religious and ethnic ties; and finally the emerging authority of institutions and communities above the nation-state (such as the European Union, the World Trade Organization, or the World Bank). (468)

The first two factors are clearly the purview of economics, but the human sciences can and should bring their expertise to bear on the study of the last four factors.

French studies in the United States ought to have a privileged role to play in global studies for two main reasons. First, France is one of the first industrialized countries to have voiced its opposition to certain aspects of globalization. In the early phases of the process during the General Agreement on

Tariffs and Trade negotiations, the French representatives, mobilized into action by a group of concerned French moviemakers led by Bertrand Tavernier, claimed that cultural productions and, more particularly, audiovisual productions (such as films, television, and radio programs) should not be treated as commodities.[8] For the French, the *exception culturelle* ("cultural exception") was not simply a way to preserve global cultural diversity and to defend French culture from the threat of United States cultural imperialism—epitomized in the French social imaginary by Disney and Hollywood. The *exception culturelle* was also an ideological opposition to the increasing commodification of all aspects of life, down to life's most sacred recesses, such as surrogate motherhood or, more recently, the human genome. There are, the French government's position implied, things that should not be commercialized; there must be, their efforts also suggested, limits to the reach of the market and to *la marchandisation du monde* ("global commodification").

This position raises the following questions: Should there be limits to the reach of the market? Is *free market* synonymous with *democracy*? What does democracy mean in a world regulated by supranational entities? How does one do politics in a global world? The debate on globalization is taking place at all levels of French society: government, trade unions or associations, the media, intellectuals. Since the questions globalization raises are rarely debated in the United States, would not teaching the French debate over globalization be the most useful thing that French studies can do today? Teaching the debate does not mean necessarily taking sides, but it can allow students to contemplate perspectives on what is happening in the world that may be different from what they hear at home. It is a paradox of our times that, however interconnected the world may be through technology (the Internet, satellite TV, cable, etc.), it is unlikely that our students will be aware of the French debate if we do not call their attention to it.

The second reason that French studies in the United States ought to play a privileged role has to do with what I call the American paradox. At a time when United States–led globalization means that more and more parts of the world are coming into contact with one another through trade, the reach of the media, and information technology, the United States paradoxically seems to be living in a period of relative cultural isolationism, quite possibly only to be increased as a result of the tragic events of September 11, 2001. Examples of this isolationism include the concentration of the media in the United States, which is owned by large corporations (GE, Westinghouse, etc.) that are at the forefront of the globalization process. It is not in these corporations' interest to open a debate on globalization, especially a debate that affects the bottom line. As a result, there seems to be a dissymmetry between United States and non–United States consumers of news. The extraordinary reach of United States–owned media companies means that information flows in mostly one way, from the United States to the outside world, with little competing information and thus few alternative perspectives available to viewers of United States news. Another example concerns cultural productions: notably, 98% of the videos watched by United States citizens are United States–made, whereas 96% of the films Canadians watch are foreign. The same dissymmetry is true for television programs and for publishing. In 1998, 1,636 translation rights were requested in France. In the same year, the number of translated books published in the United States was between 200 and 250 (see Schiller). The American public is obviously the loser in all this, since it is largely kept from new and exciting foreign creations and ideas, and in this position of ignorance it is too easy for people to believe that nothing noteworthy is created elsewhere.

My last example is the waning interest Americans have for foreign languages and cultures. Engell and Dangerfield show that since 1970,

> teaching and mastery of languages other than English have declined. The educationally intensive skill that might have a positive impact for students who will work in a global economy—namely, ability in a foreign language—has been neglected. Across the country, college entrance and education requirements in languages have been eased, even dropped. In 1960, for every 100 students in college, 16 enrolled in foreign languages. In 1970 it was 12, and by 1995, with a global economy in full swing, fewer than 8.

This waning of interest is not news to professors of French. It is in fact the very reason we are today addressing the question of the future of French studies and seeking new ways to stimulate teaching French language and literature. The paradox is that as the United States leads the way toward ever greater global integration, it remains linguistically and culturally isolationist. Under the circumstances, we may want to view the role of French studies in United States education today as a means to open up the United States intellectual market to a world of ideas. If we still believe that one of the main purposes of education is what Nussbaum describes, drawing on the etymology of the word *liberal*, as the need "to liberate the mind from the bondage of habit and custom" (8), then surely our purpose must be clear. We will have served our students and our country well if we, professors of French, can open a space in the United States curriculum where our students can attempt to understand and discuss the phenomenon engulfing the entire world. What I propose here is nothing short of turning into a new object of study the very phenomenon responsible for the crisis in which our discipline finds itself. Let's go global. What else is there?

NOTES

1. On the downsizing of United States higher education, see Engell and Dangerfield, who present the conclusion of their two-year-long study of the state of the humanities in the last thirty-five years in United States higher education: "Since the late 1960s the humanities have been neglected, downgraded, and forced to retrench, all as other areas of higher education have grown in numbers, wealth, and influence."
2. In attempting to compete with other colleges and universities for consumers, the wealthiest liberal arts schools are now also catering to more mundane needs by offering their students better recreation and exercise facilities, accommodations, dining facilities, and catering.
3. I use the word *postmodern* in Jameson's sense of the word, that is, to indicate that the conception of education put forth fits in the "the cultural logic of late capitalism."
4. France is portrayed as an economic powerhouse that, although it cannot rival the United States in economic, military, political, or cultural power, remains one of the major players on the global scene. We learn from Bob Peckham, for example, that France "ranks fourth in terms of world power" (whatever "world power" may measure here: the size of its economy? its international clout? its military force?). The importance of the French language in global trade and international organizations is also stressed, and Peckham provides numbers and ratios as evidence of that importance. Even the value of French literature is quantified. Reason number 5 is that "France has the world's greatest number of Nobel Prize winners in literature": twelve. Given the context in which this fact is used, however, reason 5 points less to the quality of French literature—let alone the importance of reading French writers—than to the size of France's cultural capital and thus to the prestige, power, and influence that France still enjoys on the world cultural scene. Power, then, is what reason 5 is about, not literature or, least of all, the power of literature.
5. According to government statistics, Hispanics are now the largest minority group in the United States (see Miller). In southern California, where I live, the creation of Spanish TV channels, radio stations, and newspapers is so frequent that it no longer makes the news. Nationally, Latin pop music, once heard only on Spanish radio stations, has now become mainstream.
6. Press and Washburn ask, "Do we care any more whether colleges and universities are custodians of collective, diverse cultures—whether they record, teach, and transmit traditions, and give us the linguistic and symbolic tools to express our veneration, criticism, and contribution to our culture, to make connections within its variety, to examine its checkered past to imagine the possible future? If our institutions of higher education don't do this, who will?".
7. See, for example, Jill Forbes ("Conclusion") and Kelly.
8. For a useful and succinct history of globalization, see Riché.

Globalization, the New Regionalism, and Foreign Language Studies

Melanie Hawthorne

At the beginning of the twenty-first century, the status of language and literature study in institutions of higher education in the United States is in crisis. This crisis is manifested in persistent concern about enrollments in language study; in the cutting of both graduate and undergraduate programs and entire departments, dramatically illustrated at Drake University (Schneider); and in the widespread sense that scholars in language and literature no longer have anything insightful to say about higher education, which has the effect of delegitimizing them in the eyes of their peers. While lip service about the importance of foreign language study remains strong, in practice this commitment does little to further the field. A recent study published in the *Chronicle of Higher Education* ("Prime Numbers") reports that 57% of students in the United States express an intent to pursue foreign languages in college, but only 8% actually do so. Thus, although there is a rhetoric of verbal support for the importance of foreign language study, when pressed to make difficult choices about what they can fit into the average undergraduate degree program, students seem to find languages dispensable. Their commitment to foreign language study is all talk, no action.

To many of us involved in the field of languages and literatures, this dramatic fall in the professional prestige has come as a surprise. We have heard institutions of higher education announce the need for something described variously as the internationalization or globalization of the curriculum. These are the new buzzwords of higher education, and we have assumed, rather naively it turns out, that our field was central to the concerns they describe. We thus sat back and waited for our colleagues to come knocking on our door, so we could advise them in their internationalization or globalization plans. Then we learned that language study (and the study of related cultures and literatures) was marginal at best—and sometimes, when viewed as a set of skills acquisitions that could be outsourced to Berlitz, dispensable—to the enterprise of internationalization. What seemed to be a window of opportunity has instead shut us out.

To illustrate this point, let me provide an example from Texas, where the verbal commitment to the principle of internationalization in public education is unquestioned, even by the state legislature. This example inevitably oversimplifies a complex situation but illustrates the place of language study when defining essential elements of education. The state recently defined the core curriculum for all its institutions of higher education. In the process, it in effect dropped the language requirement from the core curriculum and mandated that a university could not implement a requirement unless each department voted to require it—unless, that is, the department of chemistry, the department of electrical engineering, and so on all agreed that a language requirement was an essential component of an undergraduate major in their field. Thus, while a language requirement remains a theoretical possibility, it is not important enough to be mandated, despite the rhetoric of globalization. At the same time as the state effectively dropped the language requirement, it chose to retain a kinesiology (physical education) requirement for the undergraduate curriculum. Arguably, in Texas it is more important to know how to two-step than to know how to speak Spanish. More action, less talking.

I cite Texas as the example I am most familiar with, but my guess is that Texas is no exception, that colleagues will recognize the same prioritization at work in their own state or institution. Thus, in this article I explore the ideological underpinnings of the apparent contradiction that internationalization and globalization do not involve the study of other languages and cultures.

Many professionals are puzzled as to how exactly "foreign" languages came to be consistently marginalized, and some have offered answers. Bill Readings, for example, argues in *The University in Ruins* that there has been a paradigm shift in the way we understand the role of universities in society, as well as in the way we understand the role of the subjects taught at universities. The decline in what he calls "the national cultural mission" (3) has brought about a crisis for the humanities in general. In the old paradigm, students studied and majored in "American literature" or "French literature," and literature was important in the university curriculum because it suggested (and reproduced) a "unified national culture." In this model, "the study of a tradition of national literature comes to be the primary mode of teaching students what it is to be French, or English, or German" (16). Thus, we knew who we were because we belonged to a people that produced *Moby-Dick*. The activity of reading things produced by our tribe taught us what it meant to belong to that tribe. The justification for studying foreign languages and cultures was that learning about an other was a way of learning about yourself.

The study of other cultures and languages has also had an underlying nationalist rationale of control: it helped produce social and political subjects who internalized an understanding of the world in terms of nations that described the collective characteristics of other disciplined individuals (see also Chambers, "Teaching").

Writing in the 1990s, Readings maintains that "the link between the University and the nation-state no longer holds in an era of globalization" (14). The transnational trends in the global economy at the end of the twentieth century indeed challenged the ideology of national culture and had a dramatic effect on the place of the humanities in universities in the United States. A second important factor affecting the meaning of globalization—and thus the place of language study in the university curriculum—was the end of the cold war. This influence is obvious in specific shifts in fields such as Russian and German, languages whose strategic importance has declined. With perestroika and the fall of the Berlin wall, diplomatic and intelligence resources allocated to Germany and the former Soviet Union could be cut back and redirected, leading to a decline in the popularity of these languages at the college level. But the end of the cold war not only reduced well-defined national security interests that drive the need (or lack of it) for certain language skills, it also had less obvious but more far-reaching implications for the humanities in general. During the cold war, the conspicuous public funding of the humanities was ideologically important to the image the West in general and the United States in particular wanted to project. The Communist and left-wing critique of the United States was that it cared only about money, not people. To defend against this criticism, it was necessary to show that capitalism produces more than Philistines. In addition, it was important that liberal democracy be seen to allow—and even encourage, through funding—

viewpoints with which it disagreed, so it could underscore its superiority over repressive totalitarian systems. After World War II, the United States wanted to embrace whatever totalitarians "loved to hate" (Saunders 119), from the so-called decadent (i.e., modern) art scorned by Nazis to movements such as abstract expressionism that challenged the aesthetics of Soviet socialist realism. If the public, or even Congress, found avant-garde art difficult to appreciate, that was all the more reason to support cultural programs that would explain it. Abstract expressionism per se was not the issue; the goal was to show that inherently American art could survive and thrive in a capitalist state. No matter how bizarre the project seemed, the United States government could embrace it because, in the words of Laurie Anderson in her experimental performance *United States*, "these oddities were produced by a people free enough to think of making them in the first place" ("Odd Objects").

Maintaining this image of freedom was so ideologically important that not only were the humanities supported directly and overtly by government agencies but also individuals and groups that would encourage left-leaning intellectuals to reject communism were supported indirectly and covertly by the Central Intelligence Agency, which silently provided monies that could be laundered through existing funding agencies. Such is the contention of Frances Stonor Saunders, who claims in *The Cultural Cold War* that agencies such as the Farfield Foundation were given this grant money to dispense and that publications such as *Encounter* would never have been financially viable without it. A number of humanities and arts organizations received such covert funding (357): "Whether they liked it or not, whether they knew it or not, there were few writers, poets, artists, historians, scientists or critics in postwar Europe whose names were not in some way linked to this covert enterprise," states Saunders (2). My point here is not to judge this program of covert support but to ask what it might mean for the humanities in general and foreign languages in particular that such support is no longer deemed necessary today.

This essay was originally written before the events of 11 September 2001. While those events reoriented certain aspects of the trends described above, their general effect was to intensify the changes already taking place. It is true that Arabic languages have now replaced Russian and German as strategic languages of interest and therefore can perhaps attract greater funding and enrollments. It is also true that there has been a resurgence of patriotic feeling that may slow transnationalism's challenge to the way higher education affirms national identity (the role of the university as described by Readings). But these reactions do nothing to change the fundamental attitude that humanities are dispensable that has prevailed since the end of the cold war. At the beginning of the twenty-first century, "interest" is no longer about curiosity but about suspicion, which is evident in the new euphemism "persons of interest" used by policing agencies when they refer to suspects. Our desire to know about other nations is fueled not by curiosity about who they are in the world but by fear about whether they might be able to hurt us. Our interest in other nations is not the gee-whiz curiosity of *National Geographic* but the suspicious curiosity of national security. Things not easily understood (whether abstract expressionism or people saying things in languages we do not understand) are no longer to be tolerated because they represent (or are interpreted to represent) unfettered Western individualism; instead, there is safety in "transparency" (the new political buzzword). Valuing transparency implies that the opaque—the difficult or whatever cannot be immediately apprehended—must somehow be dangerous. In this climate, reading is an inherently suspicious activity, and curiosity itself is something to discourage. A government warning issued in December 2003 alerted the public to be on the lookout for people reading almanacs ("F.B.I."). There has been no specific warning about people speaking foreign languages, but perhaps there is no need to state the obvious in today's climate, when activities that demonstrate intellectual curiosity can make one not an interesting person but a person of interest.

These, then, are some of the factors that have shaped present attitudes toward foreign languages and their role in globalization. Readings's book *The University in Ruins* was published posthumously in 1996, so he cannot modify or revise his argument in the light of subsequent world events, but some of his observations and predictions continue to have relevance. Despite the resurgence in national identity that supports cultural endeavors so long as they are utilitarian and patriotic, the commitment to national culture (and its corollary foreign culture) has been superseded by a rhetoric of globalization and a domestic agenda of meaningless (according to Readings) "excellence." Educational priorities can now be set not in terms of national cultural needs but in terms of economic needs that transcend national boundaries. Higher education is increasingly viewed not as a process that equips graduates for life but as one that equips them for jobs. Therefore, what is desirable in colleges and universities is whatever employers find desirable in employees. Market concerns thus drive public educational policy. What was previously considered job training has now been outsourced by multinational corporations: it is financed by taxpayers, along with the future employees themselves, and called education.

The role of globalization as it is discussed in higher education today must be understood in this economic context, for clearly it means something different from knowledge of other languages and cultures. We can understand better how globalization is used in political and educational rhetoric from the ways it is refracted through manifestations of popular culture, such as the TV cartoon *The Simpsons*. In the show's 1999 Super Bowl special, Dolly Parton makes a guest appearance. One of the characters, a travel agent, knows her because he has worked both at Dollywood in Tennessee and at Euro-Dollywood, "which is in Alabama," he tells us. Globalization changes the understanding of national boundaries; it means that you don't have to leave the United States to have the experience of Europe. Through commodification, the other can be domesticated and reproduced in a familiar and non-threatening form: you can bring Europe home to Alabama—where you won't need a passport, you can pay in dollars, and everyone speaks English. Euro-Dollywood would be a good joke were it not for the existence of Las Vegas, which offers precisely such an experience of world travel (as well as time travel).

The flip side of this domestication of the foreign is the export of United States tastes and language. In his memoir about living in France, Adam Gopnik writes, "When people talk about globalization, what they're really saying is that an English-speaking imperium now stretches from Adelaide to Vancouver, and that anyone who is at home in one bit of it is likely to feel at home in the other bits" (98). This sense of imperium has intensified further with the beginning of the second Iraq War, in 2003, and public discussion of American "empire." If in higher education we are training students to function in such a global environment and if this imperium requires only that one speak English to feel at home anywhere, the redundancy of teaching about other languages and cultures becomes apparent. Why learn to speak French (or German or Italian) when it will in fact make you feel uncomfortable (alien, other, and not "at home") wherever you go?

Many people assume that such globalization is a benign force, because one day English will unite the world. They are mistaken; we are facing an era of what I call new regionalism. For globalization can also divide in insidious new ways—not along national lines, as in the old paradigm, but along arbitrary transnational lines defined by multinational economic interests. Instead of being inhabitants of countries, now we are all inhabitants of "regions." The optimists offer technology, specifically the Internet, as proof of unifying trends. However, evidence from that same source, the world of technology, also illustrates just the opposite—a troubling countertrend that furthers regionalism while appearing to be a form of globalization. I came to understand my region and my position in it by trying to incorporate DVD technology into the foreign language classroom. That French media recordings are not always playable with United States technology is a lesson I had already learned from videocassettes—PAL (Phase Alternating Line) format cassettes cannot be played on NTSC (National Television System Committee) players—but I always assumed that the incompatibility was the unintentional by-product of healthy economic competition. I imagined that the different formats came to dominate different geographic areas like variant species that survive the struggle for life in different ecosystems. But unlike its saurian antecedent video technology, which perhaps simply evolved that way, the sleek new DVD technology is quite intentionally and globally antiglobal by design. Buy a DVD in France, and you may not be able to view it in the United States. The incompatibility is not the result of economic evolution or contingency; it is intentional. I learned about my regional status from joining a DVD mail-order "club." A flier in one of the club mailings explains how the regions work: "Most DVDs are 'regionally coded' to play in machines purchased in specific parts of the world. For example, Region 1 DVDs are meant to be sold and played in what is known as Region 1: the U.S., U.S. territories, and Canada" ("ABCs of DVD"). Regions are thus not limited to countries (region 1 is both the United States and Canada), and they are also not merely geographic groupings (the United States and Canada are both part of the North American continent, but the United States territories include Asian locations such as Guam). Regions represent markets.

Different parts of the technology industry, however, have different stakes in the new regionalism. Thus, the global marketing of DVD technology pits the makers of DVD players against the makers of DVD recordings. To the makers of DVD players, having to include in their machines the region-specific decryption technology demanded by makers of DVD recordings adds to the cost of production and impedes distribution in a global market, thereby inhibiting competitive pricing and global competition. Making one product to sell in the United States market and another to sell in France is more costly than making a single player that can be sold in both countries. Makers of DVD players therefore streamline production and make all players the same way regardless of regional destination, simply adding the region-specific features as the final step in the manufacturing process (Fox). This basic similarity of all machines makes the players relatively easy to hack or reset so that they can play DVDs from different regions (as they were originally manufactured to do). Those who lack hacking ability have also created a market for code-free or multiregion DVD players, which can be purchased—apparently quite legally—in the United States, although only online for some reason (Webster 9). This curious state of affairs once again highlights the conflicting commercial interests of those who manufacture DVD players and those who manufacture the DVD recordings.

The onus for enforcing the regional coding has thus fallen on the producers of DVD recordings, the ones who wanted the regional distinctions in the first place. This industry has responded to hacking by adding what it calls enforced regional coding. The DVD club newsletter informs me that "as fans found a way to alter or disable the regional coding settings on their players, Region 1 discs began crossing borders before the movie opened overseas" and "Hollywood studios responded by implementing Enforced Regional Coding, a new technology that makes sure Region 1 DVDs only work in Region 1 players." The added restrictions are thus clearly attributed to "Hollywood studios," no doubt to deflect consumer frustration from those who sell the DVDs. Don't blame us, they seem to be saying, if you buy something that won't work; enforced regional coding wasn't our idea (even though in many cases Hollywood studios and mail-order DVD clubs are owned by the same conglomerates). The consumer is evidently supposed to know instinctively what is unfair about people in other countries being able to buy a personal copy of a movie that has not yet opened in their country, since no attempt is made to explain this part of the justification for enforced regional coding. But what passes in the flier as merely an explanation—albeit a poor one—turns out in fact to be a warning because, as a result of the Hollywood studios' tightened security, "some older region 1 DVD players may have difficulty playing discs with Enforced Regional Coding": caveat emptor ("ABCs of DVD").

Notice that profits are not being protected here against piracy, although theft of intellectual property is often the reason invoked when the industry defends these policies, as a recent article in the *Chronicle of Higher Education* illustrates (Foster). In the problem scenario (discs being played in countries where the movie has not yet opened), it is not a question of consumers illegally copying DVDs; they are perfectly willing to pay the asking price to purchase their own copy but have the misfortune of living in a region (i.e., market) where the film has not "opened." In this context, acting globally (using the Internet to purchase an imported copy of the DVD) is construed as a form of cheating.

It is instructive to compare DVD technology to print technology, to see how the new regionalism works. The existence of foreign languages works like a kind of enforced regional coding on books. If, for example, you live in France and speak only French and you want to read the latest Harry Potter book, you must wait until the translation (your regionally coded version) is published before you can read it. But you have the power to hack the system, as it were, if you learn to speak English. Then you can order a copy of the English version from an online company such as Amazon.com or have a friend in an anglophone country mail you a copy as soon as the book is published in English. (It was precisely for such reasons that the release of the fourth volume of the Harry Potter series was coordinated to occur at the same time in all anglophone countries throughout the world.) In the world of DVD, however, it would be a crime to learn a foreign language and a crime to teach it: section 1201 of the Digital Millennium Copyright Act "makes it a crime to bypass an encryption device that limits access to copyrighted material, *or to distribute decryption technology*" (Foster A45; emphasis added). Here my analogy breaks down, though, because simply learning a foreign language is not enough to circumvent the regional coding on DVDs. Thanks to the Internet, I can purchase a copy of *Le goût des autres* (to cite an example of a film that at the time of writing this essay was available on DVD in France but not yet in the United States) from the *Amazon.fr* Web site. The DVD is in a language I can understand (French), and I can pay in euros, thanks to my credit card, and have the DVD delivered to my door in the United States by international mail services. Here is the borderless unified world of the global optimists: the world is shrinking, borders of countries becoming irrelevant. But thanks to "Hollywood studios," I cannot view my new DVD (however legitimately purchased and paid for) on the DVD player I purchased in the United States. The world grows smaller every day, and it grows bigger. At the very moment that we are most cosmopolitan, using the latest DVD technology and taking advantage of the Internet to bring the experience of another country into the classroom, we are the most constrained by our regionalism.

This rethinking of globalization takes place both in the context of debates about the changing mission of the university (as proposed by Readings) and of debates about the proper field of inquiry in a specific discipline (the literature versus cultural-studies debate in French). The changing demands tacitly placed on universities make it harder to justify teaching subjects such as French, the value of which drops once its cultural capital is no longer perceived as contributing to the national project that used to shape educational policy. It is true that the internationalization of business creates demand for foreign languages, but this demand is strictly limited by practical concerns: the businessperson needs to know only enough foreign language to sell the product (the language is merely a means to an end, not a subject with intrinsic value) and if—better yet—the selling can be done in English, then no foreign language skills are necessary at all.

What would it mean for foreign language study to have intrinsic value once again? In the recent past, the discipline of "French" (whatever that is) was riven by a debate about whether we should be teaching a thing called "literature" or a thing called "culture" (see "French Studies" in *French Review* and "Literature" in *Diacritics* by Petrey, as well as the special issue of *Diacritics, Doing French Studies*). Moreover, thanks to the class politics of academia, many professionals teach neither literature nor culture but spend their time teaching a third thing called language, although there is even less consensus about what this actually is (see, e.g., Chambers, "Teaching" 52). Whether the focus of our teaching is literature, culture, or language, we thought we were already being global; clearly, however, we must rethink the definition of *global* when institutions simultaneously call for more globalization and less foreign language.

How does French (the culture, the literature, the language) migrate (in just the same way that people made stateless by the political redrawing of borders are forced to cross boundaries) into other programs? Originally prepared for a somewhat informal conference panel, where speakers circulated syllabi and the emphasis was on what we do in the classroom, this essay started out with a very practical agenda to discuss courses I have taught at my home institution of Texas A&M. These courses stressed using the rubric of comparative literature to teach French at the graduate level at an institution that has no graduate program in French and using interdisciplinarity at the undergraduate level to teach French content to nonmajors and those without French-language skills. Reflecting on these specific experiences, I formulate the following generalizations.

The first observation is that institutions usually not thought of as being on the cutting edge of the humanities may for once be in the vanguard of change, however unintentionally. Texas A&M, for example, is a large public research university (with an annual enrollment of more than 46,000, mostly undergraduates), a so-called flagship institution in a conservative state. A&M has always had more a technical than a humanities focus, so in some ways it was never much interested in the national cultural mission offered by the humanities in Readings's paradigm. Neither farmers nor soldiers nor engineers—traditionally the main products of the university—have ever had more than a passing need for ideas that do not have practical applications. The College of Liberal Arts is a relative newcomer: it has existed for only 25 of the university's 125 years. The university recently announced its plans to be "recognized as one of the ten best public universities in the nation by the year 2020" (in a report referred to as "Vision 2020"; see Texas A&M), but at the moment this vision remains a long way off, and some skeptics doubt that it will ever be reached.

Therefore, A&M today presents one version of what other institutions might look like after the humanities have been delegitimized. Readings warns that interdisciplinary programs are likely to reduce the need for individual programs: "At present [1996] interdisciplinary programs tend to supplement existing disciplines; the time is not far off when they will be installed in order to replace clusters of disciplines" (39). At A&M, then, the institutional acceptance of interdisciplinary courses makes developing individual disciplines unnecessary. Why have a formal graduate program in a specific discipline called French if the more general French studies can be incorporated into already existing graduate-level courses and programs, such as comparative literature, or into other new programs with broad aims, such as a graduate degree in teaching foreign languages aimed at producing high school teachers? When the predicted collapse of the national-identity project is complete and succeeds in delegitimizing the humanities, a process that already seems to be under way, other universities will face program cuts. At A&M, such cuts will not be necessary because certain programs (e.g., graduate programs in French) were not implemented in the first place.

We can, therefore, look at institutions such as Texas A&M to see what the future looks like today. These colleges and universities have bypassed the need for individual graduate programs and gone straight to the kind of generalized program—homogenized humanities—that everyone will end up with after more specialized programs wither away and are cut back. In economic terms, I am suggesting that the various language fields are on the verge of being deskilled in the same way that the job of secretary and bank teller went from being highly skilled (and male dominated) professions to low-paid, low-status jobs (held predominantly by women).

The second observation concerns the response to dwindling enrollments. It is often suggested that we have to "sell" or "market" our subjects to attract students. Courses are generally deemed to have popular appeal if they focus on the new rather than the old; if they involve visual media, not just the written; if they address contemporary issues such as gender and race or postcolonial perspectives; if they include consideration of popular as well as high culture; and if they address themes rather than traditional literary categories. But if we are serious about offering what the customer wants, we may have to abandon a commitment to teaching certain kinds of content. The trends at A&M suggest that literature, even when injected with contemporary content such as gender studies, does not attract as many buyers as the more general "civilization" courses. The gender and literature course introduced into the French undergraduate curriculum at A&M in the 1990s failed regularly to attract the minimum number of enrollments to "make," and consequently the course itself was dropped from the catalog. An attempt was made to revive it as a women-writers course. As I listened to Mary Jean Green describe the need to sell our courses in a paper delivered at the Sixteenth Annual International Colloquium on Twentieth-Century French Studies in the spring of 1999, I planned revisions of the course syllabus (literally on the back of the conference program) to focus on postrevolutionary women writers (the newer) to include visual (film) tie-ins, and so on. Even with these revisions and an advertising flier, the course failed to garner the minimum ten students required. Instead, the course had four students, who took it because they needed the three credit hours to graduate, not because of the topic—indeed, graduation requirements were the only reason the course was not canceled altogether because of low enrollment. It could have been about medieval French dialectology and the outcome—four students taking the course to graduate—would have been the same.

This is only one example, but it suggests to me that selling ourselves by trying to make French relevant (one of the arguments for cultural studies) may not be enough to save us. Not only is relevance locally defined but, as with all market-driven strategies, you may end up having to make unacceptable compromises to make a sale. The kind of topic that would attract students at A&M might be something like how to read the Bible in French (since our New Testament Greek course is a perennial favorite) or French for missionaries. (Of the four students who signed up for the women-writers course, one wanted to become a missionary. Of the eleven students I accompanied to France on a summer study-abroad program, two wanted to become missionaries. These are not statistically meaningful numbers, but they do suggest a pattern.) Such a course might fit all too well with the rhetoric of globalization and attract high enrollments to boot, but that does not mean it belongs in the curriculum of a French program at a public university (although it may have its place in a more specialized context). While experts may disagree about what belongs in the curriculum, it remains a matter for professionals to decide, not a popularity contest. Not sure that French as a discipline *can* be saved (at least in the forms we traditionally think of) and not wanting to let student interest dictate the content of French courses, I believe we must continue to explore ways of bringing French content into other, interdisciplinary areas at both the undergraduate and graduate levels.

There will always be a place for an ever-evolving specialist discipline called French, just as there are still academic programs at some universities in Sanskrit, classical studies, and nautical archaeology, but we need to rethink the role of French specifically and foreign languages generally in education. Donna Haraway once advanced the idea that teaching creationism might be viewed as a form of child abuse (*Simians, Cyborgs, and Women* 152). Perhaps denying children the chance to learn other languages when they are still young enough to learn them with the thoroughness of the native speaker, then forcing them to study other languages at an age when it is difficult to learn them easily (not to mention infantilizing)—as current educational practices do—should also qualify as abuse. In her preface to *What Is Found There*, Adrienne Rich describes the general inability to imagine other ways of thinking about the future that accompanied the "unraveling" of the cold war. "It seemed that a historic imaginative opportunity was passing through and that, in the stagnation and dissolution of public life, it might be grasped at weakly, if at all" (xiii). The crisis in foreign language programs brought about by the unraveling of the cold war and its replacement by a rhetoric of globalization and regionalism offers another such "historic imaginative opportunity," a moment in which to consider how things might be different—and better—not how they have always been.

Imagination, don't fail us now.

NOTES ON CONTRIBUTORS

ANITA ALKHAS is assistant professor in the Department of French, Italian, and Comparative Literature at the University of Wisconsin, Milwaukee. She has published an essay on utopianism in the writings of George Sand. Her research interests encompass foreign language pedagogy and teacher training and nineteenth- and twentieth-century French culture and literature. She currently is developing techniques for teaching culture and language through the use of DVDs.

JOHN ANZALONE is professor of French at Skidmore College. His research includes work on the fantastic, the French fin de siècle and belle epoque literature and culture, and French cinema, particularly of the 1930s and new-wave period. He is currently developing image banks on the Web devoted to the Belgian poet and illustrator Jean de Boschère and preparing new courses on film noir and pulp fiction and on literature and the graphic arts during World War I.

VÉRONIQUE FLAMBARD-WEISBART is associate professor of French and director of the European Studies Program at Loyola Marymount University. Her research includes work on contemporary French literary fiction (on Céline, in particular), French and transnational film, and technology and literary and cultural studies. She coauthored with Michèle Claude Magnin a textbook, *Scén@rios. Pédagogies du virtuel* (Thomson, 2000), which employs global-simulation pedagogy for the college French composition and culture courses.

MICHAEL GARVAL is associate professor of French studies at North Carolina State University, Raleigh. His publications include articles on Honoré de Balzac, George Sand, Jean-Anthelme Brillat-Savarin, and Alexandre-Balthazar-Laurent Grimod de la Reynière and a book, *"A Dream of Stone": Fame, Vision, and Monumentality in Nineteenth-Century French Literary Culture* (University of Delaware P, 2004). He serves as associate editor for the journal *Contemporary French Civilization* and has coedited, with Andrea Goulet, a special issue on visual culture. He has another book in progress, "A Feast for the Imagination: French Illustrated Menus, 1870–1940."

KATHRYN M. GROSSMAN is professor of French at Pennsylvania State University. Her research includes three books on Victor Hugo, Les Misérables: *Conversion, Revolution, Redemption* (Twayne, 1996), *Figuring Transcendence in* Les Misérables*: Hugo's Romantic Sublime* (Southern Illinois UP, 1994), and *The Early Novels of Victor Hugo: Towards a Poetics of Harmony* (Librairie Droz, 1986). She has also published essays on politics and poetics in postrevolutionary writers and coedited *Confrontations: Politics and Aesthetics in Nineteenth-Century France* (Rodopi, 2001). She is currently completing a book entitled "The Later Novels of Victor Hugo: Variations on a Poetics of Transcendence."

DEBORAH A. HARTER is associate professor of French studies at Rice University. Her publications include a book, *Bodies in Pieces: Fantastic Narrative and the Poetics of the Fragment* (Stanford UP, 1996), and essays on Flaubert, Baudelaire, Maupassant, Kafka, and the fantastic. Her research interests include images of excess in art and in fiction from the late eighteenth through early twentieth centuries, nineteenth-century narrative and representations of the body, literature and psychoanalysis, and the ethics of fiction. Her current book project is entitled "Imaging Excess: Portraits of Pathology from Balzac to Kafka, Géricault to *Silence of the Lambs*."

MELANIE HAWTHORNE is professor of French at Texas A&M University. Her publications include *Rachilde and French Women's Authorship: From Decadence to Modernism* (U of Nebraska P, 2001), which garnered the 2001 MLA Aldo and Jeanne Scaglione Prize for French and Francophone Studies; *Contingent Loves: Simone de Beauvoir and Sexuality* (UP of Virginia, 2000); *A Practical Guide to French Business* (Writers Club, 2003), coedited with Jon P. Alston and Sylvie Saillet; *Gender and Fascism in Modern France* (UP of New England, 1997), coedited with Richard J. Golsan; and her translation of *The Juggler*, by Rachilde (Rutgers UP, 1990). Her current project is a biography of Gisèle d'Estoc.

GARETT R. HEYSEL is assistant professor of French and director of the French program at Lycoming College. His publications include essays on sports for Frenchwomen and on fashion in Jean Lorrain and René Crevel. His ongoing projects are on Sidonie-Gabrielle Colette and Jean Cocteau. His research and teaching interests include nineteenth- and twentieth-century French literature and culture studies, film, gay and gender studies, surrealism and the avant-garde.

DORIS Y. KADISH is professor of French and women's studies at the University of Georgia. Her books include *Practices of the New Novel* (York, 1979), *The Literature of Images* (Rutgers UP, 1987), and *Politicizing Gender* (Rutgers UP, 1991).

She has edited *Translating Slavery*, with Françoise Massardier-Kenney (Kent State UP, 1994); *Slavery in the Caribbean Francophone World* (U of Georgia P, 2000); and *La famille noire* by Sophie Doin (L'Harmattan, 2002); and has published articles and translations in journals. Her current project is tentatively entitled "Black Texts and Contexts: French Tales of Slavery from the 1820s."

LARRY KUIPER is assistant professor of French at the University of Wisconsin, Milwaukee. His publications include five articles for *A Gustave Flaubert Encyclopedia* (Greenwood, 2001); an essay on the Parisian perception of regional French; and an essay, cowritten with India Plough and entitled "Classroom Based Research as a Collaborative Effort" in *Second Language Classroom Research: Issues and Opportunities* (Erlbaum, 1995). He is currently developing a French phonetics CD-ROM in cooperation with Radio France and the Center for Language Teaching and Research at Michigan State University and studying second language perception.

MARIE LATHERS is Treuhaft Professor of Humanities and French at Case Western Reserve University. She has published two books, *Bodies of Art: French Literary Realism and the Artist's Model* (U of Nebraska P, 2001) and *The Aesthetics of Artifice: Villiers'* 'L'Eve future (North Carolina Studies in the Romance Langs. and Lits., 1996), and articles. She is currently working on a book-length study of the *Venus de Milo* in nineteenth-century French culture.

GAYLE A. LEVY is associate professor of French and women's and gender studies at the University of Missouri, Kansas City. Her publications include *Refiguring the Muse* (Lang, 1999), essays in *Contemporary French Civilization* and *Nineteenth-Century French Studies*, and translations of "Le Collège de France" by Christophe Charle and "Le Grand Dictionnaire de Pierre Larousse" by Pascal Ory. Her current project is entitled "The Failed Genius: Representing Creativity in Nineteenth-Century French Literature."

ANNE E. MCCALL is associate professor of French and director of the Women's Studies Program at Tulane University. Her publications include one book, *De l'être en lettres. L'autobiographie épistolaire de George Sand* (Rodopi, 1996), and essays. She has served as guest editor for two issues of *George Sand Studies*. She is working on a book-length study on Romantic epistolarity as a practice and as a site of fin de siècle cultural conflict.

E. NICOLE MEYER is associate professor of French, humanistic studies, and women's studies at the University of Wisconsin, Green Bay. Her publications include essays in both French studies and business journals and in *Corps/Décors: Femmes, Orgie, Parodie* (Rodopi, 1999), *A Gustave Flaubert Encyclopedia* (Greenwood, 2001), *Who's Who in Contemporary Women's Writing* (Routledge, 2001), *Making Business Work: Models, Materials, Methodologies* (Kendall/Hunt, 1997), and *The Feminist Encyclopedia of French Literature* (Greenwood, 1999). She is completing a book-length manuscript, "The Questioning of Origins and Authority in Flaubert's Bouvard et Pécuchet."

KATE PAESANI is assistant professor of French and codirector of the Masters of Arts in Language Learning Program at Wayne State University. Her research and teaching interests lie in foreign-language reading and writing, language-program articulation, proficiency across the curriculum, French syntax, teacher training, and pedagogy. She has written a chapter on the *passé surcomposé* for "A Romance Perspective on Language Knowledge and Use" (Benjamins, 2003) and is coediting a volume of essays (with Catherine M. Barrette), "Language Program Articulation: Developing a Theoretical Foundation" (Heinle, forthcoming).

ADRIANNA M. PALIYENKO is professor of French at Colby College. Her publications include *Misreading the Creative Impulse: The Poetic Subject in Rimbaud and Claudel, Restaged* (Southern Illinois UP, 1997), and articles and book chapters on literary influence, nineteenth-century French psychiatry, and women poets. She is also coauthor (with Aimée Boutin) of a critical bibliography of women's poetic production in nineteenth-century France in a special issue of *Women in French Studies* (2002). She is currently writing a book, provisionally entitled "Genius Envy: Anatomies of Exceptional Creativity in Nineteenth-Century France" and is preparing a critical edition of Anaïs Ségalas's *Récits des Antilles: Le bois de la Soufrière* and selected poems (L'Harmattan, forthcoming).

LAURENCE M. PORTER is professor of French, classics, and Italian at Michigan State University. He has published *The Renaissance of the Lyric in French Romanticism* (French Forum, 1978); *The Literary Dream in French Romanticism* (Wayne State UP, 1979); *The Crisis of French Symbolism* (Cornell UP, 1990); and books on Flaubert, Freud, and Hugo. He has edited two volumes in the MLA Approaches to Teaching World Literature Series and contributed to two others. His current book contracts include a volume on great women authors from Sappho to the present and a new English-language edition of Hugo's *Les misérables*. He currently serves on the boards of *Nineteenth-Century French Studies, Studies in Twentieth Century Literature*, and *Women in French Studies*.

DAVID A. POWELL is professor of French at Hofstra University. His publications include *"While the Music Lasts": The Representation of Music in the Works of George Sand* (Bucknell UP, 2001), essays in *George Sand Studies* and *Francophonies d'Amérique*, and a chapter on Mallarmé in *Confrontations: Politics and Aesthetics in Nineteenth-Century France* (Rodopi, 2000). Current projects include a study of Verlaine's musical symbolism set to music and a critical edition of two George Sand novels for an edition of her complete works (Champion, forthcoming).

NATHALIE RACHLIN is associate professor of French at Scripps College. She has published articles on race and class in contemporary France; French intellectuals, such as Pierre Bourdieu and Alain Finkielkraut; and twentieth-century French writers, such as Patrick Modiano and Francis Ponge. She is currently working on a book that examines the radical transformation of the French working class since the 1970s and the representations of this social transformation in contemporary French culture.

CYNTHIA RUNNING-JOHNSON is professor of French at Western Michigan University. She has published recent essays on Tahar Ben Jelloun and Jean Genet (*College Literature, Romance Notes*) and Hélène Cixous (*French Forum*). Her teaching and research interests include modern and contemporary drama in French, literature and the visual arts, film and society, and gender studies. Her current projects, in film studies, are an article on Jean Renoir and Jean-Luc Godard and, in contemporary French theater, research on the work of the director Brigitte Jaques.

CHARLES J. STIVALE is professor of French at Wayne State University. He has published books on Jules Vallès, Stendhal, Guy de Maupassant, and Gilles Deleuze and Félix Guattari. His most recent book is *Disenchanting Les Bons Temps: Identity and Authenticity in Cajun Music and Dance* (Duke UP, 2003). He has guest-edited two issues of *Substance* on Deleuze and Guattari (in 1984 and 1991) and is currently editing a volume entitled "Gilles Deleuze: Key Concepts" (Acumen).

JUDITH F. STONE is professor of history at Western Michigan University. Her publications include two books, *Sons of the Revolution: Radical Democrats in France, 1860–1914* (Louisiana State UP, 1996) and *The Search for Social Peace: Reform Legislation in France 1890–1914* (State U of New York P, 1985), and recent articles and essays in *French Historical Studies, Gender and the Politics of Social Reform: France, 1870–1914* (Johns Hopkins UP, 1995), and *Gender and Class in Modern Europe* (Cornell UP, 1996). She currently is developing film courses and a study of female religious orders and their response to anticlericalism around 1900.

GAYLE ZACHMANN is associate professor of French at the University of Florida and director of the University of Florida Paris Research Center. Her publications include a book, *Frameworks for Mallarmé: The "Photo" and the "Graphics" of an Interdisciplinary Aesthetic* (State U of New York P, forthcoming); essays in *Studies in Twentieth Century Literature, L'Esprit Créateur, Romance Quarterly, French Forum*; and chapters in *Confrontations: Politics and Aesthetics in Nineteenth-Century France* (Rodopi, 2001) and *Corps/Décors: Femmes, Orgie, Parodie* (Rodopi, 1999). She is currently completing a book-length study about Claude Cahun.

WORKS CITED

"ABCs of DVD: Enforced Regional Coding." *DVD Buzz: The Official DVD Club Newsletter* 4.3 (2001): n. pag.

Acker, Kathy. *In Memoriam to Identity*. New York: Grove, 1990.

Agulhon, Maurice. "La *statuomanie* et l'histoire." *Ethnologie française* 7–8 (1977–78): 145–72.

American Assn. of Teachers of French. "Materials Center." 1 Sept. 2003. 11 Mar. 2004 <http://www.Frenchteachers.org/hq/materials/material.html>.

American Council on the Teaching of Foreign Languages. *ACTFL Proficiency Guidelines: Speaking*. Hastings-on-Hudson: ACTFL, 1999.

Anderson, Laurie. "Odd Objects." *United States*. New York: Harper, 1984. n. pag.

Antle, Martine, and Dominque Fisher, eds. *The Rhetoric of the Other*. New Orleans: UP of the South, 2002.

Anzalone, John, ed. *Jeering Dreamers: Essays on* L'Eve future. Amsterdam: Rodopi, 1996.

Apollinaire, Guillaume. *Calligrammes*. Paris: Gallimard, 1966.

Apostolidès, Jean-Marie. " 'This Group Is Both Male and Foreign.' " *Stanford French Review* 16 (1993): iii–vii.

Appadurai, Arjun. "Diversity and Disciplinarity as Cultural Artefacts." *Disciplinarity and Dissent in Cultural Studies*. Ed. Cary Nelson and Dilip Parameshwar Gaonkar. New York: Routledge, 1996. 23–36.

Arnold, Ivor. "Villiers de l'Isle-Adam and écriture artiste." *French Review* 57 (1974): 874–81.

Balzac, Honoré de. *Le chef d'œuvre inconnu, Gambara, Massimilla Doni*. Paris: Flammarion, 1981.

———. *La Cousine Bette*. Ed. Pierre Barbéris. Paris: Gallimard, 1972.

———. *Sarrasine*. Paris: Allia, 1989.

Barnes-Karol, Gwendolyn. "Revising a Spanish Novel Class in the Light of Standards for Foreign Language Learning." *ADFL Bulletin* 31.2 (2000): 44–48.

Barnett, Marva A. "Language and Literature: False Dichotomies, Real Allies." *ADFL Bulletin* 22.3 (1991): 7–11.

———. *More than Meets the Eye: Foreign Language Reading: Theory and Practice*. Englewood Cliffs: Prentice Hall, 1989.

Barthes, Roland. "Le guide bleu." *Mythologies*. Paris: Seuil, 1957. 121–25.

———. *S/Z*. Paris: Seuil, 1970.

———. *S/Z*. Trans. Richard Miller. New York: Hill, 1974.

Bataille, Georges. *Lascaux; or, The Birth of Art: Prehistoric Painting*. Trans. Austryn Wainhouse. Lausanne: Skira, 1955.

Baudelaire, Charles. *Œuvres complètes*. Paris: Seuil, 1968.

———. Le peintre de la vie moderne in Œuvres complètes. Vol. 2. Paris: Gallimard, 1975.

———. "Pourquoi la sculpture est ennuyeuse." *Curiosités esthétiques: L'Art romantique, et autres œuvres critiques*. Ed. Henri Lemaître. Paris: Garnier, 1962. 187–91.

Baum, Paull Franklin. "The Young Man Betrothed to a Statue." *PMLA* 34 (1919): 523–79.

Bazin, André. *French Cinema of the Occupation and Resistance: The Birth of a Critical Aesthetic*. Introd. François Truffaut. Trans. Stanley Hochman. New York: Ungar, 1981.

———. *Jean Renoir*. Trans. W. W. Halsey and William Simon. New York: Simon, 1973.

Bazin, Germain. *The Museum Age*. Trans. Jane van Nuis Cahill. New York: Universe, 1967.

Beale, Arthur. "A Technical View of Nineteenth-Century Sculpture." *Metamorphosis in Nineteenth-Century Sculpture*. Ed. Jeanne L. Wasserman. Cambridge: Harvard UP, 1975. 29–55.

Bell, David. *An Introduction to Cyberculture*. New York: Routledge, 2001.

Bell, David F. "Disciplining the Disciplines Means Saying What One Means." *Contemporary French Civilization* 21.2 (1997): 113–30.

Bénabou, Marcel. *Pourquoi je n'ai écrit aucun de mes livres*. Paris: Hachette, 1986.

Bénabou, Marcel, and Jacques Roubaud. "Présentation de l'Oulipo." 1996. 16 Feb. 2004. <http://www2.ec-lille.fr/~book/oulipo/info/presentation.shtml>.

Benamou, Michel, Eugène Ionesco, and Monique Callamand. *Mise en train*. New York: Macmillan, 1970.

Benfey, Christopher. *Degas in New Orleans*. Berkeley: U of California P, 1997.

Bérubé, Michael. *Public Access*. New York: Verso, 1994.

Birnbaum, Pierre. *La France imaginée: Déclin des rêves unitaires?* Paris: Fayard, 1998.

Blanchot, Maurice. *Le livre à venir*. Paris: Gallimard, 1959.

Boime, Albert. *Hollow Icons: The Politics of Sculpture in Nineteenth-Century France.* Kent: Kent State UP, 1987.

Bongie, Chris. *Islands and Exiles: The Creole Identities of Post/Colonial Literature.* Stanford: Stanford UP, 1998.

Bourdieu, Pierre. *Distinction: A Social Critique of the Judgement of Taste.* Cambridge: Harvard UP, 1984.

Bourgignon, J. C. *Simulations globales et enseignement du français en milieu non francophone.* Strasbourg: CRDP, 1985.

Brooks, Peter. *Reading for the Plot: Design and Intention in Narrative.* New York: Knopf, 1984.

Bruno, G. [Mme Alfred Fouillée]. *Le tour de la France par deux enfants.* 1906. Paris: Belin, 1998.

Butler, Judith, John Guillory, and Kendall Thomas, eds. Preface. *What's Left of Theory? New Work on the Politics of Literary Theory.* New York: Routledge, 2000. viii–xii.

Byrnes, Heidi. "The Cultural Turn in Foreign Language Departments: Challenge and Opportunity." *Profession* 2002. New York: MLA. 114–29.

Camille Claudel. Dir. Bruno Nuytten. Orion et al., 1988.

Carnevale, Anthony P., Leila J. Gainer, and Ann S. Meltzer. *Workplace Basics: The Skills Employers Want.* Alexandria: American Soc. for Training and Development and U.S. Dept. of Labor Employment and Training Administration, 1988.

Caron, David. "Re: 19th Century Queer Studies." E-mail to Garett R. Heysel. 26 Sept. 2001.

Carrell, Patricia. "Text-Boundedness and Schema Inference." *Interactive Approaches to Second Language Reading.* Ed. Patricia L. Carrell, Joanne Devine, and David E. Eskey. Cambridge: Cambridge UP, 1988. 101–13.

Chambers, Ross. "Cultural Studies as a Challenge to French Studies." *Australian Journal of French Studies* 33 (1996): 137–56.

———. "On Teaching 'French.' " *South Central Review* 15.1 (1998): 40–53.

———. "On the Language-Culture Nexus." Le Hir and Strand 49–67.

Charrière, Patrick, and Michèle Claude Magnin. "Simulations globales: Le surf et la survie." *Le français dans le monde* 292 (1997): 54–59.

Chathuant, Dominique. "Abolitions de l'esclavage, 1794–1848." *Yekrik! Yekrak!* 7 Oct. 2003. 20 Feb. 2004 <http://perso.wanadoo.fr/yekrik.yekrak/listesclavage .htm>.

Chateaubriand, François-René. *Atala; René; Les Abencérages* suivi du *Voyage en Amérique.* Paris: Didot, 1845.

Cobb, Martha K. "The Slave Narrative and the Black Literary Tradition." *The Art of Slave Narrative: Original Essays in Criticism and Theory.* Ed. John Sekora and Darwin T. Turner. Macomb: Western Illinois U, 1982. 36–44.

Collins, Patricia Hill. *Black Feminist Thought: Knowledge, Consciousness, and the Politics of Empowerment.* 2nd ed. New York: Routledge, 2000.

Compagnon, Antoine. "A la recherche d'un nouveau statut." *France-Amérique* 24 Feb. 1996: L–N.

———. "The Diminishing Canon of French Literature in America." *Stanford French Review* 15 (1991): 103–15.

———. "Why French Has Become like Any Other Foreign Language in the United States." *Traveling Theory: France and the United States*. Ed. Sophie Bertho and Ton Honeselaars. Madison: Fairleigh Dickinson UP, 1999. 29–38.

Condé, Maryse. *In the Time of the Revolution*. Trans. of *An tan revolisyon*. Trans. Doris Y. Kadish and Jean-Pierre Piriou. *Callaloo* 25.2 (2002): 454–93.

Condorcet, Marquis de. "Epitre dédicatoire aux esclaves nègres." <http://julienas.ipt.univ-paris8.fr/~aceme/toutxt.html>.

Conley, Tom. "Afterword/Identity: Never More." Ungar and Conley 272–82.

———. "Putting French Studies on the Map." *Diacritics* 28.3 (1998): 23–39.

Contemporary French Civilization. Spec. issue. 26.2 (2002): 141–346.

Coppola, Francis Ford, dir. *Apocalypse Now*. Omni-Zoetrope, 1979.

Corbin, Alain. *Les cloches de la terre: Paysage sonore et culture sensible dans les campagnes au XIXe siècle*. Paris: Michel, 1994.

———. *Le monde retrouvé de Louis-François Pinagot: Sur les traces d'un inconnu, 1798–1876*. Paris: Flammarion, 1998.

Culler, Jonathan. "The Literary in Theory." Butler, Guillory, and Thomas 273–92.

Cusset, François. *French Theory: Foucault, Derrida, Deleuze, and Cie et les mutations de la vie intellectuelle aux Etats-Unis*. Paris: La Découverte, 2003.

Daudet, Alphonse. *Femmes d'artistes*. Paris: Lemerre, 1874.

Davies, Gardner. *Vers une explication rationnelle du* Coup de dés: *Essai d'exégèse mallarméenne*. Paris: Corti, 1953.

Debouzy, Marianne. "Introduction: les études de civilisation en débat." *Revue française d'études américaines* 83 (2000): 3–12.

Debyser, Francis. *L'immeuble*. Paris: Hachette, 1986.

Décaux, Alain. *Victor Hugo*. Paris: Perrin, 1984.

"Déclaration des droits de l'homme et du citoyen, 26 Août 1789." 2 Feb. 2004 <http://www.droitsenfant.com/droitshomme.htm>.

Découvrir la France. Paris: Hachette, 1998.

De Grazia, Victoria. "Mass Culture and Sovereignty: The American Challege to European Cinemas, 1920–1960." *Journal of Modern History* 61 (1989): 53–87.

Delvaux, Martine. "Teaching AIDS: Toward a Protocol of Comparison." Antle and Fisher 17–30.

Démar, Claire. *Appel d'une femme au peuple;* suivi de *Ma loi d'avenir*. Paris: Bibliothèque nationale, 1977.

Desormeaux, Daniel. "Le roman réaliste: Faits divers et faits culturels dans l'enseignement littéraire." Nineteenth-Century French Studies Colloquium. Pennsylvania State Univ. 24 Oct. 1998 <http://www.langlab.wayne.edu/CStivale/NCFS/NCFS1998.html>.

Dijkstra, Bram. *Idols of Perversity: Fantasies of Feminine Evil in Fin de Siècle Culture.* New York: Oxford UP, 1986.

Doing French Studies. Spec. issue of *Diacritics* 28.3 (1998): 1–100.

Downing, Lisa. "Between Men and Women: Beyond Heterosexuality: Limits and Possibilities of the Erotic in Lynne Stopkewich's 'Kissed' and Patrice Leconte's 'La fille sur le pont.' " *Romance Studies* 20.1 (2002): 29–40.

Duby, Georges, and Michelle Perrot. *Histoire des femmes en occident: Le XIXe siècle.* Paris: Plon, 1991.

Dumas, Alexandre [Dumas fils]. *L'affaire Clémenceau.* Paris: Slatkine, 1996.

Duras, Claire de. *Ourika. Translating Slavery: Gender and Race in French Women's Writing, 1783–1823.* Ed. Doris Y. Kadish and Françoise Massardier-Kenney. Kent: Kent State UP, 1994. 194–216; 293–315.

Engell, James, and Anthony Dangerfield. "The Market-Model University: Humanities in the Age of Money." *Harvard Magazine* May–June 1998. 18 May 2004. <http://www.harvard-magazine.com/issues/mj98/forum.html>

Ericksen, Stanford C. *The Essence of Good Teaching.* San Francisco: Jossey-Bass, 1984.

Everett, Wendy. "Film at the Crossroads: *Les Roseaux sauvages.*" Powrie 47–57.

Faulkner, Christopher. "Teaching French National Cinema." *Cinema Journal* 38.4 (1999): 88–93.

"F.B.I. Warns of Suspicious Almanacs." *New York Times* 30 Dec. 2003, late ed.-final: A18.

Finkielkraut, Alain. *La défaite de la pensée: Essai.* Paris: Gallimard, 1987.

Flambard-Weisbart, Véronique, and Michèle Claude Magnin. "Les simulations à cheval sur les siècles et les disciplines." American Assn. of Teachers of French Annual Convention. Paris. 19 July 2000.

Forbes, Gordon, dir. *The Doors: A Tribute to Jim Morrison.* Distrib. Heartbeat Productions / Alchemical Music Co., 1981.

Forbes, Jill. *The Cinema in France after the New Wave.* Bloomington: Indiana UP, 1992.

———. "Conclusion: French Cultural Studies in the Future." Forbes and Michael Kelly, eds. *French Cultural Studies: An Introduction.* Oxford: Oxford UP, 1995. 290–95.

Foster, Andrea L. "Two Scholars Face Off in Copyright Clash." *Chronicle of Higher Education* 10 Aug. 2001: A45–46.

Fourny, Jean-François, and Lawrence Schehr. "Introduction: Haven't We Been through All This Before?" *Contemporary French Civilization* 21.2 (1997): 1–4.

Fowlie, Wallace. *Rimbaud and Jim Morrison: The Rebel as Poet: A Memoir.* Durham: Duke UP, 1994.

Fox, Barry. "Barry Fox's Q&A." *BBC Music Magazine* June 2001: 61.

Le guide vert: France. Paris: Michelin, 2000.

"French Major Requirements." Georgetown Univ. 11 June 2004 <http://www.georgetown.edu/departments/french/major.htm>.

"French Program." Yale Univ. 11 June 2004 <http://www.yale.edu/ycpo/ycps/E-L/frenchFM.html>.

"French Studies: The Major, Minor, and French Language Certificate." Univ. of Pennsylvania Dept. of Romance Langs. 18 May 2004 <http://ccat.sas.upenn.edu/romance/undergrad/frprogug.shtml>.

Frye, Northrop. *Anatomy of Criticism: Four Essays*. Princeton: Princeton UP, 1957.

Furman, Nelly. "French Studies: Back to the Future." *Profession 1998*. New York: MLA, 1998. 68–80.

Gilman, Sander. "Learning a Foreign Language in a Monolingual World." *PMLA* 115 (2000): 1032–40.

Glissant, Edouard. *Le quatrième siècle*. Paris: Seuil, 1964.

Gopnik, Adam. *Paris to the Moon*. New York: Random, 2000.

Gouges, Olympe de. "Déclaration de droits de la femme et de la citoyenne." *Opinions de femmes: De la veille au lendemain de la Révolution française*. Ed. Geneviève Fraisse. Paris: Côté-femmes, 1989. 47–62.

Goux, Jean-Joseph, and Philip R. Wood, eds. *Terror and Consensus: Vicissitudes of French Thought*. Stanford: Stanford UP, 1998.

Graff, Gerald. *Beyond the Culture Wars: How Teaching the Conflicts Can Revitalize American Education*. New York: Norton, 1992.

Grand Larousse de la langue française. Vol. 3. Paris: Gallimard, 1968.

Green, Mary Jean. "Marketing Strategies for a New Academic Economy: Can We Sell French without Selling Out?" Sixteenth Annual International Colloquium on Twentieth-Century French Studies. Univ. of North Carolina, Chapel Hill. 26 Mar. 1999.

Grégoire de Tours. *Histoire des Francs*. Trans. François Guizot. Paris: Didier, 1861.

Grossberg, Lawrence. *Bringing It All Back Home: Essays on Cultural Studies*. Durham: Duke UP, 1997.

Grossberg, Lawrence, Cary Nelson, and Paula Treichler, eds. *Cultural Studies*. New York: Routledge, 1992.

Grossman, Kathryn. *The Early Novels of Victor Hugo: Towards a Poetics of Harmony*. Histoire des idées et critique littéraire 241. Geneva: Droz, 1986.

———. "From Classic to Pop Icon: Popularizing Hugo." *French Review* 74 (2001): 482–95.

Guerlac, Suzanne. "Cultural Studies in French Departments." *Contemporary French Civilization* 21:2 (1997): 51–63.

Le guide du routard: Junior en France. Paris: Hachette, 2003.

Le guide vert: France. Paris: Michelin, 2000.

Hall, Gwendolyn Midlo, ed. *Databases for the Study of Afro-Louisiana History and Genealogy 1699–1860*. Baton Rouge: Louisiana State UP, 2000. <http.www.ibiblio.org/laslave/>.

Hall, James. *The World as Sculpture: The Changing Status of Sculpture from the Renaissance to the Present Day*. London: Chatto, 1999.

Hapax: French Resources on the Web. Ed. Angelo Metzidakis. Sweet Briar Coll. 18 May 2004 <http://hapax.be.sbc.edu/>.

Haraway, Donna J. *Simians, Cyborgs, and Women: The Reinvention of Nature*. New York: Routledge, 1991.

Harper, Sandra N. "Strategies for Teaching Literature at the Undergraduate Level." *Modern Language Journal* 72 (1988): 402–08.

Haskell, Francis, and Nicholas Penny. *Taste and the Antique: The Lure of Classical Sculpture, 1500–1900*. New Haven: Yale UP, 1981.

Haynes, Cynthia, and Jan Rune Holmevik, eds. *High Wired: On the Design, Use, and Theory of Educational MOOs*. Ann Arbor: U of Michigan P, 1998.

Hayward, Susan, and Ginette Vincendeau, eds. *French Film: Text and Contexts*. New York: Routledge, 2000.

Heilbrun, Carolyn G. *Writing a Woman's Life*. New York: Norton, 1988.

Hoffmann, Ernst Fedor, and Dorothy James. "Toward the Integration of Foreign Language and Literature Teaching at All Levels of the College Curriculum." *ADFL Bulletin* 18.1 (1986): 29–33.

Holden-Avard, Nancy C., Marlene A. Nusbaum, and Liliane Verdier. *Le français sans peur*. Fort Worth: Holt, Rinehart, 1991.

Hollier, Denis, ed. *A New History of French Literature*. Cambridge: Harvard UP, 1989.

Hope, Geoffrey R. "Assessing the Undergraduate French Major: Institutional and Individual Accountability." *French Review* 72 (1999): 456–68.

Hotêl du Nord. Dir. Marcel Carné. Universal, 1938.

Hugo, Victor. *Notre-Dame de Paris. 1482*. Ed. Léon Cellier. Paris: Garnier-Flammarion, 1990.

———. *Notre-Dame de Paris*. Ed. Michel Cambien. Paris: Classiques Larousse, 1973.

———. *Notre-Dame de Paris*. Trans. Alban Krailsheimer. Oxford: Oxford UP, 1993.

Hullot-Kentor, Odile. "Profession Forum: Breaking Ranks." *Profession 93*. New York: MLA, 1993. 68–71.

The Hunchback. Dir. Peter Medak. Salma Hayek, Mandy Patinkin. TNT, 1997.

The Hunchback of Notre Dame. Dir. Jean Delannoy. Gina Lollobrigida, Anthony Quinn. Miramax, 1956.

The Hunchback of Notre Dame. Dir. William Dieterle. Charles Laughton, Maureen O'Hara. RKO, 1939.

The Hunchback of Notre Dame. Dir. Bradley Raymond. Disney, 1996.

The Hunchback of Notre Dame. Dir. Wallace Worsley. Lon Chaney, Patsy Ruth Miller. Universal, 1923.

Hustvedt, Asti. "The Pathology of Eve." Anzalone 25–46.

Hutcheon, Linda, and Michael Hutcheon. "A Convenience of Marriage: Collaboration and Interdisciplinarity." *PMLA* 116 (2001): 1364–76.

"Information for Undergraduates." Univ. of Virginia, Dept. of French. <http://www.virginia.edu/french/ugrads/Major>.

Ingram, Mark. "Interdisciplinary Perspectives in the French Civilization Class." *French Review* 74 (2001): 1152–64.

Insdorf, Annette. *François Truffaut*. New York: Simon, 1989.

Jameson, Fredric R. *Postmodernism; or, The Cultural Logic of Late Capitalism*. Durham: Duke UP, 1992.

Kadish, Doris Y. Home page. 30 Mar. 2003. 18 May 2004 <http://www.uga.edu/slavery>.

Kelly, Mike. "The Stranger's Gaze: The Emergence of French Cultural Studies." *The Future of Cultural Studies*. Ed. Jan Baetens and José Lambert. Louvain: Leuven UP, 2000. 107–21.

Klein, Richard. "The Object of French Studies—*Gebrauchkunst*." *Diacritics* 28.3 (1998): 5–11.

Kramsch, Claire. "Literary Texts in the Classroom: A Discourse." *Modern Language Journal* 69 (1985): 356–66.

Kritzman, Lawrence D. "Identity Crises: France, Culture, and the Idea of Nation." *Substance* 76–77 (1995): 5–20.

Lacan, Jacques. *Ecrits*. Paris: Seuil, 1966.

LaCapra, Dominick. "Reconfiguring French Studies." *History and Reading: Tocqueville, Foucault, French Studies*. Toronto: U of Toronto P, 2000. 169–226.

La Charité, Virginia A. *The Dynamics of Space: Mallarmé's* Un coup de dés jamais n'abolira le hasard. Lexington: French Forum, 1987.

Lamartine, Alphonse de. "Déclaration en février 1842, lors d'un banquet organisé par le comité pour la libération des esclaves." 18 May 2004 <http://col-r.verges.ac-reunion.fr/Dossiers/Reunion/cdrEsclavage/Abolitionnistes/Ab147.htm>.

———. *Nouvelles méditations poétiques*. Paris: Hachette, 1924.

Laplanche, Jean. *Vie et mort en psychanalyse*. Paris: Flammarion, 1970.

Larson, Gary. "The Far Side." Cartoon. *The Far Side Oz Greeting Cards*. [Kansas City] 1991.

———. "On-line Use of 'The Far Side' Cartoons." Online posting 20 Sept. 1999. 18 May 2004 <http://www.creators.com/index2_anotefromgarylarson.html>.

Laster, Arnaud. *Pleins feux sur Victor Hugo*. Paris: Comédie-Française, 1981.

Lastinger, Michael. "Les saucissons chauds." *Michael Lastinger's Home Pages*. West Virginia Univ. 30 June 2003. <http://www.as.wvu.edu/mlastinger/main.htm/>. Path: Les saucissons chauds.

Lathers, Marie. *The Aesthetics of Artifice*. Chapel Hill: U of North Carolina P, 1996.

———. "The Decadent Goddess." Anzalone 47–65.

Latortue, Régine, and Gleason R. W. Adams, trans. *Les Cenelles: A Collection of Poems by Creole Writers of the Early Nineteenth Century*. Boston: Hall, 1979.

———. Preface. Latortue and Adams ix–xxx.

Le Hir, Marie-Pierre. "Bridging National Fields: Nineteenth-Century Scholarship in French and American Perspectives." *Nineteenth-Century French Studies* 24 (1995–96): 13–33.

———. "French Cultural Studies in the United States: A Case Study." *Sites* 1.1 (1997): 171–90.

———. "The 'Popular' in Cultural Studies." Le Hir and Strand 123–42.

———. "Transatlantic Solidarity in the Age of Globalization." *Contemporary French Civilization* 26.2 (2002): 232–42.

Le Hir, Marie-Pierre, and Dana Strand, eds. *French Cultural Studies: Criticism at the Crossroads*. Albany: State U of New York P, 2000.

Lentricchia, Frank, and Thomas McLaughlin, eds. *Critical Terms for Literary Studies*. 2nd ed. Chicago: U of Chicago P, 1995.

Leprince de Beaumont, Jeanne-Marie. "La belle et la bête." *Le magasin des enfants: "La belle et la bête" et autres contes*. Picquier Poche 37. Paris: Picquier, 1994. 37–54.

Levy, Gayle A. *Refiguring the Muse*. Bern: Lang, 1999.

———. "Teaching French Cultural Studies." *Contemporary French Civilization* 21 (1997): 100–11.

Lotringer, Sylvère, and Sande Cohen. Introduction. *French Theory in America*. Ed. Lotringer and Cohen. New York: Routledge, 2001. 1–9.

Lucey, Michael. "Re: NCFSC." E-mail to Garett R. Heysel. 10 Sept. 1999.

Magnan, Sally Sieloff, and François V. Tochon. "Reconsidering French Pedagogy: The Crucial Role of the Teacher and Teaching." *French Review* 74 (2001): 1092–112.

Magnin, Michèle Claude. "Fenêtres sur la France—la page pédagogique des Internautes." 3 Mar. 2002. 22 Feb. 2004 <http://home.sandiego.edu/~mmagnin/PagePedagogique.html>.

"M.A. in French Cultural Studies at Reid Hall, Paris." Columbia University. <http://www.columbia.edu/cu/frenchculturalstudies/>.

"Major." Univ. of Illinois French Dept. 23 June 2004 <http://www.french.uiuc.edu>. Path: Undergraduate Studies; Program and Degree Requirements; French Major.

"Major and Minor Program in French Studies." Univ. of Pennsylvania Dept. of Romance Langs. <http://ccat.sas.upenn.edu/romance/undergrad/frprogug.shtml>.

Mallarmé, Stéphane. *Œuvres complètes*. Ed. Henri Mondor and G. Jean Aubry. Paris: Gallimard, 1945.

———. *La première édition d'* Un coup de dés *par Stéphane Mallarmé*. Ed. David Mus. Fin de Siècle, 1996.

———. *Un coup de dés jamais n'abolira le hasard*. Paris: Nouvelle Revue Française, 1914.

———. *Un coup de dés jamais n'abolira le hasard*. Ed. Mitsou Ronat. Paris: Change/Errant/d'Atelier, 1980.

Marie, Michel. "It Really Makes You Sick! Jean-Luc Godard's *A bout de souffle* 1959." Hayward and Vincendeau 158–74.

Marks, John, and Edna McCaffery, eds. *French Cultural Debates*. Newark: U of Delaware P, 2001.

Mathy, Jean-Philippe. *French Resistance: The French-American Culture Wars*. Minneapolis: U of Minnesota P, 2000.

Matthews, Roy T., and F. DeWitt Platt. *The Renaissance to the Present.* 3rd ed. Mountain View: Mayfield, 1998. Vol. 2 of *The Western Humanities.*

Maurois, André. *Victor Hugo.* Trans. Gerard Hopkins. London: Jonathan Cape, 1956. Trans. of *Olympio; ou, La vie de Victor Hugo.* Paris: Hachette, 1954.

Maxwell, Richard. *The Mysteries of Paris and London.* Charlottesville: U of Virginia P, 1992.

McClellan, Andrew. *Inventing the Louvre: Art, Politics, and the Origin of the Modern Museum in Eighteenth-Century Paris.* Cambridge: Cambridge UP, 1994.

McGann, Jerome. "Who's Carving Up the Nineteenth Century?" *PMLA* 116 (2001): 1415–21.

McGrew, Anthony. "A Global Society?" *Modernity: An Introduction to Modern Societies.* Eds. Stuart Hall, David Held, Don Hunert, and Kenneth Thompson. Oxford: Blackwell, 1996. 466–503.

Meem, Deborah. "Lesbian Literature and Psychology." *Lesbian and Gay Studies Newsletter* 24 (1997): 7–10.

Mérimée, Prosper. La Vénus d'Ille *et autres nouvelles.* Paris: Flammarion, 1982.

Meyer, E. Nicole. "Active Learning Approaches to the Business French Course: The Business French Research Paper." *Foreign Language Annals* 28 (1995): 135–46.

———. "French and Francophone Women's Autobiography in the Twentieth Century." *French and Francophone Women from the 16th to the 21st Centuries: Essays on Literature, Culture and Society with Bibliographical and Media Resources.* Ed. Catherine Montfort and Marie-Christine Koop. Spec. issue of *Women in French Studies* (2002): 123–41.

———. "Ten Tips for the First Time Business French Teacher." *Making Business Work: Models, Materials, Methodologies.* Ed. Steven Loughrin-Sacco and Jane Abrate. Dubuque: Kendall/Hunt, 1997. 215–35.

Meyers, Helene. "To Queer or Not to Queer: That's Not the Question." *College Literature* 24.1 (1997): 171–83.

Miller, Scott. "Hispanics Replace African Americans as Largest U.S. Minority Group." *U.S. Department of State—International Information Programs.* 23 Jan. 2003. <http://usinfo.state.gov/usa/diversity/a012303.htm>.

Ministère de la Culture et de la Communication. "La grotte Chauvet Pont d'Arc." 19 Feb. 2004. <http://www.culture.gouv.fr/culture/arcnat/chauvet/fr/index.html>.

Mirbeau, Octave. L'octogénaire, La pipe de cidre: *Œuvres inédites.* Paris: Flammarion, 1919.

Molière. *Théâtre choisi.* Paris: Garnier, 1962.

Moura, Jean-Marc. *Littératures francophones et théorie postcoloniale.* Paris: PUF, 1999.

Murti, Kamakshi. "Teaching Literature at the First-Year Graduate Level: The Quantum Leap from Language to Literature." *ADFL Bulletin* 25.1 (1993): 41–48.

Musset, Alfred de. *La confession d'un enfant du siècle. Œuvres complètes en prose.* Ed. Maurice Allem and Paul-Courant. Paris: Gallimard, 1960. 65–288.

Myers, David Gershom. "On the Teaching of Literary Theory." *Philosophy and Literature* 18 (1994): 326–36.

Nesbitt, Frank. Interview with Maryse Condé. *Revolution in Discourse: Writing History in French Antillean Literature*. Diss. Harvard U., 1997. DAI 58 (1998): 3532.

Nochlin, Linda. *The Body in Pieces: The Fragment as a Metaphor of Modernity*. London: Thames, 1994.

Noland, Carrie. *Poetry at Stake: Lyric Aesthetics and the Challenge of Technology*. Princeton: Princeton UP, 1999.

Nussbaum, Martha. *Cultivating Humanity: A Classical Defense of Reform in Liberal Education*. Cambridge: Harvard UP, 1997.

Ophuls, Marcel. The Sorrow and the Pity: *A Film Script*. Trans. Mireille Johnston. New York: Outerbridge, 1972.

Oulipo. *Atlas de littérature potentielle*. 1981. 2nd ed. Folio ed. Paris: Gallimard, 1988.

———. *La bibliothèque oulipienne*. 3 vols. Paris: Seghers, 1990.

——— *La littérature potentielle: Créations, re-créations, récréations*. 1973. 2nd ed. Folio ed. Paris: Gallimard, 1988.

Ousselin, Edward. "French Cultural Studies: An Oxymoron?" *Contemporary French Civilization* 21 (1997): 87–99.

"Overview of the French Section." Stanford Univ. <http://www.stanford.edu/dept/fren-ital/frframe.html>.

Ozouf, Jacques, and Mona Ozouf. " 'Le tour de la France par deux enfants': Le petit livre rouge de la République." *Les lieux de mémoire*. Vol. 1. Ed. Pierre Nora. Paris: Gallimard, 1997. 277–301.

Paliyenko, Adrianna. *Mis-reading the Creative Impulse: The Poetic Subject in Rimbaud and Claudel, Restaged*. Carbondale: Southern Illinois UP, 1997.

Pardo Bazán, Emilia. *"El encaje roto" y otros cuentos*. Ed. Joyce Tolliver. New York: MLA, 1996.

———. *"Torn Lace" and Other Stories*. Trans. María Cristina Urruela. New York: MLA, 1996.

Pavel, Thomas. "Les études culturelles: Une nouvelle discipline?" *Critique* 545 (1992): 731–42.

———. Letter. *PMLA* 112 (1997): 267–68.

———. Letter. *Profession 95*. New York: MLA, 1995. 110–11.

Peabody, Sue. *"There Are No Slaves in France": The Political Culture of Race and Slavery in the Ancien Régime*. Oxford: Oxford UP, 1996.

Peckham, Robert. "On the Importance of Knowing French." *TennesseeBob's Famous French Links*. Ed. Peckham. 27 Feb. 2004. <http://www.utm.edu/departments/french/french.html>. Path: On the Importance of Knowing French.

Pérec, Georges. *Espèces d'espaces*. Paris: Galilée, 2000.

———. *La vie mode d'emploi*. Paris: Hachette, 1978.

Pernoud, Régine. *La femme au temps des cathédrales*. Paris: Stock, 1980.

Petrey, Sandy. "French Studies / Cultural Studies: Reciprocal Invigoration or Mutual Destruction?" *French Review* 68 (1995): 381–92.

———. "When Did Literature Stop Being Cultural?" *Diacritics* 28.3 (1998): 12–22.

Pingeot, Anne. *Le corps en morceaux*. Paris: Réunion des Musées Nationaux, 1990.

———. "Sculpture and Literature in Nineteenth-Century France." *From Rodin to Giacometti: Sculpture and Literature in France 1880–1950*. Ed. Keith Aspley, Elizabeth Cowley, and Peter Sharratt. Amsterdam: Rodopi, 2000. 37–48.

Planté, Christine, ed. *Femmes poètes du XIXe siècle: Une anthologie*. Lyon: PU de Lyon, 1998.

Pluchon, Pierre. *Nègres et juifs au 18e siècle: Le racisme au siècle des lumières*. Paris: Tallendier, 1984.

Popkin, Jeremy. *A History of Modern France*. Englewood Cliffs: Prentice, 1994.

Porter, David, ed. *Internet Culture*. New York: Routledge, 1997.

Porter, Laurence M., ed. *Approaches to Teaching Baudelaire's* Flowers of Evil. New York: MLA, 2000.

———. *The Crisis of French Symbolism*. Ithaca: Cornell UP, 1990.

———. *Victor Hugo*. New York: Twayne, 1999.

Potts, Alex. *The Sculptural Imagination: Figurative, Modernist, Minimalist*. New Haven: Yale UP, 2000.

Powrie, Phil, ed. *French Cinema in the 1990s: Continuity and Difference*. New York: Oxford UP, 1999.

Prendergast, Christopher. "Circulating Representations: New Historicism and the Poetics of Culture." *Substance* 88 (1999): 90–104.

Press, Eyal, and Jennifer Washburn. "The Kept University." Atlantic *Online*. Mar. 2000. <http://www.theatlantic.com/issues/2000/03/press.htm>.

"Prime Numbers." *Chronicle of Higher Education*. 23 Feb. 2001: A10.

Proust, Marcel. *A la recherche du temps perdu*. Ed. Jean-Yves Tadié. Paris: Gallimard, 1987–89.

Pudlowski, Gilles. *Les trésors gourmands de la France*. Photographs by Maurice Rougemont. Paris: La Renaissance du Livre, 1997.

Queer Utilities: Textual Studies, Theory, Pedagogy, Praxis. Ed. Donald E. Hall, Jean Walton, and Garry Leonard. Spec. issue of *College Literature* 24.1 (1997): 1–312.

Queneau, Raymond. *Exercices de style*. Paris: Gallimard, 1956.

Raitt, Alan. Preface. Anzalone 7–12.

Rapaport, Herman. *The Theory Mess: Deconstruction in Eclipse*. New York: Columbia UP, 2001.

Read, Herbert. *The Art of Sculpture*. London: Faber, 1954.

Readings, Bill. *The University in Ruins*. Cambridge: Harvard UP, 1996.

Rich, Adrienne. *On Lies, Secrets, and Silence: Selected Prose 1966–1978*. New York: Norton, 1974.

———. *What Is Found There: Notebooks on Poetry and Politics*. New York: Norton, 1993.

Riché, Pascal. "Une brève histoire de la mondialisation." *Libération*. 27 Nov. 1999. <http://www.liberation.fr/omc/actu/991127b.html>.

Robb, Graham. *Victor Hugo: A Biography*. New York: Norton, 1998.

Robinson-Valery, Judith. "The *Rough* and the *Polished*." *Yale French Studies* 89 (1996): 59–66.

Rolin, Jean. *Zones*. Paris: Gallimard, 1995.

Rollet, Brigette. "Identity and Alterity in *Indochine*." Powrie 37–46.

Rosello, Mireille. *Declining the Stereotype: Ethnicity and Representation in French Cultures*. Hanover: Dartmouth Coll. / UP of New England, 1998.

———. *Postcolonial Hospitality: The Immigrant as Guest*. Stanford: Stanford UP, 2001.

———. "Rap Music and French Cultural Studies: For an Ethics of the Ephemeral." Le Hir and Strand 81–102.

Ross, Kristin. *Fast Cars, Clean Bodies: Decolonization and the Reordering of French Culture*. Cambridge: MIT P, 1995.

Rousso, Henry. *The Vichy Syndrome: History and Memory in France since 1944*. Cambridge: Harvard UP, 1992.

Ryan, Judith. "Skinside Inside: The National Literature Major versus Comparative Literature." *ADFL Bulletin* 22.3 (1991): 15–22.

Ryan, Marie-Laure, ed. *Cyberspace Textuality: Computer Technology and Literary Theory*. Bloomington: Indiana UP, 1999.

———. *Narrative as Virtual Reality: Immersion and Interactivity in Literature*. Baltimore: Johns Hopkins UP, 2000.

Sadoff, Dianne F., and William Cain, eds. *Teaching Contemporary Theory to Undergraduates*. New York: MLA, 1994.

Sala-Molins, Louis. *Le code noir; ou, Le calvaire de Canaan*. Paris: PUF, 1987.

Saunders, Frances Stonor. *The Cultural Cold War: The CIA and the World of Arts and Letters*. New York: New, 2000.

Savoy, Eric. "You Can't Go Homo Again: Queer Theory and the Foreclosure of Gay Studies." *English Studies in Canada* 20.2 (1994): 129–52.

Schefer, Jean-Louis. "Du simulacre à la parole." *Tel quel* 31 (1967): 85–91.

Schehr, Lawrence R. "A Queer Theory Approach: Gender and Genre in *Old Goriot*." *Approaches to Teaching Balzac's* Old Goriot. Ed. Michal Peled Ginsburg. New York: MLA, 2000. 118–25.

———. "Descant." Antle and Fisher 1–16.

———. Introduction. *Contemporary French Civilization* 145–48.

Schehr, Lawrence R., and Allen S. Weiss, eds. *French Food: On the Table, on the Page, and in French Culture*. New York: Routledge, 2001.

Schiller, Herbert. "Décervelage à l'américaine." *Le monde diplomatique*. Aug. 1999. <http://www.monde-diplomatique.fr/1999/08/SCHILLER/12381>.

Schneider, Alison. "A University Plans to Promote Languages by Killing Its Languages Department." *Chronicle of Higher Education* 9 Mar. 2001: A14–15.

Schneider, Jeffrey, and Silke von der Emde. "Brave New (Virtual) World: Transforming Learning into Cultural Studies through Online Learning Environments (MOOs)." *ADFL Bulletin* 32.1 (2000): 18–26.

Schoelcher, Victor. *Histoire de l'esclavage pendant les deux dernières années.* Paris: Pagnerre, 1847.

Schofer, Peter. "Literature and Communicative Competence: A Springboard for the Development of Critical Thinking and Aesthetic Appreciation or Literature in the Land of Language." *Foreign Language Annals* 23.4 (1990): 325–34.

Schor, Naomi. "Feminist and Gender Studies." *Introduction to Scholarship in Modern Languages and Literatures.* Ed. Joseph Gibaldi. New York: MLA, 1992. 262–87.

———. Reply to letter of Odile Hullot-Kentor. *Profession 93.* New York: MLA, 1993. 71.

———. Reply to letter of Thomas G. Pavel. *Profession 95.* New York: MLA, 1995. 111–13. Rpt. in *Bad Objects: Essays Popular and Unpopular.* Durham: Duke UP, 1995. 71–81.

———. "Pensive Texts and Thinking Statues: Balzac with Rodin." *Critical Inquiry* 27 (2001): 239–65.

———. "The Righting of French Studies: Homosociality and the Killing of 'La pensée 68.' " *Profession 92.* New York: MLA, 1992. 28–34.

Schultz, Gretchen. Telephone interview with Garett Heysel. 16 Sept. 1999.

Schultz, Jean-Marie. "Making the Transition from Language to Literature." *The Foreign Language Classroom: Bridging Theory and Practice.* Ed. Margaret Austin Haggstrom, Leslie Zarker Morgan, and Joseph A. Wieczorek. New York: Garland, 1995. 3–20.

Schulz, Renate A. "Literature and Readability: Bridging the Gap in Foreign Language Reading." *Modern Language Journal* 65 (1981): 43–53.

Schwartz, Stephen Adam. "Everyman as Übermensch: The Culture of Cultural Studies." *Substance* 91 (2000): 104–38.

Schwarz-Bart, André. *La Mulâtresse Solitude.* Paris: Seuil, 1972.

Sedgwick, Eve Kosofsky. *Epistemology of the Closet.* Berkeley: U of California P, 1990.

Séjour, Victor. "Le mulâtre." *Norton Anthology of African American Literature.* New York: Norton, 1997. 286–99.

Serres, Michel. "Erres dans les cimetières." *Statues.* Paris: Bourin, 1987. 55–77.

Shattuck, Roger. "Baudelaire as an Unknown." L. Porter, *Approaches* 57–64.

Shook, David J. "Foreign Language Literature and the Beginning Learner-Reader." *Foreign Language Annals* 29 (1996): 201–16.

Showalter, Elaine. *Teaching Literature.* Malden: Blackwell, 2003.

Silin, Jonathan G. "Teaching as a Gay Man: Pedagogical Resistance or Public Spectacle?" *Gay and Lesbian Quarterly* 5 (1999): 95–106.

Smith, Barbara Leigh, and Jean T. MacGregor. "What Is Collaborative Learning?" *Collaborative Learning: A Sourcebook for Higher Education.* Ed. Anne S. Goodsell, Michelle R. Maher, and Vincent Tinto. University Park: Natl. Center for Postsecondary Teaching, Learning, and Assessment, 1992. 9–40.

Soneson, Daniel B. "Aesthetic Response to Lyric Poetry: An Interactive Approach." *Die Unterrichtspraxis-Teaching German* 24 (1991): 31–36.

Soussigne, Jean-Pierre. *Le XIXe siècle: Le siècle de Victor Hugo*. CD-ROM. N.p.: Aborescence, 1997.

Sowerwine, Charles. *France since 1870: Culture, Politics, and Society*. New York: Palgrave, 2001.

Spelman, Elizabeth V. "Gender and Race: The Ampersand Problem in Feminist Theory." *Inessential Woman: Problems of Exclusion in Feminist Thought*. Boston: Beacon, 1988. 114–32.

Staël, Germaine de. *Œuvres de Madame de Staël-Holstein*. 2 vols. Paris: Lefèvre, 1858.

Stambolian, Georges, and Elaine Marks, eds. *Homosexualities in French Literature: Cultural Contexts / Critical Texts*. Ithaca: Cornell UP, 1979.

Standards for Foreign Language Learning: Preparing for the Twenty-First Century. New York: Natl. Standards in Foreign Lang. Educ. Project, 1996.

Stanton, Domna. "Toward a Contextual Literary History: French Studies in the U.S." *Contemporary French Civilization* 21.2 (1997): 5–17.

Stivale, Charles J. "Acker/Rimbaud: 'I'-dentity Games." *Angelaki: Journal of the Theoretical Humanities* 3.3 (1998): 137–42.

———. "A la recherche des 'bons temps': Teaching and Learning (in) French Cultural Studies." *Contemporary French Civilization* 26.2 (2002): 253–62.

———. "Becoming-Cajun." *Cultural Studies* 14 (2000): 147–76.

———. *Disenchanting Les Bons Temps: Identity and Authenticity in Cajun Music and Dance*. Durham: Duke UP, 2003.

———. "Monsieur Jordain Meets Cultural Studies." Nineteenth-Century French Studies Colloquium. Pennsylvania State Univ. 24 Oct. 1998.

———. "On Cultural Lessons, French and Other." *Contemporary French Civilization* 21 (1997): 65–86.

———. "*(Se) Rendre Compte*: Orienting Graduate Students to Market (Un)Realities." *French Review* 72 (1999): 1049–59.

Stone, Oliver, dir. *The Doors*. Carolco, 1991.

Strand, Dana. "Place and Identity in Cultural Studies: Confessions of a Revised Postmodern Critic." *Contemporary French Civilization* 26 (2002): 170–78.

"Student Handbook. Romance Languages." Harvard Univ. Faculty of Arts and Sciences. <www.registrar.fas.harvard.edu/handbooks/student/chapter3/romance.html>.

Sudweeks, Fay, Margaret McLaughlin, and Sheizaf Rafaeli, eds. *Network and Netplay: Virtual Groups on the Internet*. Cambridge: MIT, 1998.

Swaffar, Janet K. "Major Changes: The Standards Project and the New Foreign Language Curriculum." *ADFL Bulletin* 30.1 (1998): 34–37.

Swaffar, Janet K., Katherine M. Arens, and Heidi Byrnes. *Reading for Meaning: An Integrated Approach to Language Learning*. Upper Saddle River: Prentice, 1991.

Texas A&M Univ. *Vision 2020: Creating a Culture of Excellence*. 27 June 2003 <http://www.tamu.edu/vision2020/culture/>.

Tondeur, Claire-Lise. *Voix de femmes: Ecritures de femmes dans la littérature française du XIX–XXème siècle*. Lanham: UP of America, 1990.

Tremblay, Michel. *Des nouvelles d'Edouard*. Montréal: Babel, 1989.

———. *Thérèse et Pierrette à l'école des Saints-Anges*. Montréal: Babel, 1980.

Triggs, Jeffery A. "The Legacy of Babel: Language in Jean Renoir's *Grand Illusion*." *New Orleans Review* 15.2 (1988): 70–74.

"Undergraduate Announcement 2001/2002." Princeton Univ. Program in European Cultural Studies. <http://www.princeton.edu/pr/catalog/ua/01/176.htm>.

Undergraduate Catalog. 1993–94. New Orleans: Tulane Univ., 1993.

Ungar, Steven, and Tom Conley, eds. *Identity Papers: Contested Nationhood in Twentieth-Century France*. Minneapolis: U of Minnesota P, 1996.

Vaid, Urvashi. *Virtual Equality: The Mainstreaming of Gay and Lesbian Liberation*. New York: Doubleday, 1995.

van Orden, Kate. "On the Side of Poetry and Chaos: Mallarméan *Hasard* and Twentieth-Century Music." *Meetings with Mallarmé in Contemporary French Culture*. Ed. Michael Temple. Exeter: U of Exeter, 1998. 160–79.

Verne, Jules. *Le tour du monde en 80 jours*. Paris: Hetzel, 1873.

Villiers de l'Isle-Adam, Auguste, comte de. *L'Eve future:* Ed. Pierre-Georges Castex and Alan Raitt. Paris: Gallimard, 1986. Vol. 1 of *Œuvres complètes*. 2 vols.

———. *Eve of the Future Eden*. Trans. Marilyn Gaddis Rose. Lawrence: Coronado, 1981.

———. *Tomorrow's Eve*. Trans. Robert Martin Adams. Urbana: U of Illinois P, 2001.

Vincendeau, Ginette. "Designs of the Banlieue: Mathieu Kassovitz's *La haine* (1995)." Hayward and Vincendeau 310–27.

Les visiteurs. Dir. Jean-Marie Poiré. Miramax, 2003.

Webster, Robert M. "DVDs in French." *American Association of Teachers of French National Bulletin* 29.3 (2004): 9.

Web Support Site for Modern French Literary Studies in the Classroom: Pedagogical Strategies. Ed. Charles J. Stivale. 13 Dec. 2002. <http://www.langlab.wayne.edu/Romance/MLAPedStrategies/Index.html>.

Welles, Elizabeth B. "Foreign Language Enrollments in United States Institutions of Higher Education, Fall 2002." *ADFL Bulletin* 35.2–3 (2004): 7–24. Forthcoming. <www.adfl.org/resources/enrollments.pdf>.

Wylie, Laurence. "The Civilization Course." *Société et culture de la France contemporaine*. Ed. Georges Santoni. Albany: State U of New York P, 1981. 1–17.

Yaari, Monique. "Culture Studies: A French Perspective." *Transculture* 1.1 (1996): 21–60.

———. "Toward a Cultural Curriculum for Graduate Studies: The Case of French." *ADFL Bulletin* 33.2 (2002): 33–49.

Yaari, Monique, and Vera Mark. "Approaches to French Civilization: A Graduate Theory and Methods Course." *French Review* 66.3 (1993): 433–52.

Ziolkowski, Theodore. *Disenchanted Images: A Literary Iconology*. Princeton: Princeton UP, 1977.

Zola, Emile. *L'œuvre*. Paris: Flammarion, 1971.

———. *Les Rougon-Macquart*. Vol. 4. Ed. Armand Lanoux and Henri Mitterand. Paris: Gallimard, 1966. Vol. 4 of *L'Œuvre*. 5 vols.

INDEX OF NAMES